Barriers and Boundaries

CPA Seminar Series

Barriers and Boundaries

The Horoscope and the
Defences of the Personality

Liz Greene

CPA

Centre for Psychological Astrology Press
London

First published 1996 by The Centre for Psychological Astrology Press, BCM Box 1815, London WC1 3XX, GB, Tel/Fax 0181-749-2330.

2nd printing 1998.

1st paperback edition 2002.

BARRIERS AND BOUNDARIES

Copyright © 1996 by Liz Greene.

Liz Greene asserts the moral right to be identified as the author of this work.

ISBN 1 900869 00 4

British Library Cataloguing-in-Publication Data. A catalogue record for this book is available from the British Library.

Printed in Great Britain by Antony Rowe Ltd, Chippenham, Wiltshire, SN14 6LH.

All rights reserved. No part of this book may be reproduced or transmitted in any form or by any means, electronic or mechanical, including photocopying, recording, or by any information storage and retrieval system, without permission in writing from the publisher.

Table of Contents

Part One: The Psychology of Defences and their Astrological Significators

Introduction... 1
Psychoanalytic interpretations of defences...5
    Oral defences... 6
    Anal defences..13
    Oedipal defences..17
    Dissociation as a defence... 23
Defence mechanisms in the zodiac signs...24
    The element of earth..24
    Taurus and Capricorn.. 25
    The polarity of earth and fire.. 30
    Capricorn (continued).. 38
    Virgo.. 39
    The element of water: Cancer... 43
    Pisces... 47
    Scorpio... 48
    Other types of water sign defences....................................... 50
    The element of fire: Leo..53
    Aries.. 57
    Sagittarius.. 57
    The element of air: Gemini... 61
    Libra.. 64
    Aquarius..69
Planets and planetary aspects as defence systems............................. 73
    Martial defences... 76
    Lunar and Neptunian defences... 77
    Mercurial defences.. 78
An example chart.. 80
    Aspect dynamics..87
    Violence as a defence... 90
    Plutonian defences.. 94
    Defences and projection..102
More example charts and group discussion................................... 105
    Example chart 2... 105
    Example chart 3... 111
Chart sources.. 120
Bibliography...120

Part Two: Saturn and Chiron as Defence Mechanisms

An overview of Saturn and Chiron... 121
Saturn.. 124
    Denial and deprivation.. 124
    "Fake" compensation as an unconscious defence..................... 130
    Avoidance as a defence... 132
    Projection as a defence... 134
    Scapegoating as a defence.. 135
    Contempt... 137
    Pride and envy.. 138
    Dissociation as a defence against Saturn's pain....................... 141
    Creative compensation... 143
    Saturn unaspected... 150
    Saturn and taboos... 155
    Saturn as a symbol of natural law.. 159
Chiron.. 163
    Wounding and spoiling... 163
    Bitterness and cynicism.. 165
    The myth of Chiron... 166
    Chiron's poisoned wound... 171
    Chiron and Pluto.. 173
    Chiron's morality... 175
    Chiron and Saturn... 178
    Chiron's violence.. 181
    Chiron's quest for understanding.. 184
    Chiron and the helping professions...................................... 187
    Chiron and the Moon's Nodes... 189
    Chiron and Asklepios.. 190
    The discovery of Chiron... 192
    Chiron and Saturn in aspect... 194
    Chiron's relationship with Sagittarius.................................... 196
    Chiron as outlaw.. 198
    Chiron and suicide.. 199
Example charts and group discussion... 202
    Example chart 1... 202
    Mars-Chiron aspects.. 209
    Example chart 2... 212
    Chiron in the 2nd house.. 219
    Pluto transiting in aspect to Saturn....................................... 225
About the CPA... 230
About the CPA Press... 233

Part One: The Psychology of Defences and their Astrological Significators

This seminar was given on 30 October, 1994 at Regents College, London as part of the Autumn Term of the seminar programme of the Centre for Psychological Astrology.

Introduction

I would like to first make some general observations about the theme we are dealing with today. An unusually large number of people have enrolled in this seminar, which makes a very interesting comment on the relevance of the theme. Defences are usually discussed in the context of pathology. We can find some very good descriptions of them, for example, in Anna Freud's book, *Ego and the Mechanisms of Defence;* and Freud himself spent a lot of time exploring various characteristic defences which arise during particular stages of childhood and which, if they do not evolve into the next stage of development, may produce problems in the adult. So normally we tend to think of defences in an adult as something negative, something fundamentally inappropriate or destructive.

I think this is an unfortunate connotation, exacerbated by the ways in which we use the word in ordinary conversation. The psychologically semi-literate will often accuse someone who doesn't agree with them, or isn't interested in their advances, or who is expressing perfectly justified anger, as "defensive"; and even psychotherapists and psychoanalysts, who ought to know better, may be caught indiscriminately telling their clients and analysands that they are being defensive if the client dares to disagree with an interpretation. We might be wise to remember that the whole of life operates on the basis of defence. Everything we do is in some way affected by our need to preserve life and defend ourselves against death – whether the death is physical, emotional or spiritual. Defences are not intrinsically negative; they are the organism's way of ensuring survival on every level.

So lest we think that defences are purely pathological, we might reflect for a moment on the fact that we, in company with every animal and plant on this earth, reproduce ourselves in order to defend ourselves and our species against extinction. We create communities and social laws in order to defend ourselves against violence and chaos. Everything we human beings have invented, everything we have created – from our most brilliant scientific discoveries to our greatest works of art – has, among other motives, an element which attempts to preserve and protect us from injury, loneliness, sickness, pain, meaninglessness, or any other of a myriad dimensions of existence which have the power to destroy us. If we did not have defences, we would not exist at all.

If we look more closely at this very fundamental purpose of defences, we find ourselves in some very mysterious terrain. For example, we create images of God (whether God, or the gods, exist, is beside the point), and formulae by which to reach God, because we are attempting to defend ourselves against the abyss of purposelessness and the threat of nothingness after death. We may look at the whole of religion and spiritual aspiration as, in part, arising from the need to defend ourselves against utter meaninglessness. We can look at our creation of families and relationships as a defence against the torment of isolation. We can also look at cosmologies, and cosmological systems such as astrology, as a defence against a chaotic universe; at its core, this is precisely what astrology is. Whether or not it works is beside the point. If we understand something about natural cycles, and can learn how to read them, then perhaps we can defend ourselves against doing the wrong thing in the eyes of the gods, and build bastions against the inevitable punishment or disintegration which ensues when we transgress natural or divine law. When we choose to study astrology seriously, we may need to ask ourselves, "Why did I really take up this study?" Amongst the many attractive motives – self-exploration, spiritual and psychological growth, a better understanding of the choices available in life – we may also discover an element of defending ourselves against destruction. If it is possible to understand and foresee – even if the foreseeing is psychological rather than literally predictive – then life might not hurt us so much. We may need to start thinking about defences as an essentially creative, positive and necessary dimension of human life. This will help us to explore the astrological patterns of defence mechanisms from a more objective and useful perspective.

We use the term "defence" in very careless and inappropriate ways. When we tell someone they are being defensive, most of the time we really mean that they are not seeing things our way. When therapists tell their patients or clients, "You're being defensive," it might be translated as, "You're not accepting my interpretation of how you feel or what your dream was about." There are, of course, defences which become destructive in therapeutic work, because they are so tight or rigid that they make an honest dialogue impossible. But when such defences are displayed, there is usually a very good reason for them, in the client's eyes if not in the therapist's; and we must always respect the vulnerability of any individual maintaining a defence in therapy, even if we also need to help them achieve a more open and flexible relationship. If we tell a loved one, "You're being defensive," what we really mean is, "You're not giving me what I want." This is rather like our use of the word "selfish". We wield it as a weapon when someone else has the audacity, as Ambrose Bierce once put it, of believing that he or she is more important than we are. So before we proceed further with our theme, I think we must resist the temptation to use the term "defensive" as an insult toward those people who are not responding to us in the way we think they should.

A somewhat more sophisticated approach to the subject of defences might be to consider that, in many ways, defences are the instinctive definitions of what we need and value most, as individuals and as a collective. If we wish to understand how defences work in terms of the astrological chart, we need to recognise this fundamental fact first. We defend ourselves to protect what we love and need, for our physical and/or psychological survival. An understanding of defences provides us with a key to what is of greatest value to any living thing, whether purely instinctively or on a more conscious level. We do not defend what we do not care about. We only defend what matters most to us – what we feel we will not be able to live without if it is taken away.

On the most basic level, we all possess biological defences of a similar kind. These are not unique to any particular horoscope or personality. We have defences against disease which are reflected by the lymphatic system. We have physical defences which give us a chance to heal our bodies even if we don't admit they need healing. If you have been up for three nights partying, or cramming for exams, and you are so tired that you can't stay awake any longer, that is the body's defence against further damage. If you kept going any longer without rest, you would become ill. Fatigue may a defence against a dangerous encroachment on the body's reserves. Fatigue leading to excessive sleep may also be a defence against emotional misery, which is why chronic tiredness is often one of the symptoms of depression. Or it may be a defence against a bacterial or viral illness which the body can only fight if there is sufficient rest. On this fundamental level, there is no appreciable difference between individuals.

When we move beyond the biological level – the defences which ensure physical survival – then our defences begin to become variable and even unique, because people are highly individual in terms of what they need to protect themselves on emotional, intellectual and spiritual levels. If the human body cannot defend itself according to its innate protective mechanisms, it dies. Medicine has always been concerned with finding ways of reawakening or replacing defences which the body can no longer muster. Antibiotics, an obvious example, provide an artificial compensation for the body's inability to fight off infection. Psychological survival, although it may be linked subtly and deeply with physical survival, has its own very special mechanisms of defence. We can each tolerate particular levels of psychological stress in particular areas of life which other people might not be able to bear.

So when we begin to examine defences on levels other than the purely physical one, we have arrived in the realm of the mystery of individuality. Each person's survival needs on these subtler levels will differ from the next person's. We cannot say, for example, that the same amount of physical affection is necessary for every person's emotional survival. It isn't, not even for a baby. A certain amount of touching and holding is undoubtedly a requirement for all infants at the beginning of life, if the child is to feel welcomed into the world and safe in the immediate environment. But babies are different from each other. They have different birth charts and different inherent natures, and they need different degrees of comfort and security, and in different forms. We cannot assume that everyone needs the same amount of love, or the same kind of love; nor can we assume that every child possesses the same need for self-expression or a desire for the same degree of intellectual stimulation. These needs vary enormously.

Throughout our lives, our personality defences will always be related to what we care about and need most. Although we may discover that painful experiences or deprivation of one kind or another have exaggerated or inflamed a defence mechanism, the mechanism itself is a healthy aspect of the whole personality. We do not become defensive because we have been deprived of something we never wanted in the first place. We only hurt if we are vulnerable, and we are only vulnerable if we need something and are threatened with denial of the life-giving thing. How we define our internal survival needs is infinitely variable. What I am saying ought to be obvious; and yet it sometimes seems very difficult for us to understand that other people's defences may be absolutely appropriate for them while proving uncomfortable for us if our own needs collide with those defences.

To use a simplistic astrological example, the person with Sun, Moon, Jupiter and Pluto conjunct in Cancer may need to recognise the validity of the emotional defences of his or her partner or child with Sun in Aquarius trine Moon conjunct Saturn and Uranus in Gemini. These defences may appear to the water sign individual as cold, unfeeling, and self-absorbed – and therefore "pathological". Yet to the airy nature they may be absolutely necessary to ensure privacy, emotional balance, and urgently needed protection against feeling overwhelmed or invaded by others' demands. Depending upon his or her own horoscope and individual nature, the astrologer or counsellor may side with the water sign client, declaring that the defences of the air sign person are destructive to the relationship and that this individual is in need of therapy to cure the problem. But one could also argue that the water sign's needs are in themselves a defence against the terror of loneliness, and that they equally might need curing. This is one of the reasons why I feel we must exercise care in how we use and understand the term "defences". What constitutes a life-threat to one individual may not look that way to another, and no person, however astrologically or psychologically knowledgeable, is in a position to decide for others whether defence mechanisms in a particular area of personal life are "normal" or "abnormal". When defences become extreme and are expressed through destructive behaviour toward self and others, we may have to do what is necessary to try to rectify the situation. But we may need to refrain from the delightful indulgence of moral certitude.

Any therapist who has experience working with people will recognise, as I have already pointed out, that one should never attempt to break down a client's defences simply because one thinks they shouldn't be there. The same applies to the astrologer. Such defences exist for a reason, and they may be absolutely necessary to the client – at least for a time – because they are protecting something extremely vulnerable which the therapist himself or herself might not personally consider so important. Defences should always be approached with great respect, because they are so highly adapted to the individual psyche and the individual's survival needs.

Psychoanalytic interpretations of defences

I would now like to look at the basic kinds of defences, and their corresponding childhood stages, according to the traditional psychoanalytic framework. Although we may wind up having to discard some of the more literal dimensions of these interpretations as we go along, they are nevertheless worth exploring; and the understanding of defence mechanisms as aspects of adaptation to life is essentially a Freudian view. We can learn a great deal from Freud in developing our astrological insights. Although Jung is generally more pleasing to astrological students because his psychological approach is inclusive, symbolic, and more closely related to the astrological world-view, Jung didn't spend a lot of time exploring the important issue of defences. Freud has much finer, more delicately tuned insight into individual behaviour and individual suffering on the everyday level, and consequently his work on defences can be of great value to us. So if any of you have prejudices against Freud, try to put them aside. His models of the psyche are as valid a psychological model as any other. His scope may be limited, but it is very thorough and very deep.

In Freud's work defences are divided into three basic types, linked with particular periods of childhood. Whether his model of childhood development is "true" or not is an arguable issue. There is undoubtedly much truth in it, but it doesn't provide the whole truth. No psychological model can. But these three types of defences are clearly related to certain astrological significators, which you will no doubt recognise as we go along.

Oral defences

The earliest and most primal form of defence is the oral defence. Freud related this to early infancy and to that fundamental stage of experience in which everything in the baby's world is focused on feeding. The word "oral" is obvious – it is connected with mother's breast and with the life-giving nourishment that the breast provides. Freud understood the longing for the breast as a defence only if this initial life-urge becomes a mechanism of protection at a later stage of development for which it is no longer appropriate. One might become "fixated" at the oral stage – in other words, one develops oral defences – if things go wrong in the initial process of bonding with the mother. During later stages of personality development, the need for a constantly nourishing breast may remain as a defence against loneliness and extinction. We can see this pattern in later childhood in compulsive habits such as thumb-sucking, which may be a problem even in a pubescent child. When oral defences translate themselves into adulthood, and we view them from a broader perspective, we can see that they are apparent in the compulsion to ensure that there is a source of emotional as well as physical nourishment close by, all the time.

So oral defensiveness (a clumsy term, but you must admit that it's descriptive) means that we set up patterns whereby we can be guaranteed a constant supply of metaphorical milk. When we encounter stressful

Part One: The Psychology of Defences and their Astrological Significators

experiences, or reach junctures in life where unpredictable or painful events, or the threat of such events, make us panic, we will respond according to the defences which come most readily and naturally to us as individuals. As I've already said, the variety of these defences is vast, and reflects the multitude of different patterns and emphases one can find among different birth horoscopes. For many people, the oral defence is the most effective defence. Therefore it becomes absolutely necessary to make sure that a supply of milk is always available.

Now what constitutes a supply of milk? Symbolically, milk can be represented by a great range of things. For someone who is desperately seeking it, it may appear in just about anything that comes to hand. And that doesn't just mean something one can eat, drink, or put in one's mouth. For some people, the life-sustaining milk can be provided by a close relationship. In this sense, human relationships are utilised as a defence against death by emotional starvation. The infant inside the adult perceives the loved one as the source of life, without whom no existence is possible. Clearly this is not the same experience as a relationship which is happy and fulfilling because two people like, love, and respect each other. Nor is it the same as a relationship in which the satisfaction of ordinary human needs – for affection, closeness, companionship – provides a sense of security and contentment. When a relationship is enlisted as an oral defence, the beloved is essential for the continuity of life. We are looking at hunger, rather than love. If the loved one is not there, one is threatened with extinction.

There are certain kinds of anxiety states which afflict some people if their partner simply goes around the corner to buy a loaf of bread. This type of panic is triggered by the physical absence of the partner. One can't let the beloved out of one's sight. If he or she goes too far away, anxiety and rage may set in. Some displays of possessiveness are rooted in oral needs, and are not really concerned with jealousy about a rival. If a baby is hungry but is not being fed, terrible rage and panic ensue, and the baby will begin to scream. There is a particular note to this scream, which gives voice to a combination of great terror and great anger. When babies scream in this way, they often trigger a corresponding rage and panic in many adults who happen to be within earshot – particularly in a cinema or restaurant, or on an aircraft. But the scream may not be so obvious in adulthood. It may not be audible at all, although some people do indulge in such panic-driven screaming tantrums – usually about something trivial, such as one's partner coming home from work half an hour late, or forgetting to telephone as promised. We may unconsciously use our loved ones as sources of milk. If we do this, we must make sure they remain constantly present in our lives. We may even try to sabotage their independence, or prevent them from developing career interests or friendships that take them too far away from us, in order to ensure that the breast is eternally there.

This is Freud's oral defence when we view it at work in ordinary life. We don't normally think of these behaviour patterns as a pathology. They are very common and very human expressions of a defence which is sometimes disguised as, or blends with, feelings of love. Another form of milk can be provided by one's work. Some people experience their job, the company they work for, or the group or institution to which they belong, as a breast. They may dislike the work itself, and find it boring and meaningless; they may have to subject themselves to humiliating restrictions and put up with appalling colleagues or employers; they may feel their personal values are ignored or violated by what they are required to do; they may have to sacrifice creative potentials or cherished dreams. But the steady job with a large organisation, particularly if it is a giant amorphous institution like the Civil Service or the National Health Service, may be a kind of breast. As long as one is attached to it, in however humble a capacity, one will get fed.

Oral defences can make us channel our energies in directions which are not really of our own conscious choosing, and which may be inappropriate or sadly inhibiting to our talents and temperaments. For those imprisoned within such defences, the idea of leaving the kind of work situation I have just described can constellate terrible panic. A concerned friend's or counsellor's suggestion that they could do something more fulfilling with their lives may fall on stony ground. It is very interesting to consider this sort of defence pattern in the context of economic climate. We all tend to seize on and exaggerate certain situations in the outer world according to what is in our inner world; and it is sometimes the case that those who are most discouraged by high unemployment figures, depressed housing markets, and other published prognostications of economic gloom, may feel hopeless about their chances for a more rewarding life in part because they cannot leave the security of the breast – however poor the quality of the milk.

So if somebody says, "I couldn't possibly go and look for another job now – there are no jobs, I'll never find any work, I have no special talents, why should anyone prefer me when there are five hundred applicants?", this may not be practical wisdom, nor even ordinary garden-variety insecurity. He or she may be stuck in an oral defence. We may see, for example, a male client whose birth chart is full of cardinal signs – the Sun and three planets in Aries, a Capricorn Ascendant or Moon, a very strong Mars or Uranus, and a nature that

Part One: The Psychology of Defences and their Astrological Significators

clearly hates having to answer to somebody else's authority. He may be well educated, or bright enough to complete an education which was left unfinished. He may have many dreams and aspirations. Yet that individual may have put himself in a position where he is being utterly crushed by an institutional hierarchy or tyrannical employer, and he may be full of resentment and rage which manifests as depression or illness. He simply cannot leave the security of the breast, even though it is obvious – to him as well as to the astrologer – that it would be better if he took the gamble and set up a business or consultancy of his own.

Oral defences may lurk in areas of life where we might not expect to find them. If we are at all psychologically sophisticated, we might expect them to colour many human relationships – perhaps even all close relationships to some extent, although not necessarily destructively. With earthy things, however, such as houses, jobs, salaries and pensions, we may be surprised to see how strongly oral defences may subtly influence our conscious choices. We may be even more surprised to discover how oral defences can shape our political and social views. The state can be a breast for some people. It is not perceived as a government run by a group of ordinary humans of whichever party; it is a magical source of sustenance, and it should miraculously, like mother's breast, be able to go on producing milk, without one's having to think seriously about where the revenue is going to come from. Like infants, such people may assume that the state is there to look after them, and any sense of personal responsibility is terrifyingly absent. One's realism about the external world may disintegrate in the face of powerful unconscious defence mechanisms. If defences begin to occlude one's perceptions, then one's entire relationship with reality becomes distorted. That is when defences cease to be creative, and begin to look distinctly pathological. When they get so big that they start amputating other, equally important aspects of the personality, and begin to reshape reality to the point where we cannot interact with it any longer except through the intermediary of the defence, then we are no longer protecting ourselves with defences. We are destroying ourselves.

Oral defences, according to Freud, are in everyone. We all have some area of our lives in which we reach for the comfort of the symbolic breast. In itself, this is not in the least pathological. As any existential psychologist knows, we have good reason to be anxious. Life is dangerous; we are not here for very long; and a lot of dreadful things can happen to us, whether we have merited them or not. The desire for comfort, and the use of oral defences to create a bastion against anxiety, are simply human. For some individuals, oral needs may provide a fundamental line of defence. For others they may be one of a range of defences which are mobilised in times of distress.

Addictions of one kind or another can be a form of oral defence. Compulsive eating may be linked to oral defences, as many of you will have realised; so may smoking; so may drinking. Chewing gum may be a form of oral defence. So may biting one's nails, or nibbling the ends of pencils. It all depends on the compulsiveness with which these things are done, and the level of anxiety which fuels the compulsion. Even kissing can sometimes be an oral defence, because we are back at the breast. Now that may sound dreadfully unromantic, and kissing may obviously mean many other things as well. But the sleepy eroticism of a long kiss, like the sleepy eroticism of a delicious bar of creamy chocolate, may be linked with the infant's sleepy eroticism after a really good feed. Clever advertisers know this and play on the sensual delights of ice cream and chocolate, and even yoghurt. There are elements in all adult sensual contact which echo the early days and weeks of life. I don't need to elaborate on this, do I? It should be obvious that sensuality is not restricted to adults. Our mouths, from infancy onward, are erotic organs, and eroticism and oral defensiveness go together. The life-sustaining power of milk, and the warm sensuous pleasure of the breast, are linked together, and both form part of the attractions of oral defences.

Audience: Could you explain a bit more about this link between eroticism and oral defences?

Liz: Babies are very sensual. Their feelings, as well as their bodies, respond to being touched and stroked. We must differentiate between sexual and erotic feelings. An infant's eroticism is not focused on penetration, nor does it reflect passion or attraction as we experience it between two individual adults. Freud called infants "polymorphous perverse", which means that they respond to a wide variety of pleasurable erotic stimuli as passive recipients, regardless of the identity or nature of the stimulus. Infantile eroticism is really a state of physical and emotional fusion with the source of pleasure. Fusion on the emotional level is also a highly sensual and physically pleasurable experience. This unity of physical and emotional delight is one of the most striking aspects of eroticism, which differentiates it from the adult experience of purely physical release, and also from the adult enjoyment of close emotional exchange devoid of physical contact. Mistaking one for the other may be why so-called "erotic" films are so rarely erotic. There is no feeling content, nothing to draw the viewer into a merged emotional state. Some of the most erotically stimulating films are those in which sexual scenes are not explicit.

Certain kinds of music are highly erotic, and produce the same combination of physical and emotional delight combined with a sense of being "taken out of oneself". I might be extremely heretical and suggest that some religious services, particularly those which use incense and sensuous music such as Latin chants, can be highly erotic – although the participants usually refer to the experience as "uplifting". One can experience erotic feelings with one's pet. This doesn't mean that one is turned on by one's cat, dog, or rabbit in a sexual way (although some people are), but it is soothing and beautifully sensuous to stroke a warm, furry animal. If one is very tactile, there is also something highly erotic about fabrics like velvet or silk; they not only feel lovely, but even the sound they make, and their flowing movements, are erotic. Erotic feeling is both emotional and sensual. Sex without eroticism can be boring and soulless. But eroticism doesn't have to be sexual, in the sense in which we ordinarily understand sexual experience.

The process of breast feeding is erotic for both mother and baby. Many mothers speak openly of their pleasure, and it is clear that for the baby it's an erotic experience as well – an emotional and sensual fusion. In adulthood we tend to blend our erotic needs with our sexual desires. What we ask for from a lover is not just an orgasm; one can do that for oneself, without all the difficulties involved in making a relationship with another human being. We also want the erotic sensuality, the emotional and physical fusion-state, of the very young child. So when we affectionately touch people that we love, it often reflects this very fundamental level of early eroticism, as well as being a mature conscious gesture expressing love. Oral defences can be highly sensuous, because they take us back, not only to the safety of the baby at the breast, but also to the erotic pleasure of the fusion-experience.

If we are to believe Michael Douglas, a condition exists called sexual addiction. By his own public testimony, this mysterious affliction appears to be the means by which he justifies some of his more unruly behaviour. Although one might well be sceptical about interpreting this as a disease, which apparently exonerates the sufferer from any personal responsibility, in fact he is deeply compulsive in his pursuit of sexual objects. He is an example of the use of the sexual act as an oral defence. The person with whom the act is performed is not particularly important. It is the oblivion, the delicious fusion-state, the escape from life, which is so addictive. This is why men like John F. Kennedy and Michael Douglas can work their way through a startling number of women in the course of an average working week. Perhaps a plastic inflatable would do as well, because the identity of the woman doesn't matter. However, a plastic inflatable would not be quite as conducive to a glamorous public image. There is something about this compulsive quest for erotic oblivion which is deeply linked to the primal oral experience of the infant.

Oral defences are present, to a greater or lesser extent, in all of us. They become a source of concern and pain when the person feels that he or she has been taken over by the defence mechanism. We can only assess an oral defence as pathological if it is making an individual suffer, or if the individual is compulsively making other people suffer because of it. We have no other measure. There is no base line of defined "normality" in these realms. When does an oral defence cease to be creative and life-preserving, and when does it become destructive? And why? Often the astrologer or psychotherapist meets the oral defence in the client when it has become so compulsive that it is destroying other aspects of life. Then the person arrives in the consulting room to ask what can be done about it. Up to that point, oral defences may provide contentment, stability and security, and may be absolutely appropriate for the individual – even if his or her partner has difficulty in responding.

I part ways with Freud when he assigns oral defensiveness in adulthood to traumatic experiences that occurred in the first year of life. Certainly some experiences – such as an abrupt separation from the mother due to illness or death – can "freeze" the defence and ensure that it assumes compulsive proportions later in life. But if we look at the creative and life-sustaining dimensions of oral defences, as well as their compulsive and destructive dimensions, we can already recognise certain astrological factors which describe a certain temperament inherently prone to such patterns. The defence reflects what is important to the individual. Something traumatic may have happened in childhood. In fact, something traumatic probably happened to all of us in childhood. But we are all selective in terms of what we remember and react to, and we come back in the end to the great mystery of subjective reality. What one person experienced in childhood as utterly devastating, another might shrug off as unpleasant but certainly not "traumatic" in the full-blown psychoanalytic sense of the term. Our responses reflect an inherent temperament which is naturally attuned to certain stages and experiences in childhood, and transforms them into the fabric of adult reality.

We will not get very far trying to link oral defences with interruptions in breast feeding, or other literal events in childhood. We need to approach the issue from another angle. Oral defences may be particularly emphasised in a person because the experience of erotic and sensual fusion is of enormous value to that person, both in infancy and in adulthood. To have such an important source of pleasure and fulfillment taken away doesn't just mean death to the infant; it may also mean a black and soul-destroying loneliness to both the infant and the adult. Oral defences are our great human bastion against the terror and darkness of isolation. Loneliness afflicts everyone sooner or later, and no one enjoys it. For some people it is life-threatening, because it eats at the core of why they wish to be alive. For others, it is painful but can be endured, because other life experiences can provide sufficient joy and meaning.

We are entering deep waters if we adopt this perspective, because our reasons for wanting to live are reflected in how we defend ourselves and what we defend ourselves against. I think many of you will have already worked out by this time that the way I prefer to work with defences is to explore the defence as a means of gaining insight into what matters most to the individual. It may be also be relevant to discuss painful events which have contributed to the rigidity of the defence. But recalling unpleasant circumstances is, in itself, not sufficient to shift the individual's focus away from who did what to whom, and toward who they actually are. And without the latter, it is doubtful whether any healing can occur. Defence mechanisms are present because something matters so much that we don't want to live without it. We need to find out what this most precious thing is. Many of us don't know why we want to live, which is another way of saying that we don't know who we are.

Anal defences

Many psychoanalysts enjoy accusing each other, as well as their patients, of being "anal". This extremely up-market insult may be translated as, "You're withholding something I want." Freud understood anal defences to be linked with the time when a child begins to learn to control his or her faeces. Anal defences in adulthood, in classical psychoanalytic texts, are related to difficulties in early toilet training. Although you may fall about laughing at this, in fact controlling faeces is a big psychological event in childhood. One suddenly discovers that one can, by an exercise of will, decide whether to make this turd come out or not. One can thwart one's mother by refusing to defecate. Or one can produce something that she will admire; she might say, "How wonderful! What a nice big one! Well done!". Through this simple exercise of sphincter control, the child has begun to assert his or her will over the environment. The beginning of toilet training is the beginning of a child's sense of individual power. That is why Freud paid so much attention to it. On a symbolic level it is a very important issue, because it is the first time that the child can feel something other than helpless dependency.

Anal defences are related to the exercise of the will and the use of the power of withholding. If we can withhold something – an object, an emotion, an idea – we are establishing the fact that we are independent beings who cannot be dominated or controlled by someone else. We have something to say about what we give or do not give; we protect ourselves from physical or psychological invasion and robbery. We are not going to sit on the pot and produce something just because someone has told us to. Anal defences may be linked with what we are pleased to call "authority problems" in adulthood. They reflect a deliberate withholding, a resistance against others' demands, in order to demonstrate power, autonomy and an independent will.

Like oral defences, anal defences may be life-supporting and healthy. It is obviously fundamental to all of us to be able to exercise the power of decision-making and maintain some degree of control over ourselves and our lives. Anal defences are the child's natural response to the vulnerable dependency of the oral phase. Without these defences, we may live in a state of utter helplessness, easily exploited and victimised, and unable to say, "No." We must in some way assert who we are, even if it is in a very small way. Anal defences are another way of understanding boundaries, without which we cannot exist as independent beings or respect the independence of others. And if you think about it, you will realise that, although excessive anal defensiveness may lock an individual into a tight, inaccessible emotional prison, for many people this important system of defence is not developed enough. How many of you feel that you have a problem in saying, "No!" to other people? Ah, I see at least a third of you have your hand up.

Anal defences are a positive and necessary mechanism of defence. But the anal defence may be so ferocious that the necessity of having to demonstrate control may entirely block other needs that are trying to be expressed. This is the "cut off your nose to spite your face" defence. Pride is a powerful ingredient. This ought to give us some insight into how important pride can be for a child, and how easily parents can trample on the child's pride because they find it amusing, don't take it seriously enough, or feel their own pride – and their own anal defences – are being threatened by the child's assertion of will. Where we find powerful anal defences in the adult, we will usually encounter a Luciferian pride which perceives any emotional need as a chink in the fortifications, and any compromise as a humiliation.

Withholding can take place on the material level. This is the most obvious expression of anal defences, and the one which Freud explored most exhaustively. Money and personal possessions are a wonderful arena in which anal defences may exhibit themselves. Another word for "anal" is "mean". We may be so defended against anyone trying to take what is ours that we are no longer capable of enjoying what we have. We may use money to wield power over a dependent child or partner. Therapeutic clients may withhold paying their weekly or monthly bill, giving a variety of excuses, but usually exhibiting this defence after the therapist has taken a holiday, or asked too probing a question. In the therapeutic situation anal defences may conceal great rage, as well as asserting power over the therapist. Material possessions thus become a symbol of aggressive control. This is the Howard Hughes syndrome. We may not even want the objects we hoard. Anal defences pay no heed to personal tastes; they are a compulsive mechanism designed to fight the threat of losing one's soul. I have met many people who hoard things because they might be "useful" one day. The garage is full of empty paint tins, used nails, bits of wood, dried-out paintbrushes, and the remains of the wheelbarrow that rusted to pieces ten years ago. The desk drawer is full of pieces of string, used envelopes, letters that are long past answering, and other bits that cannot be thrown away because in some way they symbolise the bits of one's life. Nothing can be discarded. If one throws them away, one has lost a bit of oneself. But then there is no room for anything new, and no renewal, no growth, can take place.

One can also be anal with emotions, and the defence can be expressed very subtly on that level. Once again, anality can be a positive and healthy means of ensuring that others do not rob or abuse one's emotional resources. We have to be able to say, "No!" to people who want too much from us emotionally, as well as maintaining our boundaries on the physical level. But withholding emotion can also be an expression of anger and a means of wielding power. When a loved one wants a compliment or badly needs reassurance, just at that moment the anal defence ensures that one is not going to give it. Anal defences make us emotionally mean, ungenerous, and petty. That subtle little moment of withholding, so easily overlooked or unnoticed, becomes a means of taking revenge and exercising control.

Anal defences can be very destructive to other people. Cruelty, physical or psychological, is often bound up with this system of defence, as is the desire to demean or belittle others. This is another area Freud looked at very carefully. The urge to humiliate or pick apart another person – in effect, to reduce that person to shit – is a characteristic expression of anality. It is part of the compulsive need to prove that one has control over the environment and over other people. It is also a form of projection; the individual usually feels like shit himself or herself, impotent and powerless, but tries to alleviate these feelings of self-loathing by making someone else feel even worse. Sadly, this defence may be so powerful that it dominates an individual's ability to interact with others. Relationships may be severely damaged as a result. Such people must withhold everything, but at the same time that they make others suffer, they are suffering terribly themselves because they are isolated within the walls of their defences.

If one spends time around someone who is defensive in this way, one may begin to feel put down all the time. If we are unconscious of the dynamic, we may not realise that we are the recipient of an anal defence; we may simply feel strangely unattractive, unworthy or uninteresting in that person's company. Astrologers often get clients who utilise anal defences in very obvious ways. They come in and immediately let one know that they don't "believe in this nonsense", but are there because somebody else insisted they come. One has already been put down, before one has even opened one's mouth. Behind this all-too-common common greeting lies a deep primal fear of being controlled, which many clients experience when encountering astrology for the first time.

The experienced therapist is usually very familiar with anal defenses in their subtler forms. Whatever one says, the insight or interpretation is not good enough; one is not helping the client; he or she is feeling worse; the therapy is not worth the money being invested; the client went to see a spiritual healer or a reflexologist last week and felt so much better. "Where were you trained?" they want to know. "Oh, that qualification isn't recognised by the BPS, is it? How long have you been practising? Oh, that isn't very long, is it?" This is the anal defence at work. It is sometimes hard to empathise with the terrible pain and fear behind such antics, because it is so unpleasant being at the receiving end. The message is, "I'm going to withhold my vulnerability, but I'm going to expose yours." What begins as a life-sustaining, positive statement of autonomy is transformed into a weapon of destruction. In the same way oral defences, which begin as a life-sustaining impulse toward emotional intimacy and warmth, can become so extreme that the level of dependency destroys individual autonomy and self-respect, and smothers everyone else in the process.

As usual, Freud interpreted exaggerated anal defensiveness in adulthood as a reflection of traumatic experiences occurring during the period of toilet training in childhood. Once again, we need to adopt a different perspective. There are particular zodiacal signs, planets, aspects, and horoscope emphases which seem to gravitate toward this method of defence because it is most natural to them. Childhood traumas such as systematic humiliation, suppression by an authoritarian parent, or manipulation by an overly dependent parent can inflame and exaggerate the defence in some individuals. But anality is a natural, healthy defence system which belongs to certain kinds of people, or certain attributes within people. Functioning in balance with the rest of the personality, it can provide the valuable qualities of tenacity, self-sufficiency, and self-control. If it runs out of control, it can blight the individual's life.

Oedipal defences

Many of you may know, or think you know, what an Oedipal complex is. But what is an Oedipal defence? The basic theme of the Oedipal pattern in childhood is rivalry, and Oedipal defences are concerned with turning everything into a competition in which one's victory defines one's worth. By beating the rival, one demonstrates that one possesses greater strength, power, intelligence, creative talent, sexual attractiveness, or spiritual wisdom. Freud defined Oedipal urges in context of the child trying to win the beloved parent of the opposite sex, through competing with the parent of the same sex. We may need to view this powerful and fundamental human dynamic in a broader context. To begin with, I am not convinced that it is always the parent of the opposite sex who is the "treasure hard to attain"; it may be the parent of the same sex. Nor am I convinced that the real object of the exercise is the claiming of the prize. It may be the besting of the rival. Oedipal defences are not limited to setting up painful triangles in human relationships. They may occur in other spheres of life, often disguised as professional rivalry; and sometimes they are even disguised as disagreement with another person's point of view, expressed with a particular and unmistakable aggressiveness. Envy is the great motivating force behind Oedipal defences. Beneath all the various manifestations lies the compulsive need to win as a means of affirming potency and specialness. Oedipal defences affirm the individual through beating the opposition.

You can see how enormously positive this defence system can be. Envy is not just a nasty feeling of personal inadequacy and resentment toward someone who has what we wish we had. It can also be a potent force for the development of talents and the pursuit of excellence. Oedipal defences make us creative because we must prove that we are unique. If we didn't have this driving need to compete and win, we would do nothing to affirm or encourage individual expression. But if Oedipal defences dominate the personality to the exclusion of other needs and drives, then everything is turned into a battleground. One cannot do something simply because it is relaxing, pleasurable, inspiring or fun; and it becomes impossible to genuinely respect and co-operate with other human beings. If one decides to study something, one is not studying to learn the subject. One must be the best student in the class, and all the joy of learning vanishes in the smoke of battle. If one wishes to write something, one is not writing in order to communicate an important idea. One tries to build a reputation on the systematic attack of others' ideas. Creative efforts no longer spring from the heart, and we constantly look around us to see whether anyone else has come up with something better.

In relationships, compulsive Oedipal defences may be displayed in different ways, which we might not immediately recognise as arising from the same source. One may imagine that everybody else wants one's partner (even if, to the disinterested observer, it is patently obvious that the partner is quite uninteresting and displays no visible charms). Then one is in a constant state of tension and hostility, and must go around checking to see where the potential rivals are. No relationship is secure, no friend can be trusted, because sooner or later someone will come along whose greater potency ensures one's defeat. Usually someone does come along – someone equally trapped in an Oedipal defence pattern, but exhibiting a compulsive urge to conquer everyone in the vicinity. No matter if one has a happy relationship at home – one must have as many admirers as possible, preferably admirers who have been pried loose from an existing relationship, even if one is not remotely interested in pursuing the conquest to its usual end.

Oedipal defences usually attract the services of other people who are also Oedipally defensive. They may operate on many different levels, and when they run amok they can create enormous pain and suffering in human relationships. Yet without them we are about as interesting as mushrooms, with the creative sparkle of a duvet, because we have nothing which we can truly call our own. The Oedipal defence makes us get up and do things, and want to better ourselves. But when it dominates the personality, the battling may become an all-out conflagration. In its darkest form it can generate states of paranoia and pathological jealousy, which may lead to violence – the *crime du passion* so beloved of novelists and filmmakers.

Freud placed the Oedipal stage roughly between the ages of three and six. He understood the problem of a fixated Oedipal defence in adulthood as a reflection of traumatic experiences in the father-mother-child triangle during those years. Once again, we need to broaden our perspective and consider the testimony of the astrological chart. Oedipal defences seem to be related to particular astrological figures, whether or not there have been traumas. And how do we measure a true Oedipal trauma? What differentiates it from an ordinary garden-variety experience of envy? It may be that the child with a particular astrological make-up experiences a particular defeat at the hands of the parent-rival as a complete and permanent devastation of self-esteem, while another child might feel hurt and envious, but can find the necessary confidence to get up and try again. The Oedipal defence comes naturally to certain kinds of people. Traumatic experiences may indeed "fixate" it; but the predisposition must exist in the first place. We only become defensive about what matters most to us.

In the normal run of things, we all tend to display all three of these classic Freudian defences at various times and in varying degrees, because they all represent basic natural human defences. These defences protect different areas of the personality. The lack of any one of them, or the extreme exaggeration of any one of them, can create great suffering. As we explore these defences it may seem rather like reading a medical text book; by the time one has finished, it is clear one is afflicted by every known form of disease. Before much longer you will no doubt all wind up feeling that you are horribly defensive and every area of your life is riddled by oral, anal and Oedipal compulsions. This may well be true, but it's not the point.

As I have worked my way through this brief summary of the Holy Trinity of oral, anal and Oedipal defences, it will no doubt be clear that particular signs and planets are related to the psychoanalytic model. Although I want to discuss one more defence before we move on to the astrological significators in detail, it might be worth looking at an example. Aries is a naturally Oedipal sign. This is really another way of describing the fundamental qualities of the sign, which we already recognise but perhaps have not thought of in the context of defensive behavioural patterns. The things that matter most to Aries are bound up with the need to experience a sense of personal power and uniqueness, and a feeling of being effective in the world. A person who has an emphasis in Aries in the birth chart, whether it is the Sun, Moon, Ascendant, or a stellium of planets, must have this experience of individual potency in order to feel fulfilled, alive, and worthwhile. It is what makes life worth living – the great vernal cry of "I'm here!". Inevitably, defences will be mobilised against anything that threatens to undermine or destroy that feeling, and Aries' natural line of defence is to beat the competition to affirm its own uniqueness. If one needs to be first, it presupposes the existence of someone else whom one must beat. A winner cannot exist without a loser.

Life is perceived in this way through Aries eyes. I am not suggesting that Aries individuals go around consciously adopting such a perspective. Some might be horrified at the suggestion. Such a world-view is instinctive and innate, and most people are quite unaware of the fact that they observe and evaluate life through tinted spectacles. They assume that life is really like that. Naturally Aries gets Oedipal when threatened. Often in childhood there are intense rivalries with one or both parents, as well as with siblings and sometimes friends. Aries may insist that it is the fault of the other family members. But who has initiated the competitive ambience in the first place? Aries in adulthood may also insist that a broken friendship is the fault of the friend's envy, or a failed relationship the fault of the partner's disloyalty. The disinterested observer, however, may draw a different conclusion. While we may or may not get the parents we deserve, we certainly get the parents we perceive. The Oedipal pattern, viewed archetypally rather than as a literal sexual enactment, is the life pattern which underpins this sign of the zodiac.

The film industry is a wonderful showcase for observing defences at work, since the personal lives of actors tend to be larger than life. One Aries actor who comes to mind is Warren Beatty. He has not merely had a vast number of women. That might be said of a great many people. He has found it necessary to inform his viewing audience that he has had a great number of women. Here we can observe the Oedipal defence. Why is it so necessary for him to make his private life public, unless he experiences a deep need to prove his potency before as many witnesses as possible?

Audience: What about Marlon Brando? He's another Aries. But he's given up.

Liz: Brando may be a very sad example of an Aries who feels he has been defeated, and can't bear it. What has defeated him is unclear; but apart from the personal tragedies he has experienced, it may be the simple horror of ageing. Many actors can grow old gracefully. They move into mature character parts, and lose none of their magnetism. A number of them have achieved this brilliantly – John Gielgud, John Mills, Laurence Olivier, Ralph Richardson. In America we might think of Burt Lancaster, or Paul Newman. These men were able to relinquish being youthful "heart-throbs", and developed depth and maturity in their later performances. But certain actors experience the youthful body as the symbol of potency. Aries can be a very physical sign, and tends to identify with the body's vigour and strength. Perhaps age and mortality defeated Brando.

Audience: His defeat seems to be reflected in his obesity.

Liz: Yes, that is one way of viewing his dilemma. He is an Oedipal fighter who lost the fight to Father Time, and for him the defeat is terrible. If a particular defence mechanism becomes the person's only way of relating to life, and then fails, the experience may be crushing. That is one of the reasons why, in therapeutic work, one should proceed slowly and carefully with defences. If an individual can only relate through an oral defence, and is then rejected very abruptly by the object of his or her dependency, the terror of extinction can be utterly overwhelming. It is not simply a rejection; it is the annihilation of all that makes life worth living.

If an individual relates only through an anal defence, and suddenly loses all his or her material security, that too can be overwhelming. Understanding how shattering such an experience can be may help us to realise why, for some people, violence or suicide seem the only solution to a disappointment which you or I might feel should never merit such a response. Before a defence mechanism is "dismantled", it is important to help the person discover other ways of defending himself or herself. Before we can be vulnerable, we need to feel we have some resources by which to defend ourselves if our vulnerability comes under attack. It's quite silly to expect anyone to behave otherwise. All the basic defence patterns I have been discussing are necessary and valid in different situations. But sooner or later all defence systems will fail. Oral defences cannot guarantee that loved ones will never leave us; anal defences cannot guarantee that material disaster will never occur; Oedipal defences cannot guarantee that we will always win. Time, if not a rival, will ultimately defeat even the most seasoned Oedipal fighter.

Moreover, there is no single defence system that will protect us from everything. They are all good for certain things and not others. Identifying with one particular defence, and building one's whole life pattern around it, will inevitably lead to trouble. But many people do it anyway, at least until mid-life, because our most frequently used defences tend to be based on what we have discovered works for us in the early part of life. By the time Saturn arrives at its first return, certain defence systems have been tried and proven and are assumed to be reliable. They are the ones that come most naturally, and which are often shattered at midlife when Uranus opposition its natal place, and Saturn opposition its natal place for the second time, challenge all the personality structures we have built.

Many instances of early marriage and early parenthood, for example, are motivated in large part by oral defences. One can often see the compulsive element – the blind rush to create a family before one has any idea at all of who one is or what one wants. It can be a way of ensuring that there will be an emotional source of milk to replace the parental source. If such a setup falls apart (and it often will under one of the difficult Saturn transits, such as Saturn returning to its own place, or opposition its own place for the second time), it may feel like the end of the world. Some people can get up, dust themselves off, and get on with life. Others, whose only defence is oral, seem to disintegrate into a morass of total defeat. Other defences then urgently need developing. For example, if one can learn to withhold a little bit, materially and emotionally, then when a relationship breaks down one still has the sense that one has preserved something of oneself.

Audience: What about grief? Could that be seen as a defence?

Liz: Grief is an archetypal human experience, connected with separation and loss. In itself it is not a defence; it is a direct emotional response to and processing of a particular kind of experience. But grief, like many other fundamental emotional responses, can be utilised as part of a defence system.

Audience: Some people spend years in mourning.

Liz: Each individual has his or her own time scale for working through experiences on the emotional level. We are all made differently. When painful experiences are suppressed, grief can take much longer to heal. Unless feelings are conscious, they don't have the opportunity to change or transform. They remain static. For this reason the loss of a parent when one is very young can generate a state of grieving which can last for thirty years, buried deep in the psyche, if the child is not allowed to acknowledge or voice his or her grief at the time of the loss. Perhaps for some people many years are needed to learn to live with a deep loss. But I think you are right; sometimes grief, although it may be genuine, can also be a protection against the possibility of future loss, through ensuring that the person cannot become emotionally involved with anyone else.

Later on I want to talk about the way we can use many different kinds of feelings and perceptions as defences. I have begun with Freud's Holy Trinity because it is so fundamental. But any human activity can become a defence. Not only grief, but also joy, can be put in the service of self-protection. Think of those strenuously cheerful people who can never show any anxiety, pain, weakness, or depression. Even death can be a defence. That may sound absurd, but we can use death as a defence against death. If one seeks oblivion voluntarily, it is an assertion of free will. Death then hasn't come surreptitiously and unexpectedly, so one is exercising power over death by choosing the time and manner oneself. This may be one of the factors motivating certain suicides. Self-destruction may be the one act of will the individual has been able to affirm in the whole of his or her life. It may be a positive statement, even though we find it hard as a society to comprehend the importance of it. Have a look at James Hillman's *Suicide and the Soul*, in which he deals very eloquently with the issue of voluntary death as an affirmation of the self.

Dissociation as a defence

I would like to suggest a fourth basic defence mechanism, which Freud implied but didn't really discuss. I can't think of a "sound-bite" term like anal or oral, but the mechanism of disengagement or dissociation is a fundamental human defence. It is sometimes referred to as "denial", which Freud did recognise. But he didn't relate denial to a particular stage in childhood. Perhaps it has something in common with what he termed the "latent period", between the Oedipal phase and puberty, when all the erotic conflicts which arose in the earlier period seem to go underground until the body's changes invoke them again in new and powerful ways. Dissociation is not limited to a particular person's pathology. It is a universal means of preserving life and equilibrium, and it consists of unplugging the psychological telephone so one does not hear it ringing.

In certain Eastern teachings, and in certain esoteric circles in the West, what I am calling dissociation is called nonattachment, and it is not seen as a defence. Rather, it is a path to inner development. I don't doubt that nonattachment is indeed a valid path for those who have been born into, and are part of, the archetypal spiritual and psychological framework of the East. But I have some question about it when the term is used in our own culture in the context of a frenetic attempt to "transcend". It may be valid for the Western individual too, both as a path and as a defence system; one might expect to find a great deal of healthy dissociation, for example, in the priest, the doctor, or the psychotherapist. Dissociation, and its ally, sublimation (which Freud dealt with extensively), can be an immensely creative way of dealing with life. It is one of the most important defence systems we possess. And we must be able to express it, because if we remembered every single thing that hurt us, if we were aware of all the suffering in life, we could not exist. Life would be intolerable.

Did any of you see the recent BBC production of *Middlemarch?* Do you remember the ending? If we were able to feel all of the suffering going on around us, we could not bear it. We must sometimes numb ourselves, particularly after the sixteenth TV documentary on Rwanda, or the thirty-second on Bosnia. The mechanism of dissociation allows us to cope with grief and suffering. In some people it takes over. When it dominates all other aspects of the personality, we call it psychopathy. There is no feeling of any kind left, and no capacity to relate to any living thing. When dissociation works in balance with other factors, we have the ability to disengage from suffering and view it impersonally.

Audience: Perhaps dissociation is a particular problem among psychoanalysts.

Audience: And astrologers.

Liz: In one sense you are both right. The whole edifice of psychoanalysis is itself a form of dissociation, because concepts are used to define, contain, and depersonalise primitive forces which would otherwise be terrifying to contemplate. And astrology, as I said earlier, can be utilised – and perhaps was even created – as a defence against cosmic chaos. All conceptual and symbolic systems can offer us a form of dissociation. The intellect is often, although not always, the vehicle through which this defence is mobilised. If we know the name of something and can embed it in a more or less objective framework of ideas and information, it has less power to hurt us.

Defence mechanisms in the zodiac signs

Now we can begin to look more carefully at the basic defence mechanisms in relation to the astrological elements. Because each element within a chart describes, among other things, the ability to adapt to life in a particular way, looking at the balance of elements in the horoscope can give us some idea of which defences come most naturally to the personality.

The element of earth

A preponderance of earth, for example, tells us many things about the individual, and one of the most important is the manner in which that individual will protect himself or herself from hurt and harm. Earth, as you have no doubt already worked out, tends to utilise characteristic anal defence mechanisms – withholding, control of the material environment, and control of the emotions. If any of you find Freud's word "anal" offensive, you can replace it with the word "control". This is the most natural defence mechanism of Taurus, Virgo, and Capricorn, although each of these three signs has a highly distinctive way of utilising control and withholding as a defence. Once we can grasp the relationship between a defence mechanism and what matters most to the individual, we can understand that the earth signs will invariably respond to a threat in characteristic ways which are healthy and appropriate for their nature.

When anal defences become extreme, this may be reflected in the birth chart by a dominance of planets in the earth signs, with little in the elements of water or fire. Oral and Oedipal defences, which I think are the natural mechanisms of water and fire respectively, both involve relationship, either through fusion or through competition. These two defence systems require interaction with others. But anal defences shut out others. They may also be suggested by a powerful Saturn, the chief planetary representative of the earthy trigon. There are certain dimensions of Saturn's defence mechanisms which I am not going to talk about in today's seminar, and these relate to the sense of inferiority and inadequacy which often accompanies Saturn's natal house and sign placement and aspects to other planets.

But when viewed in terms of healthy natural defences, Saturn responds to threat in characteristically anal ways. Saturn and Chiron are in a special category of their own. Their defensiveness is complex, and is based not only on the fundamental need to preserve and protect what matters to the individual, but also on early suffering and the individual's interpretation of and response to it. Saturn and Chiron can involve patterns quite different from what I am talking about today. But Saturn is an anal planet, apart from the issue of suffering. It likes to hold and keep what it has got, emotionally, materially, intellectually, and spiritually.

Taurus and Capricorn

What is it that matters so much to the earth signs, which, if it is threatened, mobilises anal defences? Let's take an example. You are living with someone – a man – who has six planets in Capricorn, and his habitual restraint and emotional withholding are driving you up the wall. The more you try to get him to respond to you, the more controlled he seems to become. You have some psychological insight, as well as a Moon-Jupiter conjunction in Cancer, and Venus in Leo trine Neptune, and you think he's very defended in his behaviour. What is really going on?

Audience: He doesn't want to be controlled. Showing feelings too freely might mean he's not in control; his partner is.

Liz: Yes, I think the key to this kind of behaviour is the immense importance Capricorn places on boundaries and the right to privacy and self-possession. Capricorn doesn't want to rely too much on anyone else, because this might mean being let down or humiliated at the critical moment. For Capricorn, survival depends on self-sufficiency. Showing emotional need is a form of dependency, so it's blocked or moderated by the defence mechanism. Responding on cue to someone else's demands may also make the Capricorn feel dominated and controlled. The message is, "I'll show love when I want to, not when you want me to. I'm in charge of my own feelings, and I will decide when and how to express them." Self-possession is desperately important to Capricorn. Anything which threatens it will mobilise defences. But is this wrong? Or pathological? I don't think so. I think it is healthy, provided the individual is able to let go as well, when life requires it. All three earth signs use control and withholding as defences, but they use them in different ways. What do you think might differentiate Taurus from Capricorn? What is it that matters so much to Taurus, and what does this fixed earth sign defend itself against? How many are here today who have the Sun in Taurus? Can we have a show of hands? I count three. We'll give them a chance to speak first.

Audience: It might take a while.

Liz: You mean you're going to withhold the answer? Taurus Ascendants are allowed to join in, and so are those with the Moon in Taurus.

Audience: I know I have security issues about my environment. I try to hold on to my physical place in the world. I feel secure when I know where I am and can recognise what's around me. I feel very threatened if I have to move, or make changes at home. I have the Sun in Taurus.

Liz: You seem to be saying that the stability of your physical world is desperately important to you. Your sense of security isn't necessarily connected

Part One: The Psychology of Defences and their Astrological Significators 27

with money or the price of a material object, but rather, with knowing that it is your object and that it isn't going anywhere without your permission.

Audience: Exactly.

Liz: How do you react when you feel your security is threatened?

Audience: I get very stubborn and won't go anywhere or do anything. I have constant quarrels with my husband about travelling, or even going out for dinner or to parties too often. I want to stay home. When I feel anxious I get very stuck.

Audience: I have the Moon in Taurus, and I have a terrible fear of poverty. Any kind of poverty – physical, emotional, or spiritual.

Liz: We can get a sense from both of you of certain important issues that might lie at the core of Taurean defences. I hope you can all recognise that some of what are described as "personality characteristics" in traditional textbooks are really the defence mechanisms of the sign. Survival, for Taurus, depends on an enduring and unchanging physical reality that nothing can take away or destroy. Without that base line, chaos threatens. Awful things might happen without a sense that some aspect of the physical world can be utterly relied upon. Anything that threatens the stability of Taurus' world is experienced as the enemy, and defences will be mobilised against it. What does Taurus do to protect that stability? We've heard one method – withdrawing and sitting tight, like a tortoise inside its shell. What else?

Audience: Owning property. Saving money.

Liz: Ownership can be very important to some Taureans, and money and property can be utilised as a form of defence. For others, money itself may matter less than a familiar environment into which one can retreat. This can also mean a stable job which, although uninspiring, has the merit of being secure, or a relationship which, although difficult, has the merit of being safe. The famous Taurean resistance to change can be understood at a much deeper level when we recognise that it is a defence against chaos and the terrors of the unknown. Any basic astrological textbook will tell you that Taureans don't like change. But we need to understand why, because this allows us not only to respect the defence mechanism, but also to enter into the inner world of the

Taurean and recognise what kind of fears might underpin his or her notorious intractability. This is a far more intelligent way of interacting than simply stamping one's foot and shouting, "Why are you so bloody stubborn?" or "How can you be so materialistic?" Taureans are often terrified of the destruction that might ensue if their world falls into disorder or what they identify as theirs is taken away from them.

Audience: I wonder whether the destruction that Taurus fears is symbolised by Scorpio.

Liz: That is certainly a valid way of looking at it. What we need and value most may be the very thing which is most greatly feared by the opposite sign. Scorpio fears stagnation, on every level. Stagnation is death; change and transformation are life. That is why so many Scorpios will poke at stable situations, and provoke a crisis even if they know they will be badly hurt by the consequences. They depend on knowledge – of self and others – for survival, and one cannot acquire this kind of knowledge without experience. And one cannot acquire experience without change, preferably of a dramatic and challenging kind which involves upheaval or loss. The thing that makes Scorpio strong is the thing which, for Taurus, is the greatest threat, and the same may be said in reverse.

The greatest fear of any sign can also reflect the element which is psychologically opposite. In the case of earth, the psychological opposite (which is not the same as the astrological 180-degree opposition) is the element of fire. This approach can give us additional insight. Certainly Taurus fears and defends itself against what Scorpio needs and values most, and needs and values what Scorpio fears the most. But Taurus also defends itself against the chaotic intuitive world that Aries, Leo, and Sagittarius symbolise as well. I feel it's extremely important to understand the nature of each sign's fears. When we interpret a birth chart for a client, unless they have exactly the same chart as we do (which is very unlikely), we need to be able to enter into the inner world of that person, even in a limited way, in order to offer any sort of intelligent and compassionate advice or help.

Bruno Bettelheim made this point very eloquently before he died, in a television interview about his work with disturbed children. Many of you may know that he ran a clinic in America in which he dealt with severely damaged children who were apparently incapable of interacting with the outside world on any "normal" level. He did some wonderful work with these children. The interviewer said, "How have you achieved this? What do you do?" The children had usually been carted around to every available facility before they reached the clinic, after other treatments had failed. Bettelheim's clinic was generally the last resort. He replied, "The first thing you must understand is that, from these children's perspective, from inside their world, everything in the world outside is terrifying to an extent you cannot possibly imagine." Bettelheim insisted that, if the therapist can recognise the extraordinary degree of fear in a child in this kind of state, he or she will then begin to understand why the child is behaving in such a destructive or incomprehensible fashion. It isn't incomprehensible any more. Such children are in a chronic state of terror, which activates extreme defensiveness. When we talk about defences, we are invariably talking about fear. Fear is an aspect of human existence which will always be with us. Fear is bound up with our sense of survival. If we can understand what people fear, we can understand why they behave as they do.

Earth signs like to get everything "right". They often need an external stamp of approval, even if they prefer not to admit this to others or themselves, or have internalised external authority as a tyrannical Freudian "superego". Capricorn may be particularly desirous of the approval of the collective. Capricorn likes to know its place. Do any of you remember the television sketch in which John Cleese, Ronnie Barker, and Ronnie Corbett are defining class? Cleese, in a city suit and a bowler hat, says in his plummiest accent, "I'm upper class, and I look down on him!" (pointing at Barker). Barker, in a tweed jacket with leather elbow patches, says, "I'm middle class, and I look down on him!" (pointing at Corbett). Corbett, in a tatty old jacket and collarless shirt, hunches his shoulders, looks at the ground, and says, "I'm working class, and I know my place!" The Python team were always brilliant when commenting on the British social structure, and we should remember that Britain is ruled by Capricorn.

Both England (born at the time of the coronation of William the Conqueror, 1066) and the United Kingdom (1801) were born with the Sun in Capricorn. While the two charts are different, there is no argument about the Sun-sign. Knowing one's place is a cultural defence system against collective anxiety. A class system of the British type is entirely in keeping with a collective psyche which operates along Capricornian lines, because it is a means of creating safety. If one knows one's place in society, one can feel secure – even if one's favourite pastime is blaming everyone else for the nasty consequences of the class system. If this collective defence system breaks down, as it has been doing gradually since the First World War, enormous anxiety is unleashed. Some other form of defence then becomes necessary, or social disintegration ensues. The same may be said for many Capricorn individuals. Knowing one's place, whether this is defined by social class, professional status, marriage, financial standing, ideology, or spiritual allegiance, defines one's identity. It is one of Capricorn's fundamental defences against internal and external chaos.

Audience: Have you found that the decanate in which the Sun is placed refines this? For example, would the Sun in the second decanate of Capricorn, which is Taurus' decanate, identify its "place" with material security?

Liz: Yes, I would say so. I find the decanates very useful, and they do seem to reflect subtler levels of each sign. I would expect the Taurus decanate of Capricorn to utilise material objects and money, and the status these might bring, as a defence system and a means of defining one's "place". The third decanate, the Virgo decanate, might rely heavily on facts, information, training, or a job which is useful to society. But beneath these variations the main drumbeat of the sign can still be heard.

The polarity of earth and fire

Audience: Do you think the *puer aeternus* could be an attribute of Virgo? Could it be a Virgo defence?

Liz: I would like to leave a discussion of mythic patterns of defence, like the figure of the *puer* or eternal youth, until a little later. Myths, which can be linked to particular signs and planets and configurations, can give us a lot of insight into the archetypal background of defence mechanisms and their essential meaning and teleology, as distinct from their apparent pathology. But I wouldn't associate the *puer* with Virgo. I think he is more relevant to understanding the defences of air and, to a greater extent, fire. What do you think fire is most frightened of?

Audience: Death. Mortality.

Liz: Yes, fire is frightened of mortality. But more than mortality, fire fears insignificance. The fact that we all must die one day, like the rest of nature, carries with it, for fire, the implication that as individuals we have no more significance than a rabbit, a cabbage, or an earthworm. The element of fire reflects that in us which we experience as divine – the power of imagination –

and this sense of divinity is linked to an individual feeling of specialness, uniqueness, and god-given destiny. Fire is the element of the divine child. To live and die without there being any point to it, anything special in it, is the great terror of fire. For this reason fire's natural defences tend to be Oedipal in nature, because these defences are aimed toward preserving a sense of uniqueness, specialness, and individual importance. Although there may be a wide range of what we could call pathological patterns linked with fiery defences, the *puer* is not pathological. He is a mythic image of the aspiration toward immortality, which ensures that mortal life is imbued with meaning and significance.

Grandiosity on various levels is another characteristic fire defence, and all three fire signs, to a greater or lesser extent, tend to exhibit a tendency toward self-aggrandisement or self-mythologising. Without it, what are we? Any old hedgehog, oak tree, or mushroom. What is there about one's life that is special, unless one creates that sense of specialness oneself? In order to assert the claim of being someone important and unique, fire has a great range of defence mechanisms linked with the Oedipal pattern on a symbolic level, one of which is the pursuit of immortality. The ferocious competitiveness of the Oedipal defence system is really a way of saying, "I matter, and to prove it I will show that I can win over all the competition. That makes me a hero or heroine, a child of the gods." Remember that, in myth, the great heroic figures are all parented by a god or goddess, and they are therefore in a position to claim celestial immortality, while ordinary mortals must descend into the underworld as shades. In the ancient world, the belief in celestial immortality began to emerge as a powerful religious and philosophical current in around the 4th century BCE, coincident with and focused on the cult of Apollo as the Sun-god, the Lord of Eternal Fire. Many forms of spiritual aspiration belong to fire's range of defences. This doesn't mean that such aspiration is invalid or purely defensive. But there is a defensive component in our insistence on the immortality of the soul. It is tantamount to saying, "I refuse to accept the fact that I am merely a piece of organic tissue which decays after death." Aspirations to immortality can be a defence against the insignificance of a creature of earth, which will one day return to the dust from which it came.

The issue here is not whether our spiritual convictions are true or not. It is a question of the extent to which the urgent necessity to prove one's specialness becomes so intense that it stifles other life possibilities and other means of adaptation. If one identifies too much with the *puer,* and one's self-mythologising reaches too great an extreme, one cannot live an ordinary life. One is unable to cope with the requirements of everyday existence. One can't face ageing, or dealing realistically with money, or disciplining oneself to work, or handling necessary mundane responsibilities such as cooking or washing up. Someone else is expected to do all that. One falls apart in panic at the slightest sign of illness. One can't bear it if one is ignored. Then the individual is dominated by his or her defence system, and the quality of life is damaged or destroyed in the process. We were talking earlier about Marlon Brando, and this might help us to understand, at least in part, what might have happened to him.

In the normal run of things, fire relies on a sense of immortality as a basic defence, and immortality depends on some essence that exists beyond the corporeal level of reality. Anyone here with a lot of fire in the birth chart will probably deeply resent the suggestion, generally made by the orthodox psychiatrist as well as the atheist, that actually there is no such thing as the psyche. You all know the dogma. The psyche, and indeed, the illusion of "I", are merely the product of chemicals in the brain, and the belief in an immortal spirit is pure wish fulfillment. Any belief in an afterlife is a sublimation of the longing to squeeze back into the timeless bliss of mother's womb. And so on. This is, in effect, what material science tells us, and it is the voice of earth *in extremis*. Naturally a fire sign gets angry and says, "No! I'm not the product of my brain, I'm immortal, I am a child of the gods. I am unique, there is a divine spark in me, and by God, I'll prove it to you!"

Audience: I've got a funny example of that. I used to belong to a group of Marxists. I was very depressed for a time, and very introspective. The other members of the group said these were only "social thoughts" that were passing through my mind, which had no reality. It made me extremely angry.

Liz: Well, Marx didn't have much fire in his birth chart. The Marxist vision is an extremely earthy one. Everything that happens in history is related to social and economic factors, without a thought for human imagination and aspiration. Marx had the Sun and Moon both in Taurus, with a Cancer Ascendant. There is no affirmation of the individual creative spark in Marx's thinking. In his example, you can see how political systems are created by individuals through their own particular perceptions of reality, as reflected by their birth charts. Of course there are people with Sun and Moon in Taurus and Cancer rising who feel differently about life. We cannot take these placements alone and assume that only the fire signs have any vision of immortality. But Marx is typical of an extremely defensive dimension of earth, which must provide a material explanation for everything that happens in life. If there are other reasons for events taking place, these must exist on a non-rational and non-corporeal level, and this is terrifying to the very earthy psyche.

Jung was typical of the Sun in fire. He observed people for a while and then said, "There is more than just a seething *id* in there. There is a Self. There is something unique within the individual which is godlike." Jung preferred to use a neutral word which doesn't carry obvious religious connotations. But all the same, throughout his psychology, there is an implicit and sometimes explicit affirmation that there is something immortal within the individual. Freud had the Sun in Taurus, and there is no trace of immortality to be found in his work. What we find in Freud is the implicit statement, "Look, the best you can hope for is to make peace with reality, and that means making peace with your instincts and understanding as much as you can about how they dominate your life." It is not surprising that many Freudians are Marxists in terms of their political persuasion; the psychology and the politics can be made to fit together. One cannot take Jung's perspective and make it work with Marx, however hard one tries. The two are really mutually exclusive.

As with political systems, so too with psychological systems. It is very useful to take the charts of those people whose psychological theories one most admires, and see how these relate to one's own chart. We feel affinity with other people's frameworks of ideas because they serve our particular need to create a defence system against what we fear most. Each system of thought is valid, but not for everybody, just as the defences we have are appropriate for us as individuals, but might not work for another person.

We may find a chart with, for example, the Sun in Taurus and the Moon conjunct Jupiter in Sagittarius, with Saturn in Virgo trine the Sun and the Ascendant in Aries. We cannot then say, "Ah, here is an earth sign, and therefore the defences will be anal and reflect a withholding or controlling tendency." The individual has two conflicting sets of needs, and both will claim the right to survival. The difficulty is that each one's survival is the other's threat of extinction. Everything in the horoscope wants to survive; every planet wants the right to live. These symbols describe living energies within the individual, which the ancients understood as gods. But the claim of one planet for the right to live may fly directly in the face of another planet, which says, "If I let you live, I won't survive." This is one way of understanding the dynamics at work within the horoscope.

Marx is not a bad example of this kind of conflict between different needs, each of which threatens the other. He had the Sun and Moon in Taurus, but he was born under a conjunction of Uranus and Neptune in Sagittarius.

Although this conjunction squares a Pluto-Chiron conjunction in Pisces, it doesn't form major aspects to any of his personal planets. The powerful configuration of outer planets in Marx' chart poses a threat to the personal values and thinking of the Sun and Moon in Taurus. It is interesting to reflect on how Marx viewed religion as the "opiate of the masses", an enemy which had to be eradicated. His own very powerful religious instinct, reflecting the aspirations of the collective at the time in which he was born, posed a threat to his sense of identity. Therefore it had to be crushed. He was a self-proclaimed atheist. Yet his politics constitute a kind of religion.

The Uranus-Neptune conjunction in Sagittarius reflects a powerful religious movement within the collective psyche. The collective seems to be saying, "We are in quest of a world in which God is present and divine meaning can be found." These planets in Sagittarius reflect a strong mystical urge, a desire to break through existing religious structures to a more direct and redemptive emotional and imaginal contact with the deity. Marx was born with a chart which has both earth and fire strongly emphasised, but the conscious ego is aligned with earth. He defended himself not only against the usual fears of earth, but also against something that was part of his generation and was permeating the world at the time he was born. He was terrified by these collective psychic undercurrents because they threatened his sense of personal safety and reality. His political philosophy is in large part an attempt to destroy religious aspiration in order to preserve a concrete view of reality. Whether the philosophy is right or wrong is not the point. It was Marx' individual reality.

Audience: He might have gone the other way, and been a very religious person who hated materialism. Perhaps a religious fanatic.

Liz: Some people might say that he *was* a religious fanatic. A rose by any other name would smell as sweet. But you are right; we cannot always be sure which side of the polarity will dominate, and which area of life the person experiences as most threatening. This depends on which set of values one consciously identifies with. Another example might help to illustrate this. If we look at the chart of Pope John Paul II, we find the Sun and Moon in Taurus in the 9th house – Sagittarius' house – with Saturn rising in Virgo and a Jupiter-Neptune conjunction in Leo trine Chiron in Aries. Again we can see the conflict between earth and fire, and can observe how earthy defences are mobilised against the enemy within, projected on the enemy without.

Unlike Marx, the Pope identifies with a religious world-view, and opposes materialism. But his method of opposition is unmistakably earthy. He relies on dogma, unchanging tradition, and a rejection of any inner or intuitive path which might challenge ecclesiastical authority. His condemnation of astrology and psychoanalysis, as well as Buddhism, reflects this defensiveness against the inner world, and his anachronistic stance on issues such as birth control portray the stubborn defensiveness of a double Taurus faced with a world in flux. Yet the claim to infallibility is a curious echo of the Jupiter-Neptune conjunction in Leo, and also forms part of the defence system. It is both traditionalist and self-aggrandising at the same time.

Sometimes we find the diametric opposite of these two Sun in earth examples, and see fiery people who display anal defences of a very marked kind, or earthy people who behave in an intensely Oedipal and competitive fashion. Or we might find airy individuals whose main line of defence is obviously oral. When the birth chart shows an emphasis in a particular element, this doesn't automatically mean the ego is identified with it – especially if the psychologically opposite element is also strongly emphasised. When such dichotomies appear, usually we will find an earth-fire or air-water axis strong in the chart.

An earthy temperament may exhibit characteristic defences against the onslaught of the fiery realm, but the defences themselves may be infected by the very thing they are erected against. It is a psychological truism that, the more extreme our conscious stance, the more the unconscious opposite will colour our behaviour so that, ultimately, it is very difficult to distinguish between them. We all know how Hitler, at the extreme political right, and Stalin, at the extreme political left, were interchangeable in terms of their tactics. When earth and fire are both strong in a chart, and the person creates powerful defences against one or the other, the results can be very curious. One can sometimes meet earthy people who suddenly experience a powerful spiritual call and embark upon a mission. This is not uncommon. Such people are often terrified by insignificance, which is fire's great bogeyman, not earth's. The collision of these two psychological opposites can create terrific tension. The earthy person who is strongly defended against chaos and disorder, but who carries that chaos within in the form of a good dose of fire, may suddenly decide that he or she is the vessel of God, and go out on the streets preaching. That is what we might expect fire to do. But fire signs are not usually so doctrinal in their defence against mortality and insignificance. More often they are unashamedly megalomaniacal, without resorting to dogma.

Audience: What would we find in the chart, with the sort of thing you've just described?

Liz: When an earthy person suddenly becomes the mouthpiece for God, we might find the Sun, Moon, and/or Ascendant in earth with a stellium in fire, or sometimes only one planet in a fire sign which sits as a singleton by itself in one of the hemispheres of the chart. We might also find Jupiter on an angle, or in strong aspect to the Sun. Sometimes a fiery house is emphasised, which is the case with the Pope. It is also the case with the Ayatollah, who like the Pope had the Sun in Taurus in the 9th with Virgo on the Ascendant. The Ayatollah, not surprisingly, had a stellium of Jupiter, Uranus, Chiron, and the North Node in Sagittarius. When this sort of earth-fire tension is generated, the fiery planets may be totally stifled by the rest of the chart, and then they may begin to defend themselves so powerfully that they dominate the ego and play terrible tricks with the ego's own defences.

Audience: So it is much easier to have no planets in a particular element than to have only one, or a stellium which conflicts with personal planets like the Sun.

Liz: In some respects it is easier, because then one can get away longer with pretending that this realm of life doesn't exist. If you have got one planet in an element, it will fight for its life, just as everything living fights for its life. A singleton by element may fight so hard that it creates extremely powerful defences, which are so compulsive that they completely shatter the equilibrium of the chart and the personality.

Audience: Even if the singleton is Neptune or Pluto?

Liz: Yes, even if it is Neptune or Pluto. Then the defences of the stifled planet will draw on collective yearnings and myths, and have a more global tone. We just talked about Marx, with his Neptune-Uranus conjunction in Sagittarius, unrelated to any personal planets. This conjunction isn't a singleton, but it is nevertheless isolated by the lack of aspects.

Audience: Could a progressed planet moving into an empty element produce this effect?

Liz: When planets change signs by progression it is certainly important, particularly if the new sign belongs to a weak or absent element in the birth chart. We then have a chance to experience something of this new realm which, previously, we might have suppressed, avoided, or projected. But our deepest defences are set at birth, because the inherent temperament contains a natural survival instinct appropriate to its nature. I don't believe inherent defence mechanisms alter their essential nature during one's life. Even in the cases we have been discussing, the natural line of defence is earthy; and while there might be a better way of integrating maverick fiery planets than persecuting unbelievers, nevertheless the ego's orientation is rightly and naturally that of earth. A defence system which is the product of a collision with the environment or a terrible family entanglement, and which is not natural to one's astrological makeup, may change or disappear over time, and this often happens in psychotherapy. It may also happen when an important progressed planet such as the Sun moves into a new sign, or forms a powerful aspect to another planet. But the defences which are part of our basic nature are as much a given as the colour of our eyes.

What happens is that we learn to balance and express our defences better, or sometimes worse, depending on how we respond to experiences. Inherent defences don't go away, and it is probably a dreadful mistake to try to make them do so. They are a fundamental part of one's nature. It is when they start taking over that something has got out of balance. It is quite pointless to tell a Taurean, "Stop being so stubborn!" or to tell a Leo, "Stop thinking you're so special!" or to tell a Virgo, "Don't be so critical!" It is necessary for these signs to express their fundamental strengths as a means of defence. If we tell them to abandon their natural defences, what are we going to give them in exchange? Our own way of doing it? How can one expect another person to feel safe with a defence mechanism alien to his or her nature? Or with no defences at all? So often our difficulties with other people are exacerbated by our inability to understand their defences.

We can tell Capricorn not to be so status-conscious. But while the need to get things right might be translated into other, more introverted or less inhibiting expressions, nevertheless Capricorn must get things right. If society's law is too repressive or shallow a judge, then it will have to be God's law, or the laws of science, or the laws of psychology. But law there must be, and Capricorn must get it right in the eyes of the law. Or we can tell Cancer, "Don't be so clingy." That's tantamount to saying, "Look, go and get a Sun in Aquarius at your nearest shop, please. I don't approve of your particular way of defending yourself against loneliness, because I personally find it difficult." If one simply can't bear living with another person's natural defences, fair enough; perhaps it's time to go. But that is a personal choice, not a declaration of the psychological wrongness of the defences.

If a person is so entrenched and fearful that he or she is totally identified with one frame of reference, one mode of perception, one psychological function, the psyche itself may try to create a better balance because such an extreme position may lead to a breakdown of some kind if the person is put under pressure. If one identifies totally with a single element and is heavily defended against all other spheres of life, one may be heading for serious trouble. Sometimes the sudden eruption of an isolated or suppressed planet, or a weak or stifled element, is the psyche's way of healing a potentially dangerous lopsidedness. The thing that one is not dealing with may rise up and manifest as a complex, or a highly compulsive defence system such as we have been examining. But suppressed parts of the chart may not always appear in the form of personality defences. They can appear as an illness, or project themselves onto other individuals. There is something in us that tries to achieve an optimum balance which preserves individual psychic health. If the ego walls itself in, the unlived bits must find some way of reaching the light of day, even if it is painful or destructive to one's security and stability. Usually this kind of eruption runs in tandem with an important progression or transit which involves the suppressed element or its planetary significators, such as a Neptune transit in someone very defended against feelings, or a transit or progression involving Saturn in someone very defended against the body and the earthy realm.

Capricorn (continued)

We haven't finished with Capricorn yet. Would any Capricorns like to speak about how they experience their own defences?

Audience: I am very conscious about what other people might be thinking. I suppose my defences take the form of trying to be what they expect me to be.

Liz: The need for collective approval is one of the most characteristic Capricornian defences. The antidote to an excess of it is the fiery Oedipal defence. If one can prove one is really special, it doesn't matter so much what others think. We can work with defences that have become too rigid by cultivating other defences, rather than trying to take inherent defences away. Developing an alternative mode of self-protection may in fact be very creative, and far more effective than telling a Capricorn, "Stop worrying about what other people think." That sounds great on paper, but impossible to do through a conscious act of will. But if we can encourage the fiery sense of doing something special which is truly one's own, then the criticism of the collective doesn't hurt so much. There is another resource on which one can draw.

Audience: I definitely agree.

Virgo

Liz: Shall we move on to Virgo's defences? What is Virgo's great fear?

Audience: Chaos.

Liz: And how does Virgo protect itself against chaos?

Audience: By creating categories.

Liz: Yes, Virgo desperately needs order, as a defence against chaos. Creating categories is a form of imposing order. Like the other earth signs, Virgo needs to have some sense of control over the environment. It needs to feel safe, as do the other two signs. Its methods, however, are different than Capricorn's or Taurus'. Knowledge, for Virgo, is a means of establishing order. Virgo doesn't pursue knowledge for its own sake, as Gemini might; any old knowledge won't do. Virgo seeks knowledge which can create patterns that make sense out of what is nonsensical, and can provide a structure for what is chaotic.

Virgo's defence mechanisms spring from the need to differentiate, categorise, discriminate, weed out, and separate the useful from the useless, because all these efforts serve the creation of order. If these defences become too dominant, Virgo may display what in old-fashioned psychiatric terminology is called "compulsive- obsessive neurosis". This is a clumsy term which implies a pathology, but repetitive ritualistic behaviour is not necessarily pathological. It is in fact one of the most ancient human methods of preserving the safety of the individual and the group. We are often presented with a caricature of exaggerated Virgo defence mechanisms – the person who circles restlessly around the room making sure all the pictures are exactly straight on the wall, or who, *in extremis,* may be seen constantly washing his or her hands. One of the more notorious examples of extreme ritualistic defences was Howard Hughes, the American industrialist and film producer, who toward the end of his life isolated himself in a sanitised room, wore plastic gloves, and would not let anyone near him unless they had been properly cleansed and disinfected. He died in a state of great terror, convinced that there were germs lurking everywhere which might infect and destroy him. Not surprisingly, he had Virgo rising, with a Sun-Uranus conjunction in Capricorn.

Such extreme fear can overwhelm the conscious ego, and defences such as Howard Hughes' reflect a deep terror of disorder or invasion by unknown forces. It may seem funny or absurd to the observer, but the rituals are absolutely necessary for the sufferer, who may become enraged or even violent if the ritual is forcibly interrupted or prevented. Mild ritualistic gestures of this kind are characteristic of many Virgos under stress, and are as valid a means of self-preservation as Taurus' material possessiveness or Capricorn's need for collective approval. Ordering material objects, and repetitive cleansing of the body, are meant to produce a magical effect on the cosmos. By a mysterious act of sympathy, the immaculate order of one's immediate physical reality will keep the forces of cosmic chaos at bay.

Audience: If Virgo can create order in daily life, then the universe itself is in order.

Liz: That's right. One is not making the universe orderly through an act of will, but rather, invoking its inherent natural order as a means of protection, through a kind of unconscious sympathetic magic. Virgo's obsessive punctuality and fussiness become understandable when seen in this context.

Audience: What about Virgo's perfectionism?

Liz: This question always comes up when Virgo is discussed. Perfectionism doesn't actually seem to be connected with Virgo. I think it is much more typical of Libra, and also an attribute of Aquarius. Virgo nit-picks, not in order to get something perfect, but in order to get something that works. Perfectionism implies an ideal against which all objects, people, and experiences are measured. To be a perfectionist, one must have a fantasy or ideal of something which is without flaw. The earth signs are not by nature idealistic in this way. They are too pragmatic, and often find the abstractions of the air signs meaningless or irritating, because ideal images don't exist in this world. The earthy temperament is not concerned with creating an alternative intellectual or imaginal reality against which to measure physical reality. It is not perfection that drives Virgo; it is a need to ensure that everything works with maximum efficiency. Anything that is creating disorder or inefficiency is at fault. When Virgos carp, they are not saying, "You are not living up to my ideal of perfection." They are saying, "You're threatening my sense of order; your behaviour is creating chaos. Clean up your act."

Audience: What about the pursuit of excellence ?

Liz: Excellence is only relevant to Virgo if it will in some way help to create order. If Virgo strives to get a First at University, or aims to produce a well-crafted product, the motive doesn't spring from an ideal of excellence (which is airy) or a desire to compete with others (which is fiery). Virgo will often seek results of the highest quality because this can help to create a life which is stable, orderly, refined, under control, and less likely to cock up later. There may be great satisfaction in making a beautiful object, or doing the best possible job; but this is a private satisfaction, not aimed at public display, because it creates the inner serenity Virgo needs. All the earth signs deal with and defend what is, not what might be, should be, or once was. Right here and now is the world they know. They defend themselves, not by aspiring toward an alternative reality, but by doing everything in their power to secure what they know to be safe, so that no one can take it away from them. And their world must be stable, hierarchical, and orderly. Change may be totally acceptable, but only as a planned improvement on what is known. Change which leads to the unknown is frightening.

Audience: I find very often that a particular sign shows the characteristics of the opposite sign. I know one or two Virgos who behave like Pisceans. They are very chaotic and messy. How does this sort of polarisation happen?

Liz: All signs may display examples which seem to deviate from what we might expect, mainly because no person is a pure example of a single sign. Also, although the defences may always be consistent, the level on which they express themselves may not always be the same, depending on what else is going on in the birth chart. Virgo will often express the need for order on the material level; that is the most natural arena in which earth signs can create stability. But if a particular Virgo has a strong Jupiter, or planets in Sagittarius, or a strong Neptune, or planets in Pisces, then he or she may be quite messy on the material level, because intellectual, artistic, or spiritual order may be more important than material order. In such cases you will usually find that the person's thinking is extremely orderly, or his or her world-view and spiritual convictions are tidy and arranged in precise and comprehensible categories. Also, even messy Virgos usually talk all the time about how messy they are, and how little time there is to do all the things they should be doing. They may be out of control on the material level, but they are constantly haunted by it, and torture themselves by carrying about lists of all the minutiae which haven't been dealt with. Messy Sagittarians and Pisceans usually don't even notice that they are messy; and the definition of messiness is relative, after all, depending on one's own standards. I don't think what you are describing is really the opposite sign showing through.

In many ways opposite signs echo each other, because they share a mutable, cardinal, or fixed axis, and have a similar quality of energy. Virgo and Pisces are both extremely fluid, receptive, and refined, and therefore they are both intensely vulnerable. They cope with their vulnerability in different ways, but they are the two most sensitive of the zodiacal signs. They can both display psychism, and Virgo often exhibits mediumistic qualities that ordinarily we associate with Pisces. And Pisces likewise can display the need for a safe cosmic system which can be magically invoked for protection against loneliness.

Earlier, we looked at the ways in which Taurus and Scorpio each fear the thing the other represents, and the same may be said of Virgo and Pisces. Virgo fears the emotional chaos of Pisces, which threatens to flood rational consciousness with uncontrolled feelings and fantasies. Pisces fears the discriminating intellect of Virgo, which threatens to sever the state of emotional fusion which is so important to the water signs. But each sign is loyal to its own defence mechanisms. When a Virgo behaves like a textbook Pisces, you will usually see Pisces or its two planetary rulers powerful in the chart. The individual may then display characteristic Virgo defences on a level other than the material one, or in some highly specific area of material reality, such as all the books arranged alphabetically on the shelf, or all the blue shirts hanging together in the wardrobe.

Capricorn's need for collective approval may not come out in conventional social snobbery. It may be expressed in a specific professional context, in which only the opinions of one's fellow surgeons, car mechanics, cat breeders, physicists, or astrologers matter; everyone else can go and you-know-what. It may surface in a religious context, because some Capricorns turn their backs on the material world. Their hierarchy may be a religious one. There are grades of evolution of souls, or grades of approval by God or one's fellow seekers. We might then expect to find a strong Jupiter or Neptune, or a full 9th or 12th house. Virgo's order may not always be material, any more than every

Taurus necessarily wants stability through multiple numbered Swiss bank accounts. The Pope is probably not especially materialistic, although with Jupiter conjunct Neptune in Leo he may love all the grandeur; but his stability is found in the enduring body of Mother Church. Taurus may also turn Rousseau-like (Jean-Jacques Rousseau, by the way, had the Moon conjunct Neptune in Taurus) and "go back to nature" in a completely non-materialistic environment where one eschews meat-eating, weaves one's own cloth, and despises the middle class. Such Taureans are not interested in accumulating money, but the Taurean defence against change, and the need for absolute stability in the enduring body of Mother Earth, are obvious.

The element of water: Cancer

Earlier, we looked at oral defences in relation to the element of water. All three water signs express the need for emotional fusion as a defence against loneliness and extinction. We should now look at each of these signs individually. What about Cancer? How are its defences most likely to manifest?

Audience: A sense of belonging might be a defence.

Liz: Yes, I would agree with that. Many Cancers feel an almost desperate need to belong and to be needed. Do we have anyone here today with the Sun in Cancer? Would any of you care to comment on what you fear most?

Audience: When I first came to England, one of the biggest fears I had was of the food.

Liz: That's not a defence, that's a realistic assessment of the situation.

Audience: I couldn't go into a restaurant without worrying about whether I might get food poisoning, or find the food completely inedible. Everybody said that when I came to England I would have a bad experience with the food.

Liz: You may know the joke we tell people from abroad who are thinking of visiting here. If you like the weather, you'll love the food. But evidently this was more than a joke for you, it was a real fear.

Audience: Yes. I don't usually take other people's comments so seriously, I try to find things out for myself.

Liz: What might this mean? The first thing you think of when you arrive is the potential unpalatability of the food. Many Cancers are reluctant to travel to unfamiliar places because they fear isolation. Even when Cancer does pack its bags and hit the road, one may have to endure stomach upsets, constipation, or a general state of irritability, anxiety, and sleeplessness, beneath which lies fear. Cancer may be frightened of not being able to speak the language, and therefore of not being able to communicate with or relate to anyone. This is the archetypal fear of not belonging. Cancer's defences are mobilised as a means of preserving relationships and fending off isolation. For many Cancers, the comfort and warmth of relationship are symbolised by food. Nourishment must be available. For many people food constitutes primal emotional as well as physical nourishment, and certain eating disorders, in particular compulsive eating and bulimia, may, in part, be bound up with the feeling of being emotionally starved. The Moon and its sign are both deeply connected with the emotional level of nourishment, because when we take nourishment from the breast in infancy, it is not merely physical food. We feel loved, wanted, and protected. We are at one with the source of life. Compulsive eating may sometimes reflect a desperate need for a fundamental emotional nourishment which one feels was denied early in life.

Audience: Could Princess Diana's bulimia be connected to this?

Liz: It is likely. She has the Sun in Cancer, trine Neptune in Scorpio and also trine Chiron in Pisces in the 2nd house. Here the emotional issues are related to the physical body, with Chiron's placement in Taurus' natural house. Bulimia, which involves a swing between compulsive eating and compulsive vomiting of the food, may be linked with very deep feelings of emotional hunger and deprivation, combined with great rage toward the source of nourishment one longs for so much. It is a compulsive need to get as much as one can because any moment it might be taken away. But then the humiliation of realising one's dependency hits, and rage compels the utter rejection of the thing that an hour earlier one so compulsively needed. We can see a different but related pattern in anorexia, which may reflect an attempt to forcibly disengage from overwhelming feelings of helplessness and neediness. One is going to prove that one is strong enough to do without the nourishment. It is a desperate attempt to free oneself from a powerful, humiliating, and threatening need for fusion. A Freudian might interpret anorexia as an anal defence against unresolved oral needs. Anorexia, as well as the vomiting phase of bulimia, may be a means of denying and withholding, in order to protect oneself from the intolerable pain – and potential danger – of needing something which one knows one is never going to have, or which might turn out to be poisonous rather than life-giving.

For the water signs, and for Cancer in particular, loneliness is a kind of death. We need to understand this about the sign, especially if one doesn't have it in one's own chart. Many of the less appealing Cancerian behaviour patterns which sometimes cause difficulties with other people – in particular the manipulative tactics, evasiveness, and tendency to use emotional blackmail – become comprehensible if we remember that, for Cancer, loneliness is not merely an unpleasant experience one has to put up with for a while. It is extinction. Isolation may frighten a Cancer more than anything else, and companionship may be symbolised by food because the two are the same at the beginning of life.

The identification between food and the warmth of human company is not limited to Cancer. When we want to show our friendship to someone, we invite them round for dinner. Food is our symbolic currency for the establishment of relationship. If we like someone, we go out for a meal with them. Businessmen organise lunches to court prospective clients. This establishes a human contact, and is more pleasing than inviting someone to sit in one's office and stare at one's fax machine. We even express this identification of food and relationship in a religious context, in the Mass, in which the participants actually eat the flesh of the redeemer in the form of a wafer. This digesting of the godhead as the source of life and love isn't limited to Christianity; it existed as a ritual practice in all the redeemer cults which flowered at the beginning of the Christian era. The cults of Mithras and Orpheus had communion meals during which the participants symbolically ate the body of the god, in the form of bread and wine or water. We achieve emotional fusion through taking nourishment from the other person, and giving them our own nourishment in return.

Audience: Might obesity then be a defence against loneliness?

Liz: Yes, sometimes. Not every individual with a weight problem eats for this reason, but it is a very common factor, perhaps combined with other issues as well, such as the repression of powerful emotions like rage. Obesity can also be a defence against others getting too close, or against the possibility of a sexual relationship. However politically correct one might wish to be, and however much one might complain about the tyranny of collective definitions of beauty, being very fat can in fact be an excellent way of discouraging potential sexual partners, at least in the West where we equate desirability in both sexes with a slim, fit body. Sometimes, in young girls, obesity is a way of avoiding sexual competition with the mother. Sometimes compulsive eating is unconsciously meant to preserve the primal bond with an archetypal "good" mother, particularly if the early relationship with the actual mother was experienced as insufficient or destructive. This means avoiding any actual relationships, which would require a separation from the mother which is intolerable.

Paradoxically, Cancer may actively push others away through eating problems, and it is not easy to understand if we assume that relationship always means an actual flesh-and-blood person in the here and now. Water is the element of feeling, and we assume this means needing other people in a literal sense. But if the first person we need is unavailable, rejecting, or cruel, we may never be able to stop seeking her, and then other relationships cannot compete with the imaginary fusion generated by constant eating. We will look at this issue more closely when we get to Pisces, and you will see how it can take the form of a retreat into a drug- or alcohol-induced state of fusion with an imaginary source. Many watery temperaments are deeply defended against actual relationship because they are still trying to recreate the primal relationship.

Water signs may use food as a means of defence against the kind of relationship which requires two independent individuals to recognise each other's otherness. They may also use other methods of defence for the same end. I mentioned the Piscean propensity for addictive substances. Scorpio often seems deeply defended against relationship because of its proclivity for isolation, as well as destructive behaviour which may drive the partner away. But this is not a defence against relationship; it is a clinging to the primal relationship, which must be preserved at all costs. For Scorpio, the surrogate might not be food; it might be a spiritual commitment of a peculiarly intense kind. I have seen enough examples of the intensely religious, anti-sex kind of Scorpio to recognise that God may also be a surrogate for that primal bond. Real people can constitute a threat to the primal relationship, because they require a degree of separateness that the person is not prepared to give.

Because the water signs need a sense of emotional fusion as a defence against isolation and extinction, it doesn't automatically follow that they are going to rush about throwing their arms around people. The watery defence system may seem as though it is doing the opposite to what we might expect.

But when we look more carefully, we can see that in fact some watery temperaments are doing everything in their power to defend a uroboric fantasy-relationship that they cannot relinquish. It is not the personal mother; it is a universal life-source. This is why the realm of the spirit can, with some individuals, be a kind of oral defence, and why Mother Church may provide the celibate priest with everything he needs emotionally. Real people, especially women, may be experienced as a threat to fusion, and have to be kept out.

Pisces

We know that alcohol and drugs are often Pisces' line of defence against separateness. What other defences might be characteristic of Pisces?

Audience: Music.

Liz: Can you elaborate?

Audience: I think some Pisceans can be obsessed with music, with the beat, with the rhythm.

Liz: You are talking about an ecstatic state, which is similar to the state induced by drugs. Ecstasy is a state of fusion. Whether the ecstasy is experienced through a mass of people in a disco moving to an insistent beat, or through a mother-substance that one shoots into one's arm, the feeling of being taken out of oneself – which is what the word "ecstasy" actually comes from in Greek – is a form of defence against loneliness and oblivion.

Audience: And boredom.

Liz: How do you define boredom?

Audience: Lack of stimulation.

Liz: Presumably you mean emotional stimulation. Boredom is an interesting word. We are bored by something when it lacks life, or doesn't invoke a feeling response in us. People are often boring when they communicate without any feeling. It's a bit like reading a telephone directory. There's nobody home, so we get bored and stop listening. Emotional stimulation, for you, seems to provide a connection, a sense that you are not alone. This may be true for most water signs, which need a combination of imaginative and emotional stimulation as a defence against the barrenness and bleakness of loneliness. We may get some insight here into why the creative process can also be a defence for the water signs. Immersed in the imaginal world, one is not alone. One has all the gods with one, and all the denizens of the mythic realm. Poetry, music, and drama, which are the most characteristic creative expressions of Pisces, are examples of the way in which a defence can also be the most rewarding and life-supporting thing we can do.

We can begin to understand certain Piscean defences of an extreme kind by recognising that ecstasy, even in solitude, is a defence against loneliness. Extreme Piscean defences might look like they are anti-relationship mechanisms. There is nothing particularly relationship-facilitating about locking oneself in one's room and shooting up, or falling down in an alcoholic stupor. But these may be attempts to preserve a state of ecstasy, which is really a relationship with a primal source. This state of fusion is the very first state we experience, first in the womb and then at the breast. In this blissful place there is no pain, loneliness, suffering, conflict, or mortality. It is the Paradise Garden before the Fall, and at all costs one must defend that place against the intrusion of the outside world and the suffering that actual relationships might bring. The word "Paradise" comes from the Persian, and means "a walled garden of delight". Water sign walls are aimed at keeping the serpent out, because the serpent brings time, change, death, and isolation.

Scorpio

We can view some of Scorpio's characteristic defences in this context as well. What is the nature of Scorpio's notorious possessiveness? We often use the term to describe Scorpio's behaviour in close relationships. But what does it mean?

Audience: Fear of being alone.

Liz: Yes. But all the water signs fear being alone. How is Scorpio different? Why possessiveness, rather than heroin or cream cakes?

Audience: Fear of being hurt.

Liz: Everyone is afraid of being hurt; that isn't exclusive to the water signs. Can you look more carefully at Scorpionic possessiveness, and what it is really saying or attempting to do?

Audience: It ensures that the loved one is always the same.

Liz: Yes, I think we are getting closer to it. Possessiveness attempts to create a bond that will not alter. The bond is absolute, fixed, eternal, and can never be disturbed or broken apart by betrayal or by feelings given to other people. Possessiveness is a means of defending oneself against loneliness through rendering the loved object not only absolutely one's own, but also absolutely predictable. No fluctuation in mood or feeling is permissible. Fusion for Scorpio is not a fluid state of ecstasy. It is an immobile and eternal union, impervious to time and change. Any sign of emotional energy being given elsewhere can provoke terrible vindictive feelings in a deeply insecure Scorpio. Such destructiveness comes from a place of great fear, and it is Scorpio's way of defending itself against the horror of betrayal, humiliation, and isolation. Scorpio might not fear physical death if the death is chosen, since death is only a route back to the source. But the kind of death represented by broken pride and the isolation which comes from powerlessness may be a far more threatening prospect.

All the water signs share the fear of isolation, but they utilise different means of defences. These defences can be enormously creative. Cancer's need to belong is a fundamental part of this sign's gift of empathy and nurturing. Pisces' retreat into the imaginal world can produce works of art. Scorpio's need to fix bonds in an unchanging state can produce extraordinary loyalty, commitment, and courage. But in some cases the defences are so extreme that the person is taken over by them. Then the Cancer produces hysterical symptoms or looks like a beach-ball, the Piscean overdoses on the bedroom floor, and the Scorpio goes on a rampage and murders his wife as well as her lover.

Audience: Why does Cancer produce hysterical symptoms?

Liz: Some people with an emphasis in Cancer can sometimes display a propensity for hypochondria. They may whine on endlessly about imaginary ailments, or little aches and pains which other signs wouldn't bother mentioning. When this happens, it may be a way of making sure that other people are attentive and concerned. Illness can be a means of ensuring closeness and constant company. I am not suggesting that all illnesses spring from this root. But many do, especially the ones which have no organic basis and often seem to be so carefully timed for when one's partner is about to go away on a business trip. "Don't forget me," the person is saying. "I'm here, and I'm lonely. If I'm ill maybe you will give me attention, and you'll feel too worried and guilty to go away." Many of the qualities that we find difficult about the water signs are extreme forms of a defence mechanism which is basically healthy and necessary, and preserves the human contact which these signs need so much. The earth signs can generally cope much better with isolation. It may not be fun, but earth can take it, as long as the world remains where one last left it. Water, on the other hand, can cope with chaos far better than earth. It doesn't really matter that much if everything is falling to bits around you, as long as the people you love are with you.

Other types of water sign defences

Audience: Can you talk about the refinements of these defences? I think water signs have a lot of variations on a theme.

Liz: Yes, you are right; this might be a good time to discuss the subtler levels of the basic defences we have been looking at. These refinements all spring from a central core, which in the water signs is the fundamental defence against separateness. I have mentioned addictions, and also certain aspects of hysterical behaviour. Hysteria can reflect a disintegration into emotional chaos, a state of emotional ecstasy (experienced through pain as easily as through pleasure), which creates a sense of fusion with the life-source and manipulates others into becoming caretakers. Another variation on the watery theme is idealisation. If we elevate someone, and perceive him or her as being so beautiful, good, gifted, and perfect that he or she can always be absolutely trusted and will never hurt us in any way, we are defending ourselves against recognising that individual as an ordinary, separate, limited human being. Such a recognition involves being separate and ordinary ourselves. We may idealise a lover, child, parent, teacher, friend, racial or social group, political platform, or country. We may also idealise our pets, or our bodies, or another person's body. Whatever the object, the process is the same, and we infuse the other with transpersonal, superhuman, or redemptive qualities which ultimately they cannot possibly sustain.

Idealisation preserves the illusion of a unity which doesn't exist. We can see it very clearly in people who have experienced dreadfully painful childhoods, yet idealise the parents who have hurt them so much. Often such people come for a chart reading or a counselling session, and one can see very dark, unpleasant family configurations, such as a T-cross between a Mars-Saturn-Pluto conjunction in the 10th house, Chiron in the 1st, and the Moon in the 4th. One might say, "Tell me something about your family background," and the person replies, "My parents were absolutely wonderful. I had a perfect childhood. My mother was the best of mothers." And one thinks, "Hang on a minute, have I calculated the chart wrongly, or is all of this psychological interpretation rubbish, or is this client lying through the teeth? What is happening here?" Over time, in a therapeutic situation, the idealisation begins to break down, and the real feelings connected with the family pattern come to the surface. This is invariably a critical and deeply disturbing rite of passage. Many people quit therapy just at the point where their idealisations begin to shatter, because they cannot face going through the painful, dreary process of facing the reality of their feelings. Idealisation is a means of preserving a fantasy relationship, and defending oneself against pain in the real relationship by pretending that the pain doesn't exist.

We all do a little bit of idealising with anyone for whom we care deeply, especially when we fall in love. All of us have watery planets in our horoscopes, if not watery signs. Idealisation is an inevitable part of the process of attraction. On this theme you might read Ethel Spector Person's fine book, *Love and Fated Encounters.* To some extent idealisation is healthy in a relationship. We need to see the beloved as more special than other people, and need to be seen this way ourselves; and this can make both people want to give their best to each other. But excessive idealisation is a defence system which may become too powerful, overwhelming the individual's capacity to relate to another person on a realistic, human level. We idealise gurus whom we believe to be so totally enlightened that everything they say is the absolute and final truth. We idealise children whom we believe will be the redeemers of our own disappointed hopes and unlived talents. We idealise doctors whom we believe will magically know everything that is wrong with us and cure it immediately. Perhaps most strangely, we may even idealise death itself, as a reunion with the source. Pisces and Scorpio may both display this love of death, which is not so much self-destructive as it is an act of idealisation. You can see how idealisation and addiction may play into each other, and how hysteria may be the reaction to an idealisation which has been shattered by someone else's separative behaviour.

Another favourite variation on the watery theme is guilt. Do you understand the difference between guilt and remorse? When we feel remorse, we feel deeply ashamed of what we are or have done. This shame and desire to atone arise from the instinctive knowledge of how it feels to be the person we have injured. There is no escape from the stark humiliation and humility of remorse. Remorse can be transformative; it has the power to ensure that we never repeat the destructive action again. But guilt is quite different in nature. There is no real understanding of what the injured person is feeling. One tends to tell everyone within earshot, "Oh, I feel so guilty!" but one tends to go on repeating the destructive action in spite of the ritual incantation. The incantation is meant to alleviate any feelings of shame, and then one is free of blame because one has declared one's guilt.

It's rather like saying ten Hail Mary's to expiate one's sin. If one feels remorse, one isn't redeemed by ten Hail Mary's. One lives forever with what one has learned about oneself and others, and that changes a person inside, usually for the better. If one feels guilty, then one can do the thing again, and muster up the required guilt afterward. We use guilt as a means of avoiding the acknowledgement of our separateness from others, because separateness involves a sense of responsibility toward others which we might not want to face. We cannot take responsibility for the consequences of our actions if, like little babies, we secretly perceive others as extensions of ourselves.

The water signs, especially Cancer and Pisces, tend to be prone to guilt as a means of defence. In an unhappy relationship, for example, it might be extremely hard for Cancer to say, "Look, this isn't working, I have to go." The threat of separateness and loneliness is too great. Instead, the Cancerian individual may set up a complicated emotional or sexual entanglement about which he or she then feels dreadfully guilty. The guilt is a means of punishing, as well as justifying, the entanglement, and removes the necessity of a separation which might be unbearable. Guilt is also an excellent means of obscuring deeper feelings which are too difficult to face. We tend to talk about our guilt a lot, and even advertise it, and this makes it somewhat suspect. Remorse is actually very painful to talk about, because of the unpleasant and painful self-revelation involved. There is something very facile about guilt.

Audience: Could the need to take care of others and deny the self be a form of defence? There is a lot of this in the helping professions.

Liz: The desire to help or nurture others, which is characteristic of all three water signs, is the natural outgrowth of water's sense of empathy with other people. I would not call that a defence, unless we view such basic characteristics in the widest sense, as a bastion against meaninglessness and extinction. But helping others can become a defence in a more specific and even pathological sense. I think you are quite right – many therapists use it as their defence against personal isolation. That is not necessarily a bad thing, as long as one realises the element of personal gain in the act of helping, and doesn't harbour the illusion that the motive is purely altruistic. There are a great many people in the helping professions who are there because it gives them a sense of belonging. They feel needed, and therefore they are not alone. This is not an inherently negative defence. It can be enormously creative and healing, to both practitioner and client. It is one of the components in the archetypal theme of the wounded healer. But it can become destructive if the need to be needed requires a total abnegation of one's own self. Denying the self in the service of others may be a means of making a kind of secret "deal" with those who are needy. If one is always there, then they will always be there too, and maybe they will give love in return. Behind it we may sometimes find the needy mother, who makes this secret deal with her child. If the child is always there for her, then she will give love and acceptance.

The element of fire: Leo

Shall we move on to the fire signs? We have touched on some characteristic Aries defences already. Fire's great fear, as I think I have said, is the fear of insignificance. Aries defends itself against insignificance by being first and best. What about Leo? How many Leos are here today? Would any of you like to comment?

Audience: I'm afraid of not being valued. Of not being seen as a special creature. I think a large part of my interest in astrology is based on the need to be special.

Liz: So you feel astrology can be a Leonine defence, because it makes you feel special. Actually, it seems to provide a good defence for every sign, in one way or another. It depends on how we use it. But I understand what you mean; a horoscope confirms individual uniqueness. Sometimes I have had a client say, "Is my horoscope unusual?" or "I don't think my chart looks like anyone else's." This is what you are describing – the need to have one's own special destiny and nature confirmed by astrology.

Audience: What about the fear of not being free?

Liz: I am not sure I would associate this with Leo. The fear of being trapped, controlled, or stifled may be linked to several different issues, and several signs as well as particular aspect configurations may reflect this fear. The demand for freedom then becomes a defence, although we need to look more deeply to find out what the threat really is. Gemini may fear being intellectually stifled; Aquarius may fear the loss of fundamental rights; Sagittarius may fear the loss of mobility; Scorpio may fear the loss of pride. All these signs can be heard insisting on their freedom. Also, someone with a particular emotional conflict, such as Moon or Venus in Cancer square Uranus, may use freedom as a defence against great emotional vulnerability. This is identification with one end of an aspect and projection of the other end, as a defence against internal conflict. We will look at this more carefully later.

Audience: I think the difference between Leo and Aries is that Leo seems to need approval from other people more than Aries does. Maybe recognition and fame are a Leonine defence.

Liz: It is an interesting issue. It would sometimes appear, on the surface, that Leo needs approval and affirmation from others, whereas Aries doesn't seem to give a damn. For Aries, the animosity of others may be taken as a compliment: "They wouldn't dislike me so much if they weren't jealous." But one can't win without engaging in competition. For Aries to win, there has to be somebody there to defeat, and also someone to judge the contest. So Aries doesn't exist in a vacuum either. Active courting of approval may not be Aries' style. But the sense of inner potency which is so important to Aries, as a defence against the helplessness and hopelessness of mortal existence, depends on an outer expression of potency in the world.

With Leo, potency in the world outside may not be that important. Obviously we have some glaring historical exceptions, such as Napoleon. On the surface, he seems to be an exception. We will look at him more carefully in a moment. But in the main, for Leo, it isn't a question of feeling potent; it is a question of feeling unique. These are not the same thing. Leo's need is not focused on beating the competition. In many ways Leo is not competitive at all. Other people simply aren't important enough to be considered as competition, because Leo's dialogue is really between oneself and God. This is reflected in the need to experience oneself as having a destiny, because an individual destiny implies that there is some divine power somewhere which says, "You're here for a special purpose; you are my favoured child." This is the core of the hero myth. The inner feeling of being chosen, of being the divine child, is a fundamental aspect of Leo's defence against the extinction of ordinariness. It is the antidote to mortality. Leo may seek that affirmation inwardly, rather than externally in front of a crowd. "Even if nobody else notices it," says the introverted Leo, "I know that I am here for a special purpose, even if it takes a lifetime to work out what the purpose is."

Many Leos will defend themselves fiercely against even the slightest suggestion that they are just ordinary creatures of clay like everybody else. They may live very humdrum lives, but harbour secret fantasies of greatness or superiority which reveal the defence at work on the inner level. Two very good examples, whom we should always remember when we want to understand Leo, are Napoleon and Alexander the Great, both of whom were born under this sign. It isn't their conquering propensities which reflect the Leonine vision; this is misleading. Neither man was really performing for anyone else. They were performing for the gods. There have been many conquerors and tyrants throughout history who had no planets in Leo, and two of the worst ones in this century were born under Taurus and Capricorn – Hitler and Stalin.

Audience: Napoleon and Alexander were real heroes, weren't they? In other people's eyes as well as their own.

Liz: Yes, and the operative phrase is "their own". Their power over others sprang not from any calculated effort to please, but from an absolute belief in their own destiny. This can make Leo very charismatic, but the love of the audience is the by-product, not the motive. It is the sense of mission, of a unique and god-given destiny, which is characteristic of both Napoleon and Alexander, and reflects the essential core of the Sun in Leo, as well as its essential defence system. There is a vast difference between seeking power because one feels one has a unique, divinely inspired destiny, and seeking it because one has a compulsion to dominate or win over others. Obviously these two can overlap, given the right chart configurations. No doubt Hitler's Saturn in Leo, perched at the MC of his horoscope, contributed to his own rampant self-mythologising. But Hitler's will to power sprang more from hatred and a sense of inner impotence (Saturn at the MC square Venus and Mars) than from any sense of being a divine child. It was the German people who projected that onto him, with his deliberate encouragement.

If you want to read a truly extraordinary portrait of Leo, you should read Mary Renault's trilogy on Alexander, who was born in "Lion Month".

She displays remarkable insight into the internal conviction of divine destiny which drove him to achieve what he did. He believed that he was the son of Zeus. He had a vision of a united world empire, a conjoining of Greece and Persia, in which both peoples mingled, married, and produced a mixed race which expressed the best and noblest attributes of both. He believed this was his destiny, a divinely ordained destiny. We aren't really in a position to argue with him; perhaps he was right. If we scale this vision down to a Leo living an ordinary life in Great Britain in the 20th century, the vision doesn't change in quality, only in quantity and level of expression. Opportunities to conquer Persia may be somewhat reduced, but the need to shape one's life as a vessel for divine intent – whether one calls it God, love, or the imagination – is just as powerful. Sadly, with many Leos this remains a private fantasy because of other issues and conflicts, and the gap between outer life and the inner dream may lead to severe depression.

Audience: It can also lead to domination.

Liz: Yes. This is where we may see Leo's defences becoming virulent, and then we can speak of the desire to have power over others. This occurs when the defence system dominates the personality. If the Leo individual can't experience an inner sense of destiny, or can't find any outlet – however humble – through which that inspiration can be expressed, where is he or she going to get it from? One favourite place is an adoring audience. Self-aggrandisment of a particularly obnoxious kind may reflect the lack of an authentic inner sense of specialness. It may be a defence against a terrible hollow, empty feeling within. Leo doesn't really need others to affirm his or her specialness, as long as the inner connection is there. Then the defence system works in a healthy and natural way, and provides the impetus for Leo's creativity.

Leo needs God as part of its defence system, although often another word or concept is chosen instead, such as Self, or imagination. Jung, who was a Leo, used the term Self, a good neutral word which avoids conventional religious connotations. It doesn't much matter; we can call it what we like. We can understand from this why Leo is traditionally associated with the artist, even though obviously not every artist is a Leo and not every Leo is an artist. But astrology links the creative process with the 5th house, the Sun, and Leo. Why do we make these links? In myth, the artist possesses divine fire. He may have been born to it, like Hephaistos, or stolen it, like Prometheus. The possession of divine fire means that the artist borrows a little bit of God's infinite creative power in order to make something individual. One has something unique that renders one immortal. If this subsumes other aspects of the personality, then we may see megalomania.

Aries

Aries is not content with an inner sense of divinity and destiny. It is impelled to conquer out there in the world. Although belief in a special mission or cause may be extremely important for Aries, it is actually the most pragmatic of the fire signs, and the vision must be made manifest in some way. The mission means nothing unless it is acted upon, and can change outer reality and vindicate the sense of being first and best. Aries is a crusader. Why do people go on crusades? Crusading may be seen as a defence. It is a very aggressive one, but a defence nonetheless. Why are we impelled to go and convert heathens, with or without their consent?

Audience: To assure ourselves of our own position.

Audience: Because if there is no one to convert, God might not exist.

Liz: Yes, the crusading spirit may be a defence against one's own deep inner doubts. God might not exist, or, perhaps even worse, one's own vision of God might not be the right one after all. Then one is a mere muddled mortal, and not first, best, or divinely inspired. The crusading spirit is also an affirmation of divine potency. The more people one can awaken and inspire, the more one's own potency is proven. This is the same spirit that drives Don Juan on his endless sexual conquests. The more women he conquers, the more potent he appears in his own eyes. We have come full circle, back to the Oedipal pattern so characteristic of this fire sign.

Sagittarius

What about Sagittarius? What matters most to Sagittarius, that must be defended at any price?

Audience: Freedom.

Liz: Go on. What else?

Audience: Faith.

Liz: Would any Sagittarians like to comment?

Audience: Meaning is terribly important. I can cope with anything as long as I feel it means something.

Liz: Yes, I think this is the core of Sagittarius' nature, and also its basic defence system. In common with the other two fire signs, and unlike the water signs, Sagittarius does not depend upon others for its defences. Meaning, for Sagittarius, has to come from inside; it is not sufficient to adopt a conventional religious or spiritual perspective based on someone else's definition of meaning. This intuitive conviction of a meaningful design is essential for Sagittarius as a defence against the threat of inertia and death. The mere suggestion that life has no meaning other than the personal meaning we inject into it, and that there isn't actually any divine plan, can be horrifying to Sagittarius, because this sign's capacity to maintain faith in the future is built on the idea that one is growing, one is evolving, one is always moving towards something. If the sense of the journey and the journey's goal and purpose are taken away, the inner coherence of the individual collapses.

Freedom is important to Sagittarius for very special reasons. It is not an ideologically based claim. Sagittarius doesn't go around with a Bill of Rights in hand as Aquarius might, saying, "Freedom is an inalienable human right!" Nor is it a fear of emotional involvement, as some people might think. Sagittarius does not back off from intense emotion. But it may back off from a commitment which closes the door to new possibilities. Freedom of movement and thought is essential because one must have room to pursue the next clue and discover another piece of the grand design. Sagittarius must always be ready to depart suddenly, in case the clue points to a journey. The secret to living with a Sagittarian is to join the great adventure. It is almost as though the heavens are strewn with magic glyphs, and life is like a treasure hunt. One tries to work out what a particular experience means, and what it is supposed to be teaching, and how one can grow from it. Once that experience has been wrung dry, then one finds the next clue in the next experience. Hopefully, one day it will all be revealed, which, of course, it never is. The design just gets larger and larger.

Denial of the freedom to pursue the clues is a kind of death to Sagittarius. It paves the road to a black despair. Most Sagittarians, although strongly motivated to defend their psychological survival through finding meaning in experience, are also balanced enough to be able to live without having to interpret the significance of every spilled cup of coffee or garden slug. But sometimes this defence can take over the personality, and the individual is no longer able to live in the here and now. Everything must be translated to a universal level, and everything contains a hidden significance or is connected with every other experience by secret chains of meaning. This is a very strange, rather manic world, and some Sagittarians inhabit it on a more or less permanent basis, driven by desperation into defending themselves against life as it is. They are only able to relate to life as it potentially could be, or life as a showcase of magic symbols.

If Sagittarius loses the sense that every experience is meaningful, what is the point of being alive? How can one justify the horror of life? We are born, and we struggle to grow up and survive, and just at the point when we begin to work out what's going on, we are old and then we die. Without meaning, the world of earth is a horror to Sagittarius. If this defence system is taken to its logical extreme, then we may see delusions of total knowledge and enlightenment. This is the manic state which is characteristic of Sagittarius' pathology. "I have the truth," says Sagittarius. "Never mind reality, I have the truth, direct from God. I just *know*. Don't confuse me with facts, because they are irrelevant." The spiritual or political dogmatism common to certain Sagittarians may be a defence against the loss of meaning. And certain experiences in life, such as the Holocaust or the war in the former Yugoslavia, do defy our efforts to read meaning into them. They seem like blind horrors, and no divine design is evident – only human barbarity. Once upon a time the Church taught us that we should not question the will of God when confronting such experiences; we should simply have faith. This is becoming more and more difficult as we become more psychologically sophisticated. We may exercise intellectual or spiritual gymnastics to impose a design on these events, but this often rings false, and deep down we know it. This can make us defensive and resistant to facing the reality of life's unfairness, or fanatical and intolerant of anyone who might remind us that we don't really know the answers.

As an archetypal figure, the *puer aeternus* is one of Sagittarius' lines of defence. The *puer* needs to be unattached, so that he is free to go on looking for clues. If one selects a particular goal or lifestyle, and commits oneself to it, one might miss out on finding another of those clues that could reveal the meaning of life. Sagittarius' wanderlust, restlessness, and difficulty with commitment do not reflect some inherent fickleness or incapacity to love. They reflect the terror of Sartre's *No Exit*. Do any of you know this play? It is

Sartre's vision of hell: a locked room in which three people are bound to each other unto eternity by highly destructive emotional bonds and no sense of meaning. Not surprisingly, Sartre had a Sagittarius Ascendant. "Don't close all the doors," says Sagittarius, "because if you lock me in I will lose my connection with all that unfolding meaning and purpose, and then I won't know what I'm here for, and I shall die of boredom and despair."

Sagittarius can go into quite a frenzy if all the doors are closed. These people can remain quietly happy and committed as long as one door is left open and there is no armed guard outside. One knows one can come and go. But the moment all the doors are closed, the defences are mobilised, and overwhelming anxiety and rage may ensue. It is important to understand why, just as we need to understand why Virgo gets nitpicky, Cancer gets whiney, and Leo gets pushy. It is not emotional callousness, which is an accusation often levelled at Sagittarius. There is something even more important to Sagittarius than human relationships. That is the freedom to pursue the hidden design. You will all no doubt know that if you miss one of the clues on a treasure hunt, the whole thing is blown.

Audience: Could the philosophical side of Sagittarius also be a defence?

Liz: Yes, I think I touched on this. Sagittarius' propensity to philosophise and put everything in a universal context can be a mode of defence against the banality of personal existence. It can be infuriating if one is very earthy. One might say, "My cat caught a mole this morning," and Sagittarius says, "Ah, I was reading that in Egypt the cat was symbolic of whatnot," and suddenly one has been plunged into mythology and archetypes, when one only wanted to talk about one's cat. It is a defence, sometimes a very obsessive defence, against the horror of banality and meaninglessness. When fire becomes pathological in its defences, it can go manic. Manic behaviour is a special favourite of Sagittarius, but Aries and Leo can also move down this path. Mania, and the manic phase of manic depression, are a defence. We haven't really explored the serious disorders arising from defences, but we could interpret severe psychological disturbances as extreme and desperate defence mechanisms. Manic depression is one of these, and is a characteristic defence of the element of fire.

Mania is understandable enough as a fiery defence. In the manic state one is immortal, and everything seems unbearably significant and connected with everything else by threads of meaning which ordinary mortals cannot perceive. I don't know if any of you have any experience of the manic phase of manic depression, either personally or in clients or loved ones, but once the person begins to "go high", the whole cosmos becomes a kind of hieroglyphic code which in the manic state one can suddenly read. This desperate need to find connections is usually a defence against unbearable feelings of loneliness and insignificance, and the depressive state which invariably follows is the crash that occurs when the treasure hunt runs out of energy and one finally collides with reality. This depression can be crippling, and one may feel quite suicidal. It is as low as the mania was high. At its core, the quest for meaning is a healthy and creative defence, and it forms the basis of many individuals' search for knowledge through astrology and spiritual disciplines. It can also generate a high degree of tolerance and understanding of many different worldviews. But once this cosmological vision becomes inflated with helium and loses all contact with the earth, it can become deeply destructive to the individual's life.

The element of air: Gemini

I talked quite a lot this morning about disengagement and dissociation, which are the main line of defence of the air signs. What do you think Gemini's defences are about? Would any Geminians care to comment?

Audience: I can think of two fears.

Liz: You're entitled to two, being a Gemini. If you were an Aquarian you would only be allowed one.

Audience: I have a terror of being committed. I also have a terror of being limited in my speech and thinking.

Liz: I'm not sure whether these aren't actually the same. You seem to be describing a kind of mental claustrophobia. But what happens when you experience being limited in this way? What limits you? What is the real fear?

Audience: I don't want to be held down. I'm afraid of stagnation, of losing my freedom. Being stuck, not being able to communicate, to circulate.

Liz: You are describing the defence. You want the freedom to think your own thoughts, to communicate as you wish, to move about freely. I'm not yet clear about what you are defending yourself against. I wonder whether it has something to do with being trapped by emotional needs. Freedom on the intellectual level depends on a certain degree of detachment from other people. The moment we need another person, our thinking, our mobility, our speech, are all compromised. This kind of bondage can be a source of great suffering to all three air signs. Ironically, Libra is traditionally associated with marriage. This is quite funny in some ways, since Libra, as an air sign, has little to do with marriage as an emotional commitment. The air signs are often deeply defended against the kind of emotional bondage that a deep relationship involves, and the compromises that are so often required.

Audience: Information is very important to me. If I know what's going on, I can cope.

Liz: For Gemini, information can be a way of preserving independence and maintaining detachment. It is a healthy defence. Gemini needs to be in touch. The more one knows about the world outside, the less likely one is to be trapped in an emotional quagmire. I know many Geminis, and people with Moon or Ascendant in Gemini, who simply must watch the news on television every night, or must have a newspaper to read in the morning. Gossip can provide the same satisfaction to some Geminians. If one isn't in touch with everything that's going on, one might sink down into a terrible swamp. One's mind can no longer provide an escape route from difficult emotions. One's orientation is gone, and one may be at the mercy of things one can't see. If Gemini doesn't have names for things, it can be attacked and hurt from behind, like Siegfried, who was stabbed in the back. The vulnerable place is from behind, from the secret emotional needs and conflicts which one can't see and doesn't understand.

Audience: Then it's a form of control.

Liz: Yes, it's a form of control. It is control through knowledge rather than control through withholding, so we cannot call it an anal defence. It is something quite different. If we are needy and vulnerable, we can be destroyed by other people. The realm of feeling, for Gemini as well as Libra and Aquarius, can seem like the Creature from the Black Lagoon, or Jaws. One can be suffocated, trapped, destroyed. We are at the mercy of other people, who might eat us alive because we need them too much to get away quickly enough.

Audience: But the air signs need feedback from other people. That is a kind of dependency.

Liz: Up to a point, yes. But a desire for feedback isn't the same as emotional need. Libra is notorious for asking advice from everyone, but in the end the Libran will usually do what he or she wanted to do in the first place; the feedback serves the purpose of helping to clarify a half-formed idea, and also gives the Libran a good sense of how to present it in a manner best suited to enlisting cooperation. Aquarius also likes to be involved with others, and share ideas and ideals. But once again, the need is not based on an emotional dependency or a desire for emotional closeness. It is based on a need for defining truth, and the more viewpoints one examines, the closer one can get to something which stands as an objective truth. The affirmation of others gives validity to the truth of the idea, and also confirms its universal or general application. Feedback gives the air signs a chance to achieve a higher level of objectivity. It is in fact the opposite of emotional dependency. Also, some air sign people are very introverted, and formulate concepts independent of any collective validation. An extroverted air sign may want constant input from others, because he or she may not feel equipped to accept an idea as true without this support. An introverted air sign may reject input because it contaminates the inner purity and truth of the idea.

The air signs may seek to create a system of knowledge as a means of defence against the unknown depths. This system may not involve information in the sense of collecting data about the world outside. Gemini is often concerned with information of this kind, but Aquarius is not. Aquarius is a researcher rather than a collector of news, and the sphere to which this sign applies its intellectual powers may be inner rather than outer. But Aquarius too will seek a system of knowledge, as a healthy and creative mechanism of defence. The Saturnian element in Aquarius wants to know what underlying laws are at work in life. That is why Aquarius is traditionally associated not only with astrology, but also with psychology, sociology, and science in general. This is probably an overly simplified association, because there are aspects of these fields which require approaches other than that of the thinking function. But that aspect of astrology, psychology, physics, or any other sphere of knowledge, which involves the creation of a system and the definition of the basic laws which underpin that system, may be of great interest to Aquarius, and may be enlisted as a defence. If the laws of reality are understood and clearly mapped, then one cannot be attacked from behind by unknown, anarchic, or invisible forces.

Libra

For Libra, relationships themselves provide a system of knowledge. Understanding the dynamics of relationship, and the creation of harmony out of conflict or disparity, are for Libra like a Pythagorean exercise in imposing cosmic order and harmony on the disorderly and frightening world of human emotion. "How do relationships work?" Libra asks. "How can harmony be established, how can balance be maintained? How can symmetry be created? What are the laws that govern human interaction? How does society work? How can all the nasty dark bits be eradicated or incorporated into a perfectly functioning system?" In Libra we may find a powerful need to understand and define the principles of human relationship, because then order can be established and there may be fewer unpleasant emotional surprises.

Audience: Sagittarius also creates cosmic systems.

Liz: Not quite. Sagittarius seeks to get a glimpse of a divine order which is already implicit, so that experiences can be correctly interpreted and yield their meaning. Sagittarius doesn't enjoy the careful and painstaking building of a system; it loves "surfing" all the existing systems, in order to extract the connections and intuit the underlying unity. Sagittarius also doesn't mind being surprised, because even a painful experience can contain meaning and contribute to growth and development.

Audience: I think that for Libra, the message is to be fair in any circumstances. That means one has to detach from one's feelings. It imposes an ethical code onto a situation which otherwise might get out of control.

Liz: The moment we postulate ideal concepts of human behaviour, such as fairness, we are dissociating ourselves from human feelings, which will never obey such abstract precepts. When Libra enters a relationship, it enters with a set of preconceived ideal concepts. As you say, one should be fair. One should not be possessive. One should be kind. One should be clear and communicative. One should share responsibilities. Equality should always be recognised. But our feelings don't behave like that. Human beings do not respond in such an orderly fashion on the emotional level. They never have, and they probably never will. Our hearts and groins will always ignore these ideal concepts, because an ideal concept may be utterly inappropriate for an individual situation. Emotions have their own laws, but these are rooted in the immediate situation and reflect the immediate responses of the living individual, who is always in a state of flux. It is this living and unpredictable flux which is so threatening to air's need for consistency. Even Gemini, which often has a reputation for being flighty, unpredictable, and changeable, is not actually all that changeable. The fluctuations in Gemini's moods are regular and cyclical, and the apparent flightiness is usually a defence against a soggy emotional atmosphere. Gemini may not like being pinned down by others, but Gemini's thinking is actually pinned down from within, by an insistent need for logic.

The air signs tend to approach other human beings with their systems of knowledge held firmly in place before them like Athene's shield, because there is nothing quite so threatening to these signs as irrationality. Irrationality means that one could suddenly be brutally hurt. The wonderful edifices of knowledge that air creates form a massive, brilliant, superbly constructed defence against the great horror in life, which is its unpredictability and its capacity to wound and destroy for no apparent reason. Nature can wound and destroy us, which is why we have developed science and technology. Science itself may be seen as a defence against the irrational powers of nature, and scientism, which turns science into a religion, is a very extreme defence against those hidden and terrifying powers over which the human mind has no control. Psychology exists because of the threatening power of the human psyche, and astrology exists because of the unpredictable nature of the cosmos. All our scientific research is a means of protecting us from those elements in life that come out of nowhere and can destroy us. Knowledge of the system is a means of controlling nature in order to prevent nature from controlling us. If we translate this into more basic psychoanalytic terms, dissociation and the building of intellectual systems are a defensive means of defusing the threatening power of the mother, and the equally threatening power of one's own emotional and instinctual needs.

Audience: What is the relationship of this with Virgo? Virgo is also concerned with knowledge.

Liz: Virgo is concerned with order, which is not the same thing. Virgo's order can exist or be created on levels that don't involve the kind of knowledge the air signs seek. For example, Virgo is often deeply attuned to the order of nature. This may not be based on information or a system of knowledge, but on observation and instinct. Virgo's instincts are often highly developed, which is why many Virgos work extremely well with animals, with plants, and with crafts of various kinds which require dexterity and sensitive hands. Such things may not require knowledge, but they do require an instinctive sense of natural rhythms and a feeling for the nuances of physical reality. The Aquarian gardener may buy thirty volumes on how to grow herbaceous perennials; the Virgo gardener will simply experiment with a cutting from a neighbour and see whether it survives the winter. When Virgo is orientated towards a knowledge of abstract principles, we will usually find a lot of air in the chart. We might see Mercury and Venus in Libra, or the Moon in Aquarius, or a strong Uranus. Virgo without air may be perfectly content to remain ignorant of the construction of the plant cells and the Ph rating of the soil, because the cycle of the seasons is reliable and orderly, and if one plant dies then another sort will probably do better in its place.

Audience: Earlier you said something about wounding. That air signs fear anything which might wound them. Can you say more about this?

Liz: I am using the word "wounding" because it conveys a particular kind of experience. Wounding involves something which penetrates our boundaries against our will, which breaks the skin, which makes us bleed, which damages us, which leaves scars or an enduring ache. Experiences which injure without reason are the source of deep suffering for the air signs. Many people can accept hurt in a relationship because they know it is inevitable, and they can pass through the pain and emerge with greater empathy. They do not feel robbed or destroyed; they recognise that human nature is a very variable thing. The water signs may not like being wounded, and hurt pride may be anathema for Scorpio, but water can generally endure the pain, and can find a way of processing and releasing it. But air has a very low pain threshold. Emotional hurts hurt a thousand times more, because they are incomprehensible to air's nature. They not only hurt; they also shatter ideals, and defy those laws on which air relies to survive in life. Also, air signs are often tightly bound by their own ethical codes, and cannot indulge in the kind of emotional release which could allow them to bounce back. "How could this have happened?" says the air sign. "I can't find the reason. I didn't do anything to deserve it. It isn't fair. Why am I bleeding?" It is the bewilderment, the incomprehensibility of the wound, the utter irrationality and amorality of it, which is so terrifying to the air signs. Water may fall about throwing an emotional scene, but behind this necessary release is an underlying attitude of, "Well, yes, people do terrible things to each other even if they love each other. The important thing is the love."

Audience: Air gets a lot of bad press as being unfeeling.

Liz: The reality is quite the opposite. The experience of powerful feeling can be overwhelming and very threatening to air. Nice, positive feelings can just about be tolerated, provided they don't get too messy. But painful ones, particularly primal emotions such as desperate need and global rage, are intolerable. Each element is equipped to work best with one area of life. No person is just one element, so we are of course not talking about individual people. But every element has its own particular domain, and its own range of skills through which it adapts to life. If an element – or, speaking psychologically, a function of adaptation – is faced with experiences which lie out of its domain, it doesn't know what to do. It doesn't cope well, and this is what triggers anxiety and, in turn, the mechanisms of defence. Fire does not cope well with the details and routines of everyday life. This ordinary, solid world can be a place of terror for fire. Those who are earthy and lack fire in the chart may fail to understand the intensity of this fear, and may accuse fire of being lazy and self-centred. But the defence mechanisms of fire, which, as we have seen, usually involve some degree of self-aggrandisement or self-mythologising, do not spring from laziness or selfishness in the ordinary sense. They arise from the fear of being trapped and suffocated in the darkness of matter, which, for earth, is not dark at all, but feels like home.

Equally, earth does not cope well with fire's world. The earth signs may experience deep panic when confronted with the ever-changing, seemingly chaotic flux of fire's invisible reality. If earth is unable to see what it is dealing with, it may defend itself through the virulent negation of anything other than the tangible. "What are you talking about?" says earth. "What inner self? What cosmic design? Where is it? How can it help you earn a living?" Fiery people may not understand earth's resistance, and may accuse earth of being obtuse and unimaginative. Failure to read the cosmic clues is not, of course, a reflection of any lack of intelligence or imaginative ability. There are, in fact, some very idiotic people running about proclaiming intuitive truths, and some extremely intelligent and creative ones who prefer, quite sensibly, to tread very carefully in the domain of the archetypes.

Water, as we know, does not cope well with separateness. It cannot bear being alone and apart. Airy people may not understand how unbearable loneliness can be to the water signs, and may accuse water of being manipulative and on a power trip. But while manipulation may be one of water's weapons of defence, the goal is not domination; it is emotional closeness. And air, as we have seen, cannot cope with emotional suffering for which there is no rational explanation. Naturally it disengages in defence, but this does not reflect a lack of feeling. It is a fear of feeling too much.

Audience: What is the link between the kind of disengagement which Neptune and Pisces practise, and the disengagement of air?

Liz: Pisces doesn't disengage. It may withdraw from individual human company, but that is in order to fuse with something much larger, deeper, and more inward.

Audience: I am a Pisces, and I experience myself as disengaging.

Liz: I don't know what other mechanisms come into play when people get too close to you. There may be other factors in your chart, such as a hard Moon/Uranus or Venus/Uranus aspect, which are triggered when you feel yourself emotionally invaded. But my experience of Piscean withdrawal is that it is not disengagement or dissociation in the airy sense. It may be a dissociation from people outside, and others may experience it that way. Even the Pisces may wonder why he or she is suddenly emotionally distant from a partner or friend and just wants to retreat. But usually this retreat inward is meant to facilitate some kind of internal communion. It is not usually conscious or deliberate. But there is an oceanic inner world into which Pisces may regularly withdraw. This world is full of feeling, but to those outside, the Piscean is emotionally out to lunch. Many Pisceans need periodic retreats of this kind, which serve a renewing and refreshing function, especially if they are artists of one kind or another. One goes "home", and then one returns to external reality cleansed and ready to take on all comers. Such retreats can also be very regressive, in a damaged personality. In an extreme form, they may reflect a narcissistic infantile state, a union with an imaginary Great Mother. Hence we may find drugs and alcohol employed to create this state, as they are surrogate Neptunian mother-substances. Some Pisceans find the meditative state very necessary on a regular, rhythmic basis. They remove themselves from the world of *maya,* and they are at one with an inner reality which no one else can see. They are not alone. Everyone else might feel lonely around the Pisces, but the Pisces isn't lonely. How can one be lonely when one is connected with everything?

If the inner connection is lost, then Pisces may head for the nearest bottle, or the nearest guru. When the wellsprings of the inner source are unavailable, Pisces may find it unbearable, and suicide may seem preferable to that state of existential isolation in which there is no god, no source, toward which one can turn.

Aquarius

Shall we look at Aquarian defences now? Would any Aquarians care to comment?

Audience: I am afraid of dependency.

Liz: Why? What is so threatening about dependency? What do you need so much, that depending on others might threaten or destroy?

Audience: My freedom.

Liz: Freedom for what, and from what?

Audience: Freedom from bondage.

Liz: What kind of bondage? Can you explain more? It is important that we can be precise in understanding what words such as "freedom" and "bondage" mean to each individual. Freedom is something which a number of signs value, but there are many kinds of freedom and many different things which might curtail it, depending on the nature of the zodiac sign.

Audience: It's hard to put into words. But I think it is connected with a fear of forces "out there", irrational forces which might hurt me if I'm not able to be free to defend myself.

Liz: And how do you defend yourself?

Audience: By being very controlled. By insisting that everyone around me is also very controlled. I suppose I use the words "selfish" and "irrational" a lot when someone starts behaving in a way that frightens me. Dependency for me means I don't have the power to control myself.

Liz: Thank you, that is very helpful, and I think we can all understand what you mean. This is the archetypal terror of the air signs, and of Aquarius in particular – unknown, irrational forces that might rise up and wreak havoc. For Aquarius, these forces may range from the forces of nature to the forces of the human psyche, in both individuals and the mass. What, then, is the characteristic line of defence likely to be? We have looked at this in some depth already. The development of a body of knowledge which defines the laws by which things work can provide a defence against the unknown, which then becomes predictable. Psychology and astrology can both offer this service. A code of ethics can also be used as a defence, because it allows the Aquarian to control his or her behaviour according to the code, and also provides the "high moral ground" from which others can be asked to behave according to the code as well. Socialisation, or civilisation, is thus the primary Aquarian defence against primitive human savagery.

Social codes and laws, from the sublime declarations of human rights to the postured maneuverings of an upper class dinner party, serve as ways of protecting both the individual and the group from the sudden invasion of primitive forces. The group is a very important line of defence for Aquarius. Any old group won't do, but a group organised according to values, ideals, precepts, or objectives which suit the individuals involved, can offer what is required. Whether the group is one's local church, one's professional colleagues, one's companions on the spiritual journey, one's racial or national collective, one's fellow students on a CPA seminar, or one's fellow Ku Klux Klan members, the laws and codes of the group provide the standard of controlled behaviour, the ethos, against which everything "outside", potentially threatening, can be measured and understood. When the group is organised and functioning according to understandable social and political laws, it is a place of safety for Aquarius – in the same way that science, astrology, psychology, or sharply defined morality can be a place of safety.

We can understand why Aquarius seeks to reform society and human nature. This is the creative dimension of Aquarius' defence system, and progress as an ideal is usually linked with the goal of civilising and controlling the irrational aspects of life. The Aquarian vision seeks to reform, transform, or eradicate those elements in the human being which are uncivilised, barbaric, and potentially destructive. The reforming impulse is very powerful in this sign. Some Aquarians turn it on themselves, and are forever denigrating themselves because they are not living up to an impossible ideal of human perfection. Some express it in a more extraverted way through political, educational, or spiritual "causes". It is extremely important for this sign to spot the places where chaos might erupt. It will then work to improve the system, so that in the future there is less possibility of an unwelcome eruption.

Aquarius finds uncivilised behaviour deeply distressing.

Aquarius usually has a clear, coherent code of ethics. One should be honest, decent, civilised, and fair. One should always be conscious of other people's rights. One shouldn't be possessive in close relationships, and one should never be vindictive even if one is badly hurt. These are civilised codes of behaviour which can prevent the unpredictable and appalling from happening, as long as everyone in the group agrees with the code. Of course everyone says they agree, because the codes are obviously honourable and good; and of course someone, sooner or later, will find he or she simply cannot follow the rules any longer. Human need and human greed invariably put a spanner in the works, and once the shock and pain have subsided Aquarius goes to work again, trying to improve the system according to what has been learned from the latest eruption. For Aquarius, the world is constantly in need of improvement. It is never totally right; and it is also never going to be totally right, because no matter how hard Aquarius works to perfect and enforce its codes, there will always be elements in human nature which defy them.

We can understand a great deal about Aquarian behaviour and motives by viewing it from this perspective. Sometimes, if the defence system occludes other aspects of the personality, Aquarian codes can become a tyranny. We should remember that Saturn as well as Uranus rules this sign, and Saturn is the quintessential tyrant of myth. When ethical codes become a matter of legal or military enforcement employing highly unethical means, we are in terrain which many people do not recognise as Aquarian. Likewise, we often don't realise that scapegoating, and the projection of inferiority onto "undesirable" social elements, may also be a manifestation of extreme Aquarian defences. This usually tolerant and free-thinking sign can sometimes display extraordinary intolerance toward anyone who does not "fit" whatever social or moral code the Aquarian espouses.

We may see certain aspects of this problem in the horoscope of America, which has the natal Moon in Aquarius. This country, which enshrined the ideal of individual freedom in its Constitution and Bill of Rights, can display the most appalling and brutish bigotry and intolerance on religious and social levels. I have met certain Aquarians who are very dogmatic and controlling in this way, particularly toward their families. They do not want to be tyrants; such behaviour is totally opposed to their ethics. But how else, asks Aquarius, can we make sure that everyone adheres to the code? We can see many elements of this dilemma in what is known as political correctness. It is rapidly becoming a tyranny, rather than an expression of respect between individuals and social groups, which was its original intention.

It isn't that Aquarian ethics are fake. They are very real, and a healthy and creative defence against elements in human nature which are wantonly destructive. The idea that there might be objective evil in the world can be terrifying to Aquarius, because one cannot reform or cure objective evil, or explain its existence in a rational way. This is why Aquarius will generally take the view that "evil" is the reflection of deep damage and suffering.

What if there is such a thing as objective evil? What if some people are simply evil, rather than redeemable souls expressing the pain of poverty or a deprived childhood in destructive ways?

Audience: I find that idea very objectionable.

Liz: Are you an Aquarian?

Audience: I have the Moon in Aquarius.

Liz: And are you involved in the helping professions?

Audience: I am a psychiatric social worker.

Liz: Presumably you deeply believe that no human being is irredeemable, and that with sufficient effort and compassion, even the most hardened criminal could change.

Audience: I am a little more realistic than that. But on an ideal level, yes. It's just that "sufficient effort and compassion" might not be available. It usually isn't.

Liz: There is, of course, a school of thought, or of feeling, primarily to be found amongst elements other than air, that human perfection is like the speed limit on Italian motorways – an ideal toward which we should always fondly aspire. I am not disagreeing with you. But this world-view which forms the core of your aspirations and commitment may be as inappropriate for others as it is right for you. It may also prove destructive if unleashed without common sense within the legal system. If Aquarian defences are balanced sufficiently by other functions and aspects of the personality, then some reasonable compromise can be achieved, without losing sight of the ideal or giving up efforts to make it manifest. Aquarius believes that there must always be a reason when dreadful things happen and people run amok. If the reason can be found, then steps can be taken to reform the conditions which produced the problem.

Aquarius depends for its psychological survival on the conviction that life operates according to comprehensible laws by which all behaviour can be explained. If if can't be explained, one is totally vulnerable, and at the mercy of absolutely anything. If it can be explained, then the source of the problem can be addressed. If human savagery is due to poverty and social deprivation, then this can be corrected on a political or psychotherapeutic level. If it is due to bad education, it can be corrected in schools. But if it is not due to anything except innate human barbarity, how then can Aquarius defend itself effectively, and still remain ethical and fair?

Planets and planetary aspects as defence systems

Audience: Do you think rebellious teenagers are expressing Uranian defences?

Liz: I think you may need to be more precise about what you mean by "rebellious teenagers". There are many different kinds of rebellion, just as there are many different kinds of freedom, and sometimes ordinary healthy self-expression in a young person is interpreted as rebellion because the older individual feels envious, or is afraid that his or her control is being threatened. The phrase is a charged one, and can conceal a multitude of sins on the part of the unrebellious. Uranus does not seem to be inclined toward rebellion for the sheer hell of it. If Aquarians do rebel, it will usually be ideological. In other words, there will be a reason for it, a general principle which justifies it. There will probably be a set of precepts which Aquarius does not agree with, and there will be a set of precepts for which it is fighting. Behind the rebellion is a collision between opposing codes.

A great deal of what is often called rebellion may reflect great personal anger, which erupts because of emotional conflicts with parents, or social constraints which are experienced as oppressive on the emotional level. Here there is no principle involved. It's a passionate cry of "What about me?" This is more the expression of Mars than it is of Uranus. If feelings of personal potency and value are being crushed, Mars may defend itself with violence. Sometimes, of course, the two get mixed up, and fighting for a general principle can mask, or be thoroughly enmeshed with, a very personal sense of humiliation and outrage. Probably this is the norm rather than the exception.

Jupiter can be very rebellious. If one tries to trap Jupiter, one of its methods of defence is to blow everything up and make a quick exit. Jupiter may also create fireworks simply in order to be noticed. In myth, Zeus-Jupiter is always rebelling against the restrictions imposed on him by his wife Hera. These are usually sexual restrictions, in the form of an insistence on monogamy. Apart from the literal enactment, which may sometimes be seen with a rampant Jupiter, this rebellion is often directed against material limits of any kind.

Pluto can also be very rebellious, although one will usually be unaware of it until the bomb goes off. Pluto's rebellion, which may be observed in society in the form of terrorist attacks, is often a last-ditch bid for survival against what the person experiences as insurmountable odds. "If I don't kill you, you'll kill me," says Pluto, "and therefore I must destroy you, and even myself in the process, if the choice is between death and slavery." Pluto's defences on the psychological level may sometimes involve wounding a person who is deeply loved, or terminating an important and much-needed relationship, because this is preferable to being controlled and humiliated. You can see that each planet has its own form of rebellion as a defence against annihilation. Uranian rebellion is not necessarily teenage rebellion. It may appear anarchic, but there is usually an ideology behind it.

We need to understand that defence systems are not mutually exclusive of compassion, love, decency, integrity, honesty, or sensitivity to other people. All the attributes which we value most highly in human nature are in some way bound up with defences. When viewing these fine qualities as part of a defence system, this doesn't mean they are false or hypocritical. By looking at Aquarius' ethical code as an aspect of its defences, I am not suggesting that therefore it is fake, or rooted in meaner motives. Defences are not artificial, nor are they a mere reaction to fear. They exist to serve life, and they belong to the soul as much as any "higher" aspiration does. Aquarius' abhorrence of savagery arises, in part, because there is a clear and compassionate recognition of what such behaviour does to people. But the Aquarian insistence on "ought" and "should" can be a little compulsive, and the compulsiveness reveals the defence system at work.

Audience: The double planetary rulership of Aquarius also shows how revolutions work. There is an established Saturnian power, and then Uranus comes to break it down. Then the new power becomes crystallised, and it starts all over again.

Part One: The Psychology of Defences and their Astrological Significators   75

Liz: You are pointing out something very important about Aquarius. The implicit tension between the two rulers is part of the reforming instinct. Saturn crystallises the law, as a defence against anarchy and breakdown. Uranus says, "This law isn't sufficient. It's not inclusive enough. It hasn't dealt with all the problems. There is still an irrational pocket here that's not right, and another one over there. We'll overthrow the existing Saturnian structure [or change it from within, because Aquarian reform is not always violent], and replace it with something better." But the newly reformed system in time becomes Saturnian, and as it solidifies, all the chaotic bits that it hasn't dealt with begin to show up. There is a constant crystallising and renewing process occurring within Aquarius. Nothing ever remains the same. Yet this is a fixed sign, and when the new system is inaugurated there is a tendency to establish it in a very inflexible way – even though one may know perfectly well that, sooner or later, it will prove insufficient or incomplete in its turn.

Planets can be understood in the context of mechanisms of defence. Each planet reflects a fundamental drive or archetypal urge, which seeks expression in life and will fight against being stifled or destroyed. But planetary defences may also be mobilised to protect the individual against experiencing other factors in the chart. One planet may be enlisted as a defence against the negative experience of another planet. We can begin to understand the psychology of planetary aspects in this way. Aggression and anger, for example, are not simply instinctive responses to attack. Certainly an animal will fight if it is under attack, and so will a human. If you pull your cat's tail, it will bite you. If you shout at me, I will probably shout back. But anger may also be a defence against other, more frightening feelings. Mars and its two signs, Aries and Scorpio, are often much more comfortable with anger than they are with tears or other expressions of vulnerability. Mars may be enlisted as a defence against the powerlessless and dependency of Neptune, or the gnawing insecurity and shyness of Saturn. Anger can protect us from many things, not least from ourselves.

If an Aries or Scorpio has been rejected, he or she is unlikely to collapse in a sodden heap of self-pity and moan, "Please, please don't leave me, I'll do anything." The individual is much more likely to become aggressive and vitriolic, and to punch back with any means that comes to hand. The Mars function is used as a defence against feeling powerless and admitting dependency. Many people find anger easier than a display of more vulnerable feelings. This may be reflected in the chart, not only by an emphasis in Aries or Scorpio, but also by a strong Mars.

Martial defences

Let's take the example of an individual who has an angular Mars, which is also conjunct the Sun and trine the Moon, with Aries on the Ascendant and Venus in Scorpio. This individual has been rejected or betrayed in a close relationship. The emotional reactions may be very complex. There may be grief at the loss, and a feeling of humiliation and worthlessness, and a fear that it will be impossible to live without the beloved. The Moon function might be saying, "What will I do in an empty house without you there?" and Neptune might be saying, "I never deserved you anyway," and Saturn might be grumbling, "I should never have got so deeply involved in the first place." Uranus might reach for the ephemeris and say, "I'm sure there is a bad Saturn transit going on." Pluto may be muttering *sotto voce*, "How can I get back at you where it really hurts?" and Jupiter may say, "What am I supposed to be learning from this?" Mercury, meanwhile, says, "Surely we can discuss this."

When something important happens to us, all of us reacts. We have many layers and levels of response to any major event. All the planets, which are really the archetypal dominants within the psyche, have their own voices and ways of responding. But depending on what the ego identifies as its recognisable characteristics, some of these voices will be habitually louder than others, and may drown the quieter ones out – especially if the responses are ambivalent. That is why sometimes we can acknowledge one feeling, but may remain unconscious of another, which rises to the surface later and comes out in indirect ways. Mars will get really pissed off, because rejection is something which is done to us, and we apparently have no choice in the matter. This activates Mars' rage. If Mars dominates the horoscope, then this voice will be the loudest, and it will be much easier for the individual to react with rage and aggression than to say, "I feel awful. You've really hurt me, you've made me feel useless and diminished." Mars can't do this, because rejection equals loss of potency, and loss of potency, for Mars, is a kind of death. To admit that someone has the power to hurt us means he or she has power over us. We can recreate a feeling of potency, however fleeting or illusory, through displaying anger.

Penetrating to the core of a person's defensive reactions can help to build a bridge, and can allow us to tolerate and even feel compassion for behaviour which we might otherwise write off. And if we feel we must fight or write someone off, then we can do so with understanding, which tends to keep cruelty in check. We can also make sense of our own inconsistent or troublesome behaviour patterns, and work more consciously with them. If, for example, one gets angry all the time, and it is clear that this is causing problems, it can make a big difference if one can see what hidden purpose this anger might be serving. What is it covering up? What is it supposed to be achieving? Defences are intelligent, and always serve a purpose, even if we are unconscious of it. They are not merely reactions. A defence is mobilised to preserve something precious and valuable, or to protect something deeply vulnerable.

Lunar and Neptunian defences

Audience: Some people seem to have the opposite problem. They can't get angry when they should be.

Liz: Yes, there are many individuals in whom Mars never gets a look in, because other defences are blocking its voice. Sometimes the main line of defence is Neptunian. Such people cannot get angry, because anger would create separateness and loneliness. The other person might get up and walk away, so instead of getting angry, one might get drunk, or stuff oneself with chocolate cake, or dissolve in tears. Guilt can also be mobilised by Neptune as a defence. Neptune says, "I'm so sorry, I'm a terrible person, I'm so unworthy, it's my fault." Neptune will even say this when one has just been punched in the face and it is clearly the other person's problem. Neptune will do anything in order to preserve a relationship, including stifling healthy anger. Sometimes we may see this pattern when Neptune and Mars are in hard aspect in the birth chart. Anger, for the Neptunian, can be a terrible threat to relationship, because when one is angry with someone, there is hatred present, even if there is also great love. A gaping hole appears in the fabric of fusion. The moment we have a quarrel with someone, no matter how close to them we are, we experience ourselves as separate. One feels it in the atmosphere, which drops several degrees in temperature and is full of jagged red sparks. The warm invisible fluid of emotional interconnection suddenly freezes. For whatever length of time it takes to get over the anger – minutes, days, weeks, years – one is with a stranger, and a horrible loneliness can descend.

The Moon doesn't exactly enjoy this state of affairs either. Not only Cancerians, but also those with an angular Moon, or a hard aspect between the Moon and Mars, may have a lot of trouble acknowledging and expressing anger. It may be easier for them to inflict pain on themselves, or to collapse under hurt, than it is for them to show anger. Emotional collapse also doesn't destroy the thing that matters most to the Moon, even if it reveals helplessness and dependency. The relationship is preserved.

Making the other person feel guilty by flagellating oneself is a favourite lunar defence, because one can communicate one's hurt without that terrible chilling of the atmosphere. A display of helplessness is not threatening to the Moon, because one has managed to protect the thing that matters. But one's anger might destroy it. As I mentioned earlier, idealisation may be mobilised by Neptune as a defence against the destructive effects of anger. Of course such efforts to preserve the emotional connection may ultimately prove illusory or ineffectual, because other people have a way of picking up an angry Mars even if it is muzzled and locked in the basement. Then the anger may erupt through the other person, who feels manipulated and comes out fighting. But the Moon and Neptune will go on trying.

Mercurial defences

Many defences are connected with one's intellectual capacities. Words can be a defence for Mercurial people. This doesn't just mean cutting words. Mercury's defences can also involve being cleverer or more articulate than others. Mercury may also use the analytic faculty as a defence. If we analyse someone's motives, or react to their display of intense feeling with a cool rationality, we may defend ourselves against feeling. We may also use Mercurial defences to protect ourselves from experiencing our own Moon, Neptune, or Pluto. Naming and categorising things can provide a wonderfully creative defence against feeling them.

Mercury may also use jargon as a defence. Many astrologers are culpable of this one, and so are many psychologists. Jargon can be a defence against expressing vulnerability in ordinary human terms. It is a concealment. If we say to a friend, "Saturn is transiting square my Moon this week," what have we actually said? We have used jargon to communicate something, because we do not dare say, "I feel incredibly low and depressed. I'm very lonely. I don't like myself much at the moment, and when I look in the mirror all I see is a mess. I have no friends, and I'm feeling really sorry for myself, and my mother just died." Understandably, there may be very few friends who want to hear all that. The jargon is preferable, because it preserves boundaries. It also serves as a defence against appearing helpless, vulnerable, and needy. But I have had analytic patients, who were familiar with astrology, try this on, rather than exposing their feelings in a therapeutic session. In some places jargon is inappropriate, and the defence is no longer constructive.

Audience: If I say, "I'm feeling lonely and miserable!" to another astrologer, they usually say "Oh, what are your transits?"

Liz: Invariably. This is partly because jargon can also be a defence against having to respond emotionally to somebody else's unhappiness. Jargon gives breathing space. Once again, it can be a constructive and creative defence, because sometimes other people simply want too much. Also, astrological or psychological jargon can help to orientate a person who is swamped by his or her feelings. Every astrologer and counsellor knows how powerfully healing it can be to have one's crisis explained in detached terms which put things into a broader context.

The defensive nature of jargon can sometimes be very amusing. Many years ago, when I went to my first Astrological Association meeting, there was a short break and everyone queued for coffee. A man got into the queue behind me and smiled and said, "Hello. Where is your Venus?". Never mind banalities like "What's your name?" or "What are you doing later?" or "I find you really attractive." Being inexperienced at the time, I told him, and he looked at me meaningfully, moved closer, and said, "Ah, it's trine my Mars."

Non-astrologers cannot possibly imagine how much obscenity can be encapsulated in such innocent phrases. But elegant though this approach was, nevertheless it was extremely defensive. What this man succeeded in doing was avoiding the possibility of rejection. If he had said "What are you doing later?" I might have replied, "Anything as long as it's not with you." Perhaps he expected that sort of response from women. I didn't ask him whether he had Venus opposite Saturn. I could have signalled my interest by saying, "Oh, my Venus is in whatnot. Where is your Mars?" We then might have continued exchanging chart placements without any risk of real vulnerability. Unfortunately, I failed to respond to what on paper clearly seemed to him a perfect match, and I didn't ask for further information. On that note the conversation ended. But you can all see how our jargon, at the same time that it communicates, also protects us from the emotional risks that astrologically illiterate people have to go through every time they find someone attractive.

Analysts sometimes use jargon to an appalling extent. A label is given to an emotional state or pattern of behaviour, and that's the end of it. One is displaying resistance, or one is involved in a negative transference, or one is displaying Oedipal behaviour. "You are projecting!" is another favourite. So are terms like anima and animus. "I couldn't help starting the affair," says the novice Jungian to his wife, "she was a hook for the projection of my anima." This is much easier and more elegant than saying, "I couldn't keep my hands off her." Putting ordinary garden-variety lust in a clinical context somehow makes it seem loftier and more defensible. Words can be a sublime and massive defence. We all need Mercury's defences, because if we exposed our innermost souls to each other, it would be unbearable.

Audience: Words are a kind of collective defence, a mutually agreed collective avoidance.

Liz: Words may be a very necessary defence system, and an enormously creative one. But we also need to know when we are overdoing it, and when we must communicate directly, with the body and from the heart.

An example chart

We should now look at what happens in an actual chart. For the moment I will withhold the name of the individual, who is male.
Let's examine the planetary configurations, and consider the kind of defence mechanisms that we might expect, and how they might show themselves in actual life. Until now, we have not been talking about real people. We have looked at the psychoanalytic categories of defences, and at how each element and sign displays its characteristic defences. But no one's chart contains only one sign or one planet. Each individual has many different defence mechanisms, and some of them collide. Also, some are more prominent at different ages and stages of life. Sometimes the need to defend ourselves in one area, or through one set of defences, conflicts violently with our need to defend something else, and in an entirely different way. We touched on this in looking at certain planetary aspects, such as Mars in hard aspect to Neptune. In the end we can only make sense of the remarkable and complex orchestration of personality defences by exploring their expression in an individual chart and an individual life.
As you can see, there are some striking configurations in this chart. First of all, there are two grand trines. One of them is in the element of water, between the Sun-Saturn conjunction in Scorpio, Pluto in Cancer, and Uranus in Pisces. Then there is another grand trine which extends over two elements, between Neptune in Leo, Chiron in Aries, and Venus at the beginning of

Capricorn. Set against these grand trines, there is a T-cross involving Jupiter, Mars, and Chiron. Pluto doesn't quite earn membership to the T-cross because it is not square Chiron or Mars, but it is opposite Jupiter. Then we must consider the Sun-Saturn conjunction square Neptune, and the square between Mercury and the Moon. This is a very energetic chart, with many powerful aspects. We need an entry point, an overview which can allow us to approach these complex configurations without getting lost.

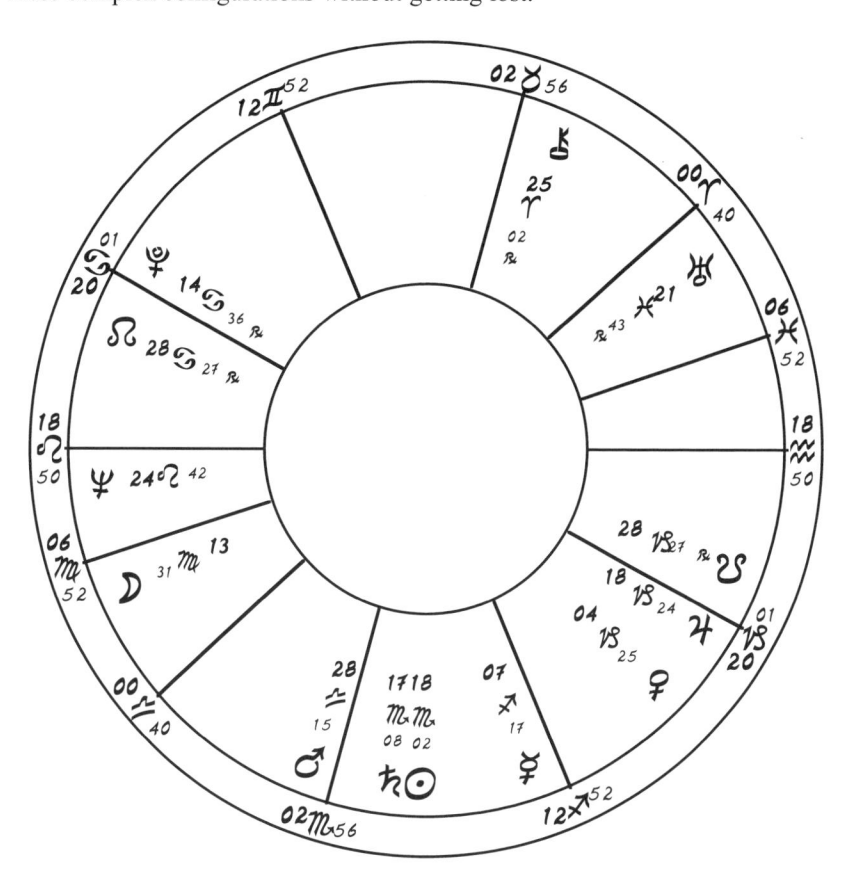

Example Chart 1
Male, 10 November 1925, 11.00 pm GMT, Pontrhydyfen, Wales

The balance of elements can tell us a great deal. Mars is the only planet in air. Water clearly dominates, with Pluto in Cancer, Uranus in Pisces, and the Sun (which is the Ascendant ruler) and Saturn in Scorpio. Neptune angular, conjuncting the Ascendant, also emphasises the importance of water. In earth and fire there are three planets each.

Audience: You don't count the Ascendant and MC.

Liz: I keep them in mind. Their testimony is not in conflict with the basic chart balance, which tells us that water is dominant and air is the weakest element. This immediately gives us a general psychological portrait. Fire is strong, and the Ascendant supports the weight of planets in fire. We can surmise that this man tends to respond to life with his feelings rather than his intellect, and that emotional intimacy and intensity are extremely important to him. We can also assume that he has a powerful imagination and a need to experience himself as special and larger than life. He may have difficulty in maintaining boundaries and containing his feelings, and the body and the material world may pose a problem because his emotional needs and fantasies might make him very indulgent or careless of mundane limits. It is in this overall context that we need to look at the planetary configurations.

I think there are several important points about defences that this chart can highlight. To begin with, configurations such as grand trines can be used as defences, and usually are. Because they are by nature harmonious, and reflect aptitudes, gifts, or natural abilities in a particular sphere of life, one feels comfortable and strong expressing the planets and element of a grand trine. Consequently they can be used as a defence, not only against a weak element, but against another planet or configuration in the chart. We use the support system of our trines and sextiles to defend ourselves against the pain and friction generated by our squares and oppositions. How might that work here?

Audience: He could find the pain of the Mars-Chiron opposition, and the feelings of sexual inadequacy which it suggests, alleviated by diving into the idealisation suggested by the Venus-Neptune trine.

Liz: Yes, that is exactly what he did. When we have a really painful aspect in the chart – and there is always going to be one, of one sort or another – we will mobilise those qualities with which we are most comfortable against the suffering of the difficult aspect. As you say, this Mars-Chiron opposition suggests deep self-doubt and feelings of sexual inadequacy. "Sexual" doesn't just mean performance in bed. It is a more general issue, and pertains to his feelings about himself as a man in many other spheres of life. I have always liked Jung's definition of masculinity: "Knowing what you want and doing

Part One: The Psychology of Defences and their Astrological Significators   83

what you have to do to get it." Mars-Chiron may have difficulty in decision-making and self-motivation. Also, Mars is in detriment in Libra. It isn't very happy to begin with. It is also retrograde, and therefore somewhat introverted in its expression. So it is not a comfortable Mars, and it is a singleton in the element of air. To complicate matters further, it is also one of the two rulers of the Sun-sign, Scorpio. So we might say that the side of Scorpio which is concerned with inner strength, self-determination, and fighting power, is going to be hampered.

In order to avoid experiencing all the difficulties of a problematic Mars, Venus-Neptune can be mobilised. The ecstasy of a passionate and idealised love affair can intoxicate him enough to forget those gnawing doubts. The Moon-Jupiter trine can also be mobilised, and indulgence and extravagance, sensually and materially, can help him to forget how inadequate he sometimes feels. The grand trine in water is especially suited to provide a defence against this unhappy Mars. Can you see how the grand trine of Sun, Pluto and Uranus could be used as a bastion against feelings of impotence and inadequacy? Here are two outer planets in trine to the Sun. What kind of defence do these planets provide?

Audience: It would have something to do with involvement with the collective. The outer planets are concerned with the collective. He might be part of a large organisation, and he wouldn't feel inundated by collective forces that might make another person feel overwhelmed.

Liz: Yes, he would have the power to channel, and perhaps also manipulate, collective forces. He is a kind of mouthpiece for the collective, and can express collective feelings and longings in a highly individual way. This would give him great charisma.

Audience: Would he repress his feelings?

Liz: No, I don't think he represses feelings in a general sense. After all, his chart is weighted in the element of water. He would be highly emotional, and not afraid to show it. But he may repress very particular feelings, especially those reflected by the difficult Mars.

Audience: I am interested in that Sun-Saturn conjunction. Would he use that as a defence, or is it something he would defend himself against?

Liz: The Saturn-Sun conjunction suggests a deep sense of isolation and separateness. Saturn throws its barriers up against the natural expression of the sign in which it is placed, and here it would try to block Scorpio's longing for intense emotional encounter because of a fear of being controlled. Saturn in Scorpio is often deeply fearful of humiliation, and of being at the mercy of someone else's domination through emotional and sexual needs. So this man may try hard to suppress his passions, or express them only in safe places. A kind of permanent volcanic bubbling is produced, which goes on under the surface of a rather suspicious and highly controlled nature. This results in isolation, because he cannot then fulfill himself with the kind of emotional closeness he craves so much. So it is a very painful aspect for a water sign personality. This conjunction, like the Mars-Chiron opposition, is one of the configurations in the chart against which his defences would be mobilised. You can see how the romantic idealising of the Venus-Neptune trine, and the charisma reflected by the two outer planets trine the Sun, might provide relief from loneliness. Sun-Saturn people often feel terribly alone, even if they are surrounded by friends and lovers. It is part of the price one pays for Saturn's strength and tenacity. Because Sun-Saturn people tend to work very hard to define themselves as individuals, and often have to do this without any help or support in childhood, they are unable to let go as adults, and can't simply fuse happily with anyone they care about. Sun-Saturn reflects a powerful need to establish a definite individuality, and this inevitably creates a lot of loneliness.

When the Sun and Saturn are trine or sextile, it may not feel like such a burden. When they are conjunct, square, or opposition, the feeling of loneliness can be extremely difficult. In a chart with so much water and a rising Neptune, it can become intolerable. So there are two aspects here that are extremely painful and likely to mobilise powerful defence mechanisms.

Audience: Is this the chart of Prince Charles?

Liz: I know Prince Charles looks a little weary these days, but he wasn't born in 1925 as this man was. Look at the birth date. However, I take your point. There are factors here which might apply to him, especially the involvement with the collective. Prince Charles has the Sun in Scorpio square Pluto in the 1st house, and also has a Leo Ascendant. The sense of being able to get many people to do what you want, or get them to feel what you wish them to feel, can be heady stuff. So can the conviction that one is meant to help, save, or transform the collective. This can provide a powerful defence against corrosive personal doubts such as Mars-Chiron and Sun-Saturn might generate. People with the Sun aspecting the outer planets may use their connection with the collective psyche as a line of defence.

Audience: Does this man try to overcome his feelings of isolation by asserting his connection with others very powerfully?

Liz: Yes. His main defence is to try to preserve a feeling of closeness, of belonging. He has a very powerful need to be loved and admired by as many people as possible. The fear of being impotent, insignificant, and unacceptable is constantly gnawing away at him. In defence he can express the magnetism of the water signs and their capacity to relate on an emotional level. And he can also use his instinctive ability to portray what the collective needs and desires. His defence is also his gift. Our gifts are developed, in part, because they help us preserve what is of greatest value to us.

Audience: If it isn't Prince Charles, who is it?

Liz: Richard Burton. Perhaps I should have waited until we had gone further into the chart. But you can see how we have begun to build up an accurate picture of the psychological dynamics, without any biographical information. I am sure some of you would have raised the issue of alcohol as we went on. Burton made a statement toward the end of his life, which is quoted in his brother's biography, *Richard Burton: A Brother Remembered*. It is one of those statements that somehow encapsulates the chart, in a profound and frightening way. I would like to read it to you.

> ...The horror is that it (alcohol) is so available, so convivial, so nice, just sitting in a bar and watching someone pour. I started to drink because I couldn't face going on the stage without one. It steadied the nerves – and later it broke them...You see, it's not really my fault: it's the valleys and the pitheads. My background is there and I'm the victim. I am the authentic dark voice of the tortured part of my world. Although I like to be thought of as all-machismo and tough Welsh rugby-playing, and able to do anything with my own two hands – and yes, take on the world too – that isn't the reality at all. The reality is that there is a fundamental weakness in me, and that whole image is merely superficial. I need a woman to pull me out of that weakness...It has taken these delicate, fragile, beautiful but strong-minded ladies to save me.

Burton possessed a great acting talent. What happened to him was a tragedy. He certainly used his gifts, and they provided one line of defence which was enormously creative. His actor's ability is connected with the grand water trine and with Neptune, as well as with the imaginative and self-mythologising qualities of fire. He had the capacity to enter into a *participation mystique* with the audience, and to mysteriously embody feelings that lie deep in everyone but cannot be articulated. But at the same time, alcohol is the other defence reflected by Neptune and the grand water trine, and this defence eventually destroyed him. His horror of loneliness was so great that in the end a rather sordid and undignified death was preferable to being alone. Alcohol served as a defence against his feelings of inadequacy. He says this himself. He started drinking because he couldn't face going on a stage without a drink. The fear of rejection, failure, and inferiority was so enormous that he could only manage to perform if he created the alcoholic's illusion of merging with others, the illusion of relationship.

Burton is a very disturbing example of defences which worked both creatively and destructively. The Leo ascendant, with its grand vision of kingly glory, also provided him with a defence. It is a long time ago now, but some of you might remember the phase he went through after he met Elizabeth Taylor on the set of *Cleopatra*. He was buying her jewels which would not have been inappropriate for the real Cleopatra. As a couple they did not simply entertain; they held court. The boundaries seemed to slip between his actual identity and the part he was playing at the time. This extravagant Leonine fantasy-world became a bastion against the horror of the poor mining village in which he grew up and saw his family emotionally and spiritually destroyed.

Audience: Wasn't Elizabeth Taylor a Pisces?

Liz: She still is, as far as I know. The Sun is in Pisces opposition Neptune, and Sagittarius is on the Ascendant. To some extent alcohol was one of her defences as well. But she seems to have greater resilience than Burton, and has managed to survive and bounce back over and over again. Burton is not the first alcoholic I have seen who has a Sun-Saturn-Neptune configuration. Neptune alone is not an automatic indicator of this problem. But when you combine it with Saturn, a terrible battle may ensue, and if the individual cannot or will not deal with the battle as an internal conflict, then Neptune may be mobilised as a defence against the loneliness and self-doubt of Saturn.

Audience: What do you think could have saved him?

Liz: I don't think he wanted to be saved. He preferred dissolution to an ordinary grubby AA-type battle with alcohol. Neptune rising in Leo, square a Scorpio Sun-Saturn, may find it somewhat difficult to stand up at an AA meeting as one of many sufferers and say, "I'm Richard Burton, and I'm an alcoholic." In the end we cannot judge people's choices when they are on this level. Burton found too much in life that was unbearable, and he was not prepared to go out into the cold world without the protective lubricant to blurr the outlines of the horror. He was also ferociously proud. I think the self-aggrandising elements in Leo, combined with Neptune's need for otherworldly fusion, made it necessary for him to be tragic rather than ordinary. It was preferable to have a short but intense life, lived on the romantic heights, than to die in his bed at eighty without being very interesting.

Burton's fame doesn't come exclusively from the status we have accorded him as an actor. It also comes from his notorious marriage to Elizabeth Taylor, which was a stage show in itself. And many people don't really know much about his stage work at all. They may never have seen him do *Hamlet*. They just remember him in *Cleopatra,* or in *Where Eagles Dare,* or in other B-grade films that were a bit silly and far beneath his capabilities. In terms of his aspirations as an actor, he never got there. He self-destructed, and made a lot of very ill-advised professional decisions in order to be able to buy jewels for Elizabeth Taylor. In some ways Burton enacted Parsifal the Fool. But he never found the Grail. His defences, which are intimately connected with his talent, eventually become so compulsive that other, life-supporting dimensions of the personality could no longer function. His defences made him famous, but in the end they destroyed him.

Aspect dynamics

If you are finding it difficult to get a sense of how planetary configurations might interact with each other, I would suggest that you try to imagine the planets as living beings. Of course this is what the Greeks did; they envisaged them as gods, complete with individual personalities, physical characteristics, and behaviour patterns. Try to get a feeling of who is friends with whom in a chart, as though this was a community of people all trying to live together and forming liaisons according to their natural affinities and antipathies. The dynamics of the group are no less applicable to the inner group, and that is what we are dealing with. It is a community of "subpersonalities" or inner needs and attributes, and each of the planets will align itself according to which others are friends, enemies, or merely neutral. The same applies to planets in signs. Each planet will feel comfortable in certain signs, and uncomfortable in others. Some configurations have friends, and sometimes one aspect or planet will be isolated or cut off. Just as a group or community may select a scapegoat or pick on one person or family who seems different, groups of planets which have affinities may gang up on a singleton or a difficult aspect which doesn't "fit". Psychologically, this means we consciously acknowledge and express the favoured configurations, and try to change, stifle, or disown the misfit.

In Burton's chart, the rising Neptune is friends with the emphasis in water, because Neptune's realm is watery. Venus trine Neptune is also friendly with the water emphasis, because it is highly romantic and seeks a mystical union with a soul-mate. Moon trine Jupiter can get on comfortably with Venus trine Neptune and with the emphasis in water, because this configuration likes excess. Although it is in earth, this trine is more concerned with pleasure and beauty than it is with structure. Mercury in Sagittarius is a friend, because it is not analytical; it is a storyteller. Mercury in Sagittarius perceives life in big, colourful, mythic terms. The Leo Ascendant can join this group because of its love of drama and its self-mythologising propensities. We can get the sense that most of this chart is well-knit. All these individual configurations support, appreciate, and blend with each other. They are the dominant force in the psychic community, and one can visualise them all having delightful parties together, eating and drinking too much, dressing extravagantly, telling wonderful stories, and indulging in passionate romantic escapades.

It should be obvious who gets to live in the slum tenement in the poor part of town. Sun-Saturn and Mars-Chiron are not welcome at any of the parties. The only friend that Sun-Saturn might possibly have is Venus in Capricorn, but most of the time Venus would prefer to spend time with Neptune, and will only occasionally nod a greeting to Sun-Saturn. These two configurations are a dead weight at jolly inner parties. They are too lonely and withdrawn, and don't know how to join in the fun. They are too conscious of life's cruel face to indulge in grand theatrical dreams. And Mars in Libra also has no friends. Who wants Mars in Libra, in a chart dominated by water and fire? What are the qualities of Mars in Libra?

Audience: He would find it difficult to assert himself or take action on his own behalf. He needs to have somebody else around to make decisions for him.

Liz: Mars in Libra needs a "We" in order to function. It does not require someone else to make the decisions. It wants a consensus of opinion to confirm that its decision is the right one. It is a very ethical Mars, because Libra is, as we have already seen, deeply concerned with "right" principles and the application of ethical codes in relationship. Mars is inhibited in Libra. Once again, try to visualise the planet as a living being, a person or personified god. In the *Iliad,* Homer portrayed Mars as a hirsute brute, three hundred feet tall, muscular, sweaty, and very boorish. He's too butch to use deodorant, and his language is pretty coarse. But the cosmos has played a trick on him, and placed him in Libra. This brave but insensitive soldier now has to go around in a pale beige Armani silk suit with a flowered bow tie, reeking of Calvin Klein's Obsession for Men, with a gold Cartier watch on his wrist. To make matters worse, he has to sit at a dinner party hosted by the Queen Mother at St James' Palace, and everyone will be watching to see how he handles his fish knife. Other people will think he looks absolutely fascinating – all that elegance, and the suggestion of brute force lurking beneath. Mars in Libra often exercises a powerful attraction over other people. But how do you think Mars feels? Very, very uncomfortable. He has to do the right thing, you see, and he's terrified he'll say something to offend, or use the wrong fork to eat his salad.

One of the reasons why Mars in Libra has trouble in spheres where Mars in Aries does so well, is that Mars in Libra is forever thinking about whether one is doing the right thing. Mars in Aries operates on an instinctive level. One acts on intuition and instinct, without hanging about waiting for approval. Mars in Aries serves Number One. But Mars in Libra says, "Right. I'm now going to make a decision. I'm going to...er...um...Now, hang on a minute. If I do it, So-and-so will be angry, and maybe he would be right to be pissed off, because it's really rather selfish of me. But if I don't do it, then Whatnot will be angry, and I wouldn't blame her, because she was counting on me. Oh, dear, I know what I want, but what should I do? I'd better ring all my friends and ask them." After several days have gone by and one has checked with numerous people to solicit their opinions, the moment has passed, and one is left with a feeling of failure and inadequacy. This highly ethical Mars, which is extremely socially sensitive and acutely conscious of fair play, is not going to please those other configurations we were looking at. Although water is sensitive to others' feelings, the dominant tone of this chart is not particularly concerned with, or motivated by, ethics.

Audience: There's a story that Richard Burton went up to Elizabeth Taylor's husband, Eddie Fisher, and said, "I'm in love with your wife and I want her."

That doesn't sound like an ethical Mars in Libra.

Liz: Doesn't it? Most people would prefer to have the wife without the hassle of informing the husband. It happens all the time. In its own fashion, this was a highly ethical thing to do. Also, perhaps he found it easier to say because he already had her. That isn't quite the same as having to fight for her. Probably he knew enough about Eddie Fisher to recognise that no real opposition would be offered.

Audience: He probably did it when he was drunk.

Audience: Wouldn't it be more civilised if he had suggested an arrangement to share her?

Liz: Perhaps he did. Perhaps she wasn't interested. Perhaps Eddie Fisher wasn't interested. Would you be, in his position?

Violence as a defence

Audience: Wasn't Burton quite violent at times? Was that an expression of his frustration?

Liz: Yes, I think so. Violence is often linked with hard Mars-Chiron, Mars-Saturn, and Mars-Pluto aspects. I have also seen it in relation to Mars-Neptune, which can reflect terrible feelings of helplessness and passivity. The violence is a defence against humiliating feelings of being controlled or dominated by others. The feelings of frustration and inadequacy which these configurations can generate internally may get projected onto someone or something in the outer world. If one can use brute force to humiliate or defeat the controlling party outside, then one can experience the illusion of potency inside. In many situations of domestic violence, the man feels impotent or castrated, and the violence he exhibits toward his wife or children may be a way of making himself feel more potent. Sometimes his feelings of impotence are totally unconnected with his family, and may come from someone humiliating him or treating him shabbily at work. Such situations may trigger the frustrated Mars in the birth chart. He has to let his rage out on someone, so he chooses those who are smaller or weaker than him, or who are less likely than his employer, or a stranger on the street, to run to the police to complain.

Sometimes the wife is in collusion, and is subtly or overtly emasculating him. Burton exhibited a fair amount of violence to Taylor, and I don't doubt that she helped to call it out of him. The violence may then be a product of the relationship itself, and often a similar problematic Mars appears in the wife's chart and is acted out by the husband. Taylor in fact has a Mars-Neptune opposition, and I suspect she coped with her own feelings of helplessness by mocking and denigrating Burton until he blew up at her. She had a habit of calling him "Pockface" in front of his friends. We don't like looking at this kind of situation, because it raises very painful issues of individual responsibility, and it is easier to simply blame the awful violent male. But whether violence is unleashed in personal relationships, or against authority figures in the outer world, it is a compulsive Martial defence against feelings of impotence and powerlessness.

There is another issue in Burton's life which has direct bearing on the problems of his ethical Mars, and therefore on his violence and alcoholism. In his first marriage he had two daughters, one of whom was autistic. She had not been diagnosed as autistic at the time. She had always had great communication difficulties, but had begun to show improvement, and was starting to talk more easily. After Burton left his wife, she withdrew completely, and never spoke again. Burton had to live with this as one of the consequences of his actions. He had done something that, to him, must have seemed deeply unethical, and had resulted in what he perceived as the destruction of his child. I think it is more complex than that, and if we wished to explore the issue more deeply we would have to consider the effect on the child of the abandoned wife's rage, as well as the original psychological roots of the autism. But the trigger for complete withdrawal was provided by his leaving. The rest of Burton's chart, apart from the singleton Mars, probably didn't reflect for very long on the morality or immorality of his actions. He followed his passions. But this lone champion of the ethical code took the burden of the terrible remorse he must have felt afterwards. I think he suffered remorse for many things he did that caused injury to others. A singleton is a very powerful force in the chart, albeit often unconscious.

Audience: So you are saying that a sign is like a suit of clothes which a planet wears.

Liz: Yes, that is one way of looking at it. It is a suit of clothes, a setting in which the clothes are worn, and a formula for behaviour which is required for that setting. It is a part in a play, already scripted, and the planet is the actor who must perform on the set, wear the outfit, and recite the lines. Hence Mars in Libra in the Armani suit at the Queen Mother's dinner. Some outfits and settings can make a planet extremely uncomfortable. Others are just right and the planet has a wonderful time. A planet in the sign of its detriment or fall is not "weakened", as older textbooks sometimes tell us. But a great many of the planet's natural qualities may be inhibited, and it may sit and seethe underneath. Of course some of the most powerful and effective performances are given by actors who are playing parts radically different from their own personalities. They must work terribly hard work to understand the strange new role, and often they do a brilliant job. But they may hate it while they are doing it. Mars retrograde in Libra, and opposition Chiron, is not a happy Mars. The refined torment and elegant, seething restraint which Burton was so good at portraying on stage and screen seem to reflect this.

Alcoholism can also be a form of aggression. This is obvious in those cases where a person gets blind drunk and exhibits a violence which is conveniently forgotten the next day. But the passive alcoholic can be an enormous burden on the people around him or her. It can provide a means of unleashing terrible anger. Partners and children can be psychologically destroyed, while the alcoholic sits about looking pathetic and harmless. Alcoholism is not just a defence against pain and loneliness. It is also a defence against impotence. Paradoxically, it usually produces sexual impotence. But the alcoholic may wield enormous power over others, because they are forced into playing the role of the caretaker.

Burton had four marriages. The two after Taylor were essentially enlisted as caretakers. The first of these gave up after a while. She was required to buy whisky for him during his binges, and then hide it when he wanted to dry out. She was forever buying it, concealing it, mopping him up, picking him up off the floor, and getting him to bed. She was expected to provide a 24-hour-a-day nursing service. The alcoholic *in extremis* can control everybody around him or her. There is no potency in terms of controlling one's own life. But one can create the illusion of potency because somebody else must be there to provide the nursing.

Audience: Burton seemed such a forbidding person. He wasn't the sort of man one could feel was approachable. He helped to create his own isolation.

Liz: Yes, this is often the effect of Sun-Saturn. It exacerbates its own loneliness. Despite his desperate need to be loved, Burton drove people away. They were always surprised to find out that he was actually a very warm-

Part One: The Psychology of Defences and their Astrological Significators 93

hearted, kind person, because he created an atmosphere of impenetrable isolation round him. He was aware of this, and wrote about it. The forbidding quality which Burton displayed may be connected with Saturn's mistrust and expectation of rejection, which can take the form of "shut them out before they shut you out". Saturn has great pride, and will not beg. And of course the same may be said of Scorpio. In contrast, some Sun-Saturn people are so defended against their loneliness that they do not know they are feeling it. They may appear to be rabidly extroverted, because they are trying desperately not to experience the Saturnian sense of solitude and separateness. Yet it is immediately recognisable by other people, on a gut level if not a conscious one, and the performance may fail to achieve its purpose. It may be far better to acknowledge and express what one is. The friendships one forms, although perhaps fewer, are more likely to be authentic, and if more voluble people are put off, they may not be the right friends in the first place.

Audience: In a consultation, how would you deal with a Sun-Saturn person who displayed extreme extraversion, and talked all the time?

Liz: It would depend on how the session was going, and how the relationship was developing with the client. I don't think I would arbitrarily attempt to break down such a defence in an astrological consultation, because beneath this kind of defence there is usually great vulnerability and anxiety. On the other hand, I have had Sun-Saturn clients who knew their extraversion was false in some way, and who admitted they felt like frauds. In such a case I would discuss it as I have been discussing it here. If I were working analytically with someone, then when the time seemed right I might tell the client that I felt all this talking was somehow covering something up. I might say that I felt talked at rather than with, and ask what was going on underneath.

We can sometimes see Mercury-Saturn exhibiting this kind of defence mechanism. But these patterns must always be viewed in the context of the whole chart. If Burton's Sun-Saturn-Neptune configuration appeared in a chart that was weighted in earth and air, with Venus trine Saturn instead of Neptune, and Mars in Taurus instead of Libra, the configuration would be the same but the internal dynamics would be quite different. The Sun-Saturn wouldn't be living in the ghetto; it would be in the biggest, best house in town. And Neptune would probably be the outcast. Burton is not afraid of Neptune because he is watery. Neptune is his friend. Many people are terrified of Neptune, and adopt a hyper-rational approach to life to defend themselves against the threat of chaos.

Plutonian defences

Pluto is often consigned to the psychological ghetto. Sun-Pluto configurations can be deeply painful aspects, because they reflect a family or ancestral inheritance of relationship patterns, often very primitive, which must be recognised and worked through. We have many defences against Pluto, not least the dissociating propensities of Mercury, Uranus, and the element of air. A hard Sun-Pluto contact in an airy chart may lead to massive defences being erected against compulsive emotions and moods which keep threatening to overwhelm the rational mind. Moon-Pluto contacts can also be very difficult for the same reason, and other aspects of the chart may be mobilised as a defence against the emotional intensity the aspects reflect.

Let's take a hypothetical example. A person has the Moon in Scorpio, square Pluto, with the Sun, Venus, and Mercury in Sagittarius and a Libra Ascendant.

Audience: The Plutonian side would be projected.

Liz: Yes, projection would probably be involved. But projection is not in itself a defence. It seems to be a natural psychological phenomenon, when any unconscious component has not yet been recognised or assimilated by the ego. This can occur, not because someone is defended against that quality, but because it simply isn't yet ready to be expressed. But sometimes projection also gets mixed up with powerful defences. Then we defend ourselves against the person or external situation on which we are projecting that bit of ourselves, and we may express these defenses quite compulsively. But what do you mean by "the Plutonian side"? Can you describe what would be projected in nonastrological terms? And what kind of defences might we expect from this person with an emphasis in Sagittarius and Libra?

Audience: I suppose by Plutonian I mean very strong emotions. Things like intense jealousy, or anger. There might be a lot of talk about wanting to be free, wanting to avoid commitment. Maybe the person would be very involved in spiritual or philosophical issues, in order to avoid the feelings.

Liz: Yes, these are all characteristic Sagittarian defences. As it is the Sun in Sagittarius in our example, the person's values and sense of purpose in life might, as you say, be very spiritually orientated. Sagittarius also tends to look at things symbolically, in order to avoid feeling them. And with the Moon in

Pluto's sign and in hard aspect to Pluto, the feelings would be very powerful and somewhat inflexible. Symbols are our door into what Plato called the "eternal realities", and they are also one of the great creative defences against direct emotional experience. Symbols allow something to enter our lives without our having to react directly and personally on an emotional level. For example, cyclical depression is characteristic of Moon-Pluto. This is partly because one's emotional responses are coloured by a profound awareness of the transience of life, the irrevocability of endings, and the power-struggles which usually accompany any deep relationship. Moon-Pluto knows too much about life, and what it knows isn't always pretty and shining. So what does our hypothetical Sagittarian do with depression?

Audience: Is it a hypothetical male or a hypothetical female?

Liz: Whichever you prefer. In practice the basic dynamics are the same. A woman may project Moon qualities onto men or other women, and a man may project them onto women or other men. In the old days it was assumed that women expressed the Moon and men the Sun. But of course it isn't that simple any more. It probably never was. A woman might just as easily express the Sagittarian hopefulness, optimism, and reluctance to face any contact with the darker elements in life and in herself. Anyway, we can't call our example "it", so let's assume it is a woman.

Audience: Might she get manic in order to avoid depression?

Liz: Yes, she might. She could accelerate either her social life or her intellectual interests, or plunge ferociously into one creative project after another, or maybe even travel in a rather compulsive and rootless way, in order to avoid sitting still and being overwhelmed by those dark feelings. Or she might try to interpret the depression symbolically. She would come along to a CPA seminar on Depression, or buy a copy of *Dynamics of the Unconscious* and read the section on alchemy and the *nigredo* as a necessary dark phase in the alchemical process. If Sagittarius can put the depression into a universal context, it isn't depressing any more. It's something to learn from, something which can help one to grow. And by the time she has finished reading and attending seminars, the cycle has passed, and she has managed to avoid feeling the depression. So when it returns, which it inevitably will, it may be stronger and darker. The Libran Ascendant will have its own set of defences against Moon in Scorpio square Pluto. Do you have some idea of how these might be expressed?

Audience: She would probably be very nice all the time.

Liz: Exactly. Because the Ascendant is concerned with the way we express ourselves to the outside world, she would probably be extremely careful to behave in a courteous, pleasant, charming, and equable fashion. Under no circumstances would the Plutonian side be allowed to show itself. We would never catch her screaming bloody murder at her partner because he flirted with someone else, or letting her friends see how enraged she feels about having her secrets betrayed. She would, in short, be an extremely likeable, pleasant, bright, and generous personality. She would probably be incredibly tolerant of others' idiosyncrasies, and always eager to understand and talk through any difficulties. She might be deeply ashamed of her dark moods and emotions, or, if she is powerfully defended, she might not even know they were there. Then we might see compulsive oral defences, such as an eating disorder, providing the only outlet for the stifled Moon.

We will often find pockets like this in a chart. The ego will usually be heavily defended against such hot places. They are the norm rather than the exception, and the frequency is partly due to the fact that Venus, which can be anywhere within 48° of the Sun, will often be in a sign which is fundamentally in conflict with the Sun sign. Many people with the Sun in Libra have Venus in Scorpio, many with the Sun in Virgo have Venus in Leo, many with the Sun in Gemini have Venus in Cancer, and so on. When these fire-earth or air-water combinations occur, we need to understand who in the chart is friends with whom, and whether Venus – or perhaps the Sun – is an outcast. Aspects can emphasise this, and gradually one builds up a picture of those dimensions of the personality against which one is most heavily defended.

Audience: Are these hot places triggered by transits?

Liz: Yes. They are also triggered by another person's natal planets touching the vulnerable point. We can often discover our defences when we are undergoing important transits which suddenly present us with something we fear very much. Since important transits also tend to be expressed through our relationships with other people, we may frequently see the two things together – a transit of Pluto to, say, the Moon in Scorpio in our example, and a relationship with someone whose natal Mars is square the woman's Moon. Then the Pluto transit will trigger both people, and the defences will be mobilised within the relationship. You can work out the consequences yourselves, I think.

Defences are mobilised against anything we find intolerable. Most of all, we find parts of ourselves intolerable. When we find things outside intolerable, it is usually because they are resonating with something inside. Although we initially looked at defences in terms of the basic patterns inherent in every zodiac sign, and then looked at specific examples of natal configurations in conflict with each other, each person's natal horoscope, as a matter of course, contains planets which represent the thing that he or she fears most. One doesn't even need to find a "pocket" such as we have been discussing. The Cancerian has Uranus in the birth chart, and the Aries has Saturn. The Taurus has Jupiter and Mars, and the Aquarian has Neptune and Pluto. These planets will sooner or later be triggered by important transits, and constellate the person's deepest fears. The enemy is always within, even if it is without as well. In any chart, we need to understand what constitutes an intolerable threat. Then we can work with transits and progressions, and with synastry, to get a sense of when and where these issues are likely to crystallise in the person's life, and how they might best be coped with in a way which honours the defences yet also allows some flexibility and change.

Audience: What do you mean by honouring the defences? Surely someone like the example we were looking at needs to learn to express her feelings.

Liz: That looks wonderful on paper. But what does "express her feelings" mean? I began the seminar by talking about the necessity of defences, and their creative contribution to the personality. A Sagittarian with Libra rising will never really find Plutonian emotions attractive, any more than an Aquarian with Capricorn rising will find Neptunian dissolution pleasant. Experiencing these planets may yield great meaning and richness, and our example might eventually find that she is glad she has this side to her nature, because it gives her depth, insight, and compassion. But Jupiter and Venus will never look at Pluto and say, "Oh, how lovely." Our lady will have to learn to live with this dichotomy, and in fact her defences against too violent or excessive a display of emotion may be absolutely appropriate. She would have a hard time living with herself afterward if she went for her partner in Medea-like fashion, especially if he didn't deserve it. Someone with such a sign combination needs to see herself as a good and ethical person.

And we should probably also remember, although we might not like it, that certain Plutonian emotions are not just destructive in the eyes of some mythic oppressive patriarchy or rigid superego. They are simply destructive. Sometimes they can't be justified by the claim that they are "instinctual" and "natural". That is idealising of a kind which is highly suspect, and which may itself be a defence against facing fundamental moral issues about how we behave to each other. Perhaps we need to create defences around certain aspects of ourselves, so that they can bubble away without being inflicted too forcibly on our fellow humans. The critical issue seems to me to be whether we are conscious of them. Consciousness of our dichotomies causes pain, and leaves us with an unanswerable conflict. But it also give us a soul.

Audience: If a client exhibited strong defences in a session, would you tell them what they were doing?

Liz: Not in a direct or accusing way, no. But I might try to get at the issue in a roundabout fashion. The defences a client shows an astrologer or therapist are going to be the same ones that person shows to others as well, and, as I keep saying, they are there for a reason, and are mobilised to protect great anxiety and vulnerability. It is important to explore any defence mechanisms which are glaringly evident in the chart and are creating problems in the person's life. The defensive isolation of an aspect like Sun-Saturn may need to be discussed, so that the person can understand why he or she is driving others away. But confrontation on the level of "You're doing this to me!" is usually, although not always, inappropriate in an astrological session, unless the defences are very bad and the astrologer isn't able to do his or her work properly. In ongoing therapeutic work a relationship of trust is built up over time, and it is almost always helpful to give the client feedback of an honest kind, when the time is right. But the relative brevity of an astrological reading precludes that kind of relationship and therefore requires more circumspection, unless, as I said, the client is so unpleasant that it simply isn't possible to continue.

Other people's defences can be very disturbing to encounter, if they have become compulsive and are blocking everything else from expression. When we meet someone who is deeply and compulsively defended, it can feel like a slap in the face. We are dismissed, shut out, treated with contempt, verbally or physically attacked or intimidated, or clawed at as a food-source. We may sense a huge reservoir of rage and aggression, which in turn can trigger our own defences so quickly that we are in the midst of a full-blown fight before we even realise what has happened. That is why defences tend to attract the very thing they are mobilised against. And the more the person unconsciously recreates the same situation over and over again, the more entrenched his or her defences become.

Burton is a good example. His defences were meant to protect him from feelings of impotence and loneliness. Yet look how he wound up: impotent and lonely. He drew down upon his own head the very thing from which his defences were meant to save him. When defences take over the personality, this seems to be the inevitable and tragic result. We create our own defeat, because our defences drive other people into responding to us in the very way which feels most threatening.

Audience: Can you say something about Venus-Pluto aspects? Would any aspect between these two create conflict and a defence mechanism? They seem to me incompatible planets.

Liz: They needn't be. Although the Libran aspect of Venus, with its aestheticism, strong ethics, and high ideals, may find Plutonian intensity threatening, the sensual, Taurean side of Venus can find Pluto a very pleasant bedfellow. In myth, Aphrodite is one of the few friends Hades has got, which is why she sets up Persephone's abduction and rape rather than allowing the girl to languish in eternal virginity. I would need to know what kind of chart the Venus-Pluto aspect was embedded in before I could get a sense of whether it was a "hot place". If these two planets have friends in the chart – say, the Sun in Scorpio, or Mars trine Pluto, or a grand water trine between Moon and Neptune and Mars, then I wouldn't assume Venus-Pluto to be the source of fear and defensiveness. The person may find passionate and even obsessive feelings exciting and enriching, rather than threatening, and the need for crisis and struggle in relationship might be accepted and appreciated. Not everyone wants a peaceful life. The world of theatre and music is full of individuals who love living life on the edge. Their larger-than-life love affairs, as well as their creative performances, may owe much to aspects like Venus-Pluto. Maria Callas, for example, had Venus in Capricorn opposition Pluto in Cancer. Her Scorpio Ascendant ensured that the two planets had a friend. Not surprisingly, her performance of *Medea* is still considered unsurpassed.

Pluto itself, however, is in a state of permanent defence. It is nature's defence against stagnation. Pluto is concerned with survival on the most fundamental level, and therefore life is seen as mortal combat, a perpetual battle between the forces of generation and the forces of decay. Either we take power, or something else will take power over us. This is life in the jungle, where only the fittest survive. There is no welfare state in the jungle to provide a safety net for old, handicapped, or unemployed animals. The weak are destroyed by their own kind for the good of the species. If we don't eat our enemy, he or she will eat us.

This Plutonian world-view enters the sphere of human relationships when Pluto is in aspect to Venus in the natal chart. Issues of survival, power, and the battle against stagnation become part of one's perception of relationship. This can intensify one's feelings for and against other people, because there is so much at stake. Every deep relationship enriches life enormously, but it also poses a threat. In the power-battle that ensues, Venus-Pluto may grow to love and respect most the person who is strong enough to fight back. Venus-Pluto may seek power in relationship, not because power is fun or because of any love of dominating others, but because Pluto instinctively knows that if there is no battle and no potential of change through crisis, love will grow cold and the stagnation of the whole personality will ensue.

Audience: I have a Venus-Pluto conjunction in the 12th house, and recently transiting Pluto squared it. I actually woke up in the middle of the night with a raging fit of paranoia. I was convinced that someone I knew, a fellow therapist, was pinching my material, and that she was going to take away all my clients. I had to literally restrain myself from lifting the telephone at four o'clock in the morning to give her hell. I struggled for a whole day with these feelings. But it was an eruption which taught me a lot, even if it was a desperate twelve hours.

Liz: Pluto often feels desperate. Life is desperate, after all. We spend our lives fighting against death. When we try to enter into this planet's state of mind, if mind is the appropriate word – or perhaps state of feeling? – the world is not a civilised place in which people can discuss their issues with each other. It is a jungle, and every emotion and sensual experience is heightened. Everything in some way reflects the eternal cycle of procreation and death, and nothing is as important as survival. So everything is pared down to its absolute basics. Paranoia is a Plutonian defence. You will know the old cliché: "Don't worry if you think people are out to get you. They are." Pluto always feels under threat, and one must always be on the alert.

Audience: How can one break that pattern if one is aware of it?

Liz: I don't think one can break it, and perhaps one shouldn't try. Even though it is primitive, unchristian, and politically incorrect, there is profound truth in it. But one can recognise that one's own perceptions may not constitute another person's reality or experience. One can try to live Pluto's values for oneself, but not impose them on others. If your partner doesn't have a strongly Plutonian dimension in the chart, you may never be able to convince him or her that your intensity and urgency are valid and necessary. And if you value the relationship, you will have to learn to contain, rather than break, the pattern.

If you perceive love as a battle of opposites – life or death, survival or extinction, dominance or submission – you may have to learn to express this vision in a context where it will not destroy. Write a really gritty novel. Or get it out through painting, or music, or theatre. Find someplace where you don't have to apologise for it, or feel forced to explain to shallower souls the depths which are so patently obvious to you. Join an amateur acting group. There is no better place for Venus-Pluto than playing Medea, or Lady Macbeth. The arts have always provided a home for Pluto, because it is the one place where we sanction savagery, apart fom war. If Pluto has at least one good creative outlet, it is less likely to turn defensively on others. Pluto, like all the planets, has got to be able to live what it is. But its nature is inimical to what we call "civilised" interaction. If you give it an outlet where it can really rip, it makes a lot less trouble on the personal level. The need for intensity and emotional confrontation will still be there, but perhaps not so compulsively.

Plutonian defences can be enormously creative and life-sustaining. Without them, we would not survive. We tend to forget, in this hyper-rational age, that without Plutonian instincts we would be missing a basic level of paranoia that might be very healthy and necessary for us. We lock our doors at night because if we don't, we may pay dearly, not just with material possessions, but with our lives as well. While the air signs sit about discussing the roots of crime and the possible social reasons why burglary and rape are on the rise, Pluto gets on with the bitter but necessary business of putting a padlock on the gate and learning simple techniques of physical self-defence. The world is like that right now, no matter how much our ideals tell us it ought not to be. And while we may be right to attempt to implement changes on the political and social level, we still have to know how to protect ourselves against human brutality.

Pluto doesn't tend to go about saying, "Oh, what a terrible state the world is in. Twenty years ago I used to leave my front door unlocked and I never got robbed. It's all the fault of the government." If Pluto isn't the burglar himself, then it's the chap who sells burglar alarms, as well as the one who has the perspicacity to install one. Like recognises like, and Pluto within us knows that Pluto outside us will be hanging about the alley at nightfall, waiting for the chance to do a spot of grievous bodily harm. There will always be Plutonian elements in society, despite the efforts of Uranus to reform them. If we fail to recognise them in ourselves, then we will have no idea of how to look after ourselves because we cannot mobilise jungle instincts as a defence. And perhaps the woman about whom you had the fit of paranoia really does harbour secret feelings of envy and hostility toward you. You would, of course, have to look hard at your own emotional issues of rivalry as well. But your jungle instincts may have been right about her secret feelings, if not her actual intentions and actions.

Defences and projection

I have two charts which have been given to me by members of the group. Before I put the first of these up on the overhead projector, are there any questions or comments?

Audience: I am interested in what you said about defences tending to attract the very thing that they defend against. How does one distinguish whether the enemy is real or not?

Liz: The enemy is always real. The problem lies in working out whether it is internal, external, or both, and on what level and to what degree. This is mysterious terrain, because we are moving in that "psychoid" realm in which we ourselves are the reality we meet outside. Jung said that a person's life is characteristic of the person. On the individual level, I believe this to be true, and it is why any placement in the chart describes both our inner reality and also the circumstances which we are likely to meet in life. It is the point where psychological and predictive astrology meet.

There are areas where this view breaks down, and we must allow for collective crises, such as wars, plagues, and revolutions, when individual destiny is superseded by impersonal or transpersonal forces of which the individual is a part. We cannot claim that every Bosnian has somehow conjured the terrible ravages of war because of some individual inner destroyer. The issue of collective culpability is a complex one, and also a great mystery. Nor is this an issue of personal blame, or personal failure. But somehow, the substance of which we are made as individuals resonates to its like outside us, and we tend to meet those people, and encounter those situations, which reflect our secret souls back to ourselves.

There may always be things within us against which we must defend ourselves, even if we are nicely analysed and very conscious of our internal fears and conflicts. There may be a deep and inherent conflict of values, and we may have to choose one over another. Or there may be destructive elements, which exist in everyone, which simply have to be contained and prevented from breaking out and injuring others as well as ourselves. But the more aware we are, and the more loyal we are to our own values, the less likely we are to constellate these inner issues in the world outside in a compulsive fashion.

The enemy may also be outside, and may mirror something within ourselves. We may still have to defend ourselves against that enemy, even if we recognise our secret affinity. Not to do so would be foolish. If I were starving, homeless, and desperate, with three small children to look after, I might well be reduced to stealing. Because of this recognition, I can also see that it would be very stupid to leave my BMW in a dark alley with the doors unlocked. Likewise, I know that if someone threatened my life, or the life of someone I loved, I would fight back, and violently if necessary. Therefore I can understand, although not condone, those people who, when abused too long and too often, become destructive.

But if I were so convinced of my moral purity and spiritual enlightenment that I could not imagine any shared humanity with the thief or the criminal, then my arrogance, which would be a defence against more primitive aspects in the horoscope, might mysteriously activate something in that strange web of connections which we call the collective psyche. Then some Plutonian would come along and do to me what I can't admit I might do to him if I were *in extremis*. He might not do it physically, in a street fight. He might do it emotionally, because I have found myself compulsively attracted to him and wound up marrying him. Or, because life is so full of strange tricks, he might be my son, and the thing which I fear within would come to meet me in the guise of my own flesh and blood. Or he may appear as the Plutonian illness which causes my body pain.

Consciousness is no guarantee of protection. We may still suffer, because life is not fair, and we are also at the mercy of our psychological inheritance and of the collective in which we live. But even without guarantees, at least we know we are doing our best to avoid an unconscious invocation of what we cannot face within. I feel we should remember, when we judge people and the sometimes terrible things they do in defence, that there, but for the grace of the gods, go the rest of us.

Consciousness can help us to avoid being compulsive, both in our reactions to others' defences, and in our defence against what we experience as a threat. Defences are not inherently pathological. But compulsiveness usually suggests that something has got badly out of balance. There is a difference between a Moon-Pluto which is dramatic and intense, and a Moon-Pluto which is compulsively paranoid. Moon-Pluto is always a little mistrustful. It is made like that, and rightly so, because if one senses so much going on beneath the surface, one is vulnerable to others' unconscious malice and anger in a way a less sensitive person isn't. To Moon-Pluto, another person's unspoken rage is as real as a physical punch, and just as painful. But when the suspicion becomes compulsive, and the person begins to avoid social gatherings because everyone seems full of aggression, or he or she starts behaving aggressively toward everyone else, then the defences have begun to interfere with reality, and that person is in trouble. We can recognise compulsiveness in ourselves when our fantasies and reactions are hugely out of proportion to the actual situation, or when we become so obsessed with defending ourselves that we forget how to trust.

The same thing might be applied to anger as a defence. We can generally recognise when our anger is justified, if we have a reasonably objective relationship to reality. And we can also recognise when that anger is pulling something much older up with it, like a fisherman who pulls up a mass of gunge from the bottom of the lake along with the fish. We can feel the difference because of the compulsive quality of the anger, and its hugeness in proportion to the trigger – even if we prefer to enjoy the indulgence of a really good conflagration. We can also learn to recognise when we are using words as a defence. I think we all know when we are talking rubbish to impress, or because we can't bear the silence. When it is compulsive, we can feel it. And we have the power, at that point, to say to ourselves, "Wait a minute. Shut up and think about why you are behaving like this." If we don't do this, we may then provoke others into treating us in precisely the way we most fear.

Audience: Yet you are saying that we need these defences, that they are part of our identity.

Liz: Yes, I believe this is so. There is a difference between expressing healthy defences, and being compulsively taken over by defences. If we attempt to give up a necessary defence, we are betraying ourselves, and attempting to live according to a concept of "right" behaviour which may deeply damage us. I doubt that it is possible to eradicate such defences – only to suppress them. I started the morning off saying that defences exist for the protection of what we most need and value. I think it is a question of balance and consciousness, rather than an issue of remodelling the human being.

We couldn't very well have walked up to Richard Burton and said, "Look, old chap, aren't you being a bit inflated? Don't you realise that being a famous actor is really a defence against your poor Welsh background? Drop the defence and stay in the coal mines. If it was good enough for your family, it's good enough for you." Do you seriously think he would have been happy? Of course Burton's self-mythologising was a defence. But it was also a fundamental part of his great gift, and ultimately he was attempting to defend his artist's soul against a corrosively meaningless existence. It might have been appropriate to say, "Look, your defences have got out of balance. They're so compulsive that you can't cope with ordinary mortal life. You can still be a famous actor and not drink yourself to death." But it is unlikely that he would have listened.

More example charts and group discussion

Example chart 2

Now we have a chart from the group. Would you like to tell us what is concerning you in this chart?

Audience: It's something I've thought quite a lot about. The strongest area of conflict in the chart seems to be between all the fire, and the Scorpio Moon and the T-cross together.

Liz: Let's begin with the balance of elements. The Moon is the only planet in water in the chart. There are three planets in earth, two of which are outer planets. Jupiter and Venus are in air. Fire is clearly the most powerful element, with the Sun and Mercury in Sagittarius trine Pluto and Chiron in Leo trine Mars and the Ascendant in Aries. There is a grand fire trine here. Although earth is the next emphasised element numerically, it is psychologically opposite to fire, and fire will undoubtedly win in any contest of values and attitudes. Air will probably be easier to express than earth, and the earth-water combination may provide the focus for a great deal of tension. So who is friends with whom in this chart?

Audience: The fire trine is connected to Jupiter in Gemini because Mercury and Jupiter are in mutual reception. So they would be friends.

Liz: Yes, they are in mutual reception, by house as well as by sign. Mercury is in Jupiter's house, the 9th, and Jupiter is in Mercury's house, the 3rd. Although they are in opposition, they are friends. Jupiter disposes of all the Sagittarian planets, and there is clearly a lot of creative mental energy and a fine imaginative capacity. And an airy Venus is comfortable with this air-fire emphasis, because the aesthetic, cultured side of Venus can be easily expressed.

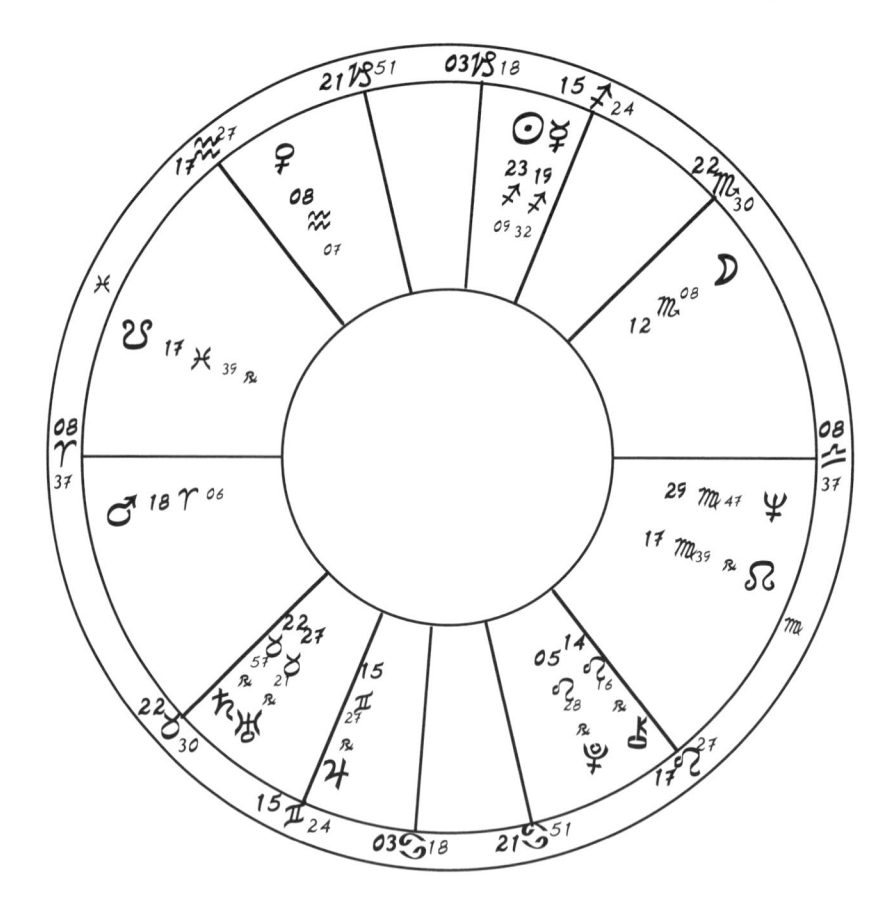

Example chart 2
Female, 15 December 1941, 1.40 pm BST, London

The Moon is clearly the social outcast in this chart. It is in the 7th house, where it is likely to be projected onto partners. It's in a difficult T-

Part One: The Psychology of Defences and their Astrological Significators 107

cross, and it's in the sign of its fall. The Moon has no friends at all. If we want to look at this chart from the perspective of defences, rather than any one of a hundred other perfectly valid perspectives we could take, we would need to recognise how vulnerable the Moon is, and how strong the internal defences are likely to be against intense emotional attachments.

Audience: My mother had the Sun in Cancer, with no planets in fire at all in her chart. I experienced her as the most claustrophobic person.

Liz: You are touching on a very important issue. Our defences are often exacerbated by childhood experiences. I don't mean this in terms of Freud's idea that defences belong to particular stages in childhood, although that is probably true enough in a general sense. But you clearly have very strong needs of a particular kind, reflected by the fire emphasis in the chart as well as the importance of the 9th and 3rd houses. In childhood as well as in adulthood, there is a powerful need for mobility, freedom of movement and ideas, and open communication. As a child you probably badly needed someone to talk to, to show interest in what interested you. Only then might you have felt comfortable enough to show your emotional needs. If the environment was unsympathetic to your basic nature, it would probably make you even more defensive and uncomfortable with any expression of feeling. It also sounds as though your mother still stands between you and your ability to understand and value your Moon, because she seemed to you a personification of the worst dimensions of it.

Audience: Wouldn't there be a lot of unexpressed rage in that Moon? Might there be a problem with showing anger?

Audience: I don't have trouble showing anger.

Liz: You might be right about the rage if Mars was involved with the Moon, but it isn't, except as co-ruler of Scorpio. Mars itself is beautifully aspected, and placed in the sign of its dignity in its natural house. Anger is not the problem. I don't think this Moon rages. I think it is just desperately lonely and hungry. Nobody listens to this Moon. The personality defences are mobilised against it to such an extent that it's virtually mute.

Audience: I am sure it is linked with depression. I suffer a lot from cyclical depression.

Liz: I think you are right. Depression is the only way the Moon can make itself known. It might be very important to know how you deal with your depression, because if you are defended against it, which Sagittarians tend to be, then it will just keep coming back. As we have seen, Sagittarius has a whole bag of intellectual and spiritual tricks to cope with depression. You might also find yourself attracted to rather introverted people who are themselves melancholic or depressed, and then you could avoid your own depression by projecting the Moon on them and getting irritated at their low spirits.

Audience: Yes, I know that one.

Liz: The rising Mars in Aries will contribute its own defences. One of Aries' favourite defences, which we haven't yet mentioned, is that it gets terribly busy. Aries must always be doing something, whether it is athletic or intellectual. This can be a great defence against loneliness and pain. Aries may violently resist inactivity. They can be appalling patients in hospital for this reason, because they often can't bear to lie quietly and wait for the body to heal. Sagittarius will resist inactivity as well. You may have to learn to be very quiet and still in order to work with the Moon.

Audience: Your description of Sagittarius' bag of intellectual tricks sums up perfectly how I deal with it. But I think it's catching up with me. There is an eclipse of the Sun on Sunday in 10 Scorpio, and I am having an operation.

Liz: Is it major surgery?

Audience: It's a bone graft. It isn't essential.

Liz: Are you in pain? When defences block the Moon, it will often somatise its suffering, which means that it will convert the emotional pain into physical distress. The Moon tends to do this more than any other planet, if defences are stifling its expression.

Audience: I had a cancer removed two months ago, which is where this present problem comes from.

Liz: When powerful feelings are denied recognition and expression, the body can sometimes suffer the pain. I am not suggesting that this is the "cause" of cancer, or any other illness, but it may be a contributing factor. Just how big the contribution is remains as yet unknown. What the body feels can be what one feels oneself, without being aware of it as feelings. It is almost as if the body becomes a dumb animal which has to carry the burden of the pain. There is a great range of symptoms and ailments that can be linked with Moon issues. It isn't one specific kind of illness; but the common denominator seems to be pain. And the pain is often bound up with loneliness.

Lunar unhappiness may somatise itself. This is not the same as illness used as a defence, although the two may sometimes overlap. In some cases, illness can have a secondary gain, particularly when the organic basis of the illness is unclear. The pain may be a means of claiming attention and care. But I think this is quite different from what you are describing. Perhaps the only way that you can experience the pain on the emotional level is to lie in a hospital bed with it. Then all that frenzied fiery activity can't be utilised to escape it. Your operation may turn out to be a very creative experience.

Audience: I don't understand how the pain of the Moon can be experienced in the body.

Liz: Body and feelings are not as separate as we think. We associate the Moon in traditional astrology with instinctual needs, and assume these are always emotional. But in Kabbalistic symbolism, the Moon represents the realm of dense matter. In a small child, feelings and body are one thing. The experience of pleasure or pain occurs on both emotional and physical levels. Of course this does not apply only to a small child. The identity of body and feeling exists in us all. But the ego has a way of perceiving the two as separate as we get older, perhaps in part because this serves as a defence against being overwhelmed. We experience differentiation, up to a point. Certainly we can be conscious of feelings that don't somatise as recognisable physical "symptoms" of a painful kind. But it may be that every emotion registers in some way as a bodily process, through the heartbeat, the blood pressure, the respiratory rate, the endocrine system, or the digestive processes. I doubt very much whether we can feel, and not reflect these feelings through the body in some way, however subtle. A child's ego does not play the same tricks of differentiation, and both emotional and bodily level are experienced at once, and powerfully. If a child is left alone crying, the loneliness and the fear are also bodily terror, because there is no one there to provide physical protection against death. Loneliness for a small child is also a physical experience of being threatened with extinction.

If a baby is hungry, it is not merely physiological hunger. The satiation of the body's hunger at the mother's breast is also the fulfillment of emotional need, and the full stomach is bound up with being loved, wanted, and protected. These are not separate experiences. When we split off from bits of ourselves, which is what can happen when defences become too entrenched, we may disconnect from the emotional level of experience, leaving the body to carry the entire load. This is not uncommon when water is weak or absent in a chart. It is also a frequent problem when earth is weak or absent.

Audience: How do you reconnect them again?

Liz: Not by an act of will. Defences exist for a reason, and if such a split occurs between body and feelings, then there is usually a deep fear of the emotional suffering involved in being conscious. The threat is too great. Connections seem to develop under the right transits, such as the Pluto transit over this Scorpio Moon. Transits are symbolic indicators of the activation of something within us which is demanding recognition and space in our lives, especially if it has been stifled before. Body and feelings are likely to try to reconnect themselves, when the time is right. However, you can't just sit back and wait for some miraculous transformation. You must make time and space for things to come to the surface, and you will need some kind of outlet for what emerges. Rushing about being ferociously busy is a defence which may have to be consciously restrained. But if you choose to remain still and quiet, and allow feelings to begin to rise to the surface, you may experience great anxiety. This anxiety needs to be recognised and contained, rather than fought by the mobilisation of defence mechanisms. Sometimes the support of a counsellor or therapist is essential for containing anxiety, so that what lies underneath can begin to show itself.

    With the Sun-Mercury-Jupiter emphasis in this chart by planet, sign, and house, learning and communicating are extremely important, and always will be. But sometimes you may use all that intuitive and intellectual energy and activity as a defence against terrible feelings of emptiness and loneliness. I suspect you are aware of the difference between a really enjoyable and productive learning time, and a compulsive page-turning session which is meant to barricade the door against your emotions. Perhaps you can find the strength not to give in to such compulsions. Take the telephone off the hook, and try to articulate in a journal, or in visual form, what you are experiencing. Don't immediately grab a book which will interpret your feelings, but try to give them expression as they are, however disturbing or unpleasant they might seem. It is possible that words are not the best medium for you, since you are

CS300

REORDER FROM CUSTOM PRODUCTS AT RAPIDFORMS, INC. CALL TOLL FREE 800-247-8394. FAX 800-422-8113

Ref. No: G 191210633

Part One: The Psychology of Defences and their Astrological Significators   111

very articulate and can manipulate language too easily.

Audience: I think you are right about not relying on words. I am a writer, and I am too clever with them.

Liz: Try painting instead, or working with clay. Body work may also help, although you would have to be very sure of the integrity and training of the therapist. But you must make the space. This kind of deep split will eventually knit itself, given half a chance and a little help. Like the body, the psyche has its own self-healing mechanisms, if only we can invoke them. Granting time and space to your feelings is probably precisely what your mother could not do when you were small; only her emotional needs mattered, not yours. You may need to become your own mother, on the level on which you first experienced the wound. I am not even sure whether "doing" things is as relevant as the attitude you take toward your feelings. You may be doing the same thing to yourself that your mother did. A genuine change in consciousness may be the thing which mobilises the healing energies within.

Thank you for giving us the chart to discuss. Perhaps we can look at a second chart from the group now. What issues did you want to discuss?

Example chart 3

Audience: I think my main defence is collecting information about others, to find out as much as I can about their feelings, in order to get close to them without having to be vulnerable myself. Maybe studying astrology is part of that defence.

Liz: Let's look at the balance of elements in the chart. The Sun and Mercury are in Pisces, a water sign, and Scorpio, another water sign, is on the Ascendant. The need for emotional closeness is probably very powerful. Yet you seem to be afraid of asking for this closeness in case you are hurt, so you use information to defend yourself against vulnerability. The more you know about other people, the more you hope to be able to pre-empt any emotional rejection or wounding. You are trying to have your cake and eat it too. The Moon is in air, in 17° Gemini, trine a Saturn-Neptune conjunction in Libra. So there are three planets in air. Venus is in Aries, opposite the Saturn-Neptune, and Mars is also in Aries. These two, with Pluto in Leo, indicate three planets in fire, plus the Midheaven. Jupiter and Chiron are in earth. The elements are

Barriers and Boundaries

quite balanced in this chart, and it isn't simple to work out where the weight is; but if we look at the aspect configurations we can get a good sense of who is friends with whom.

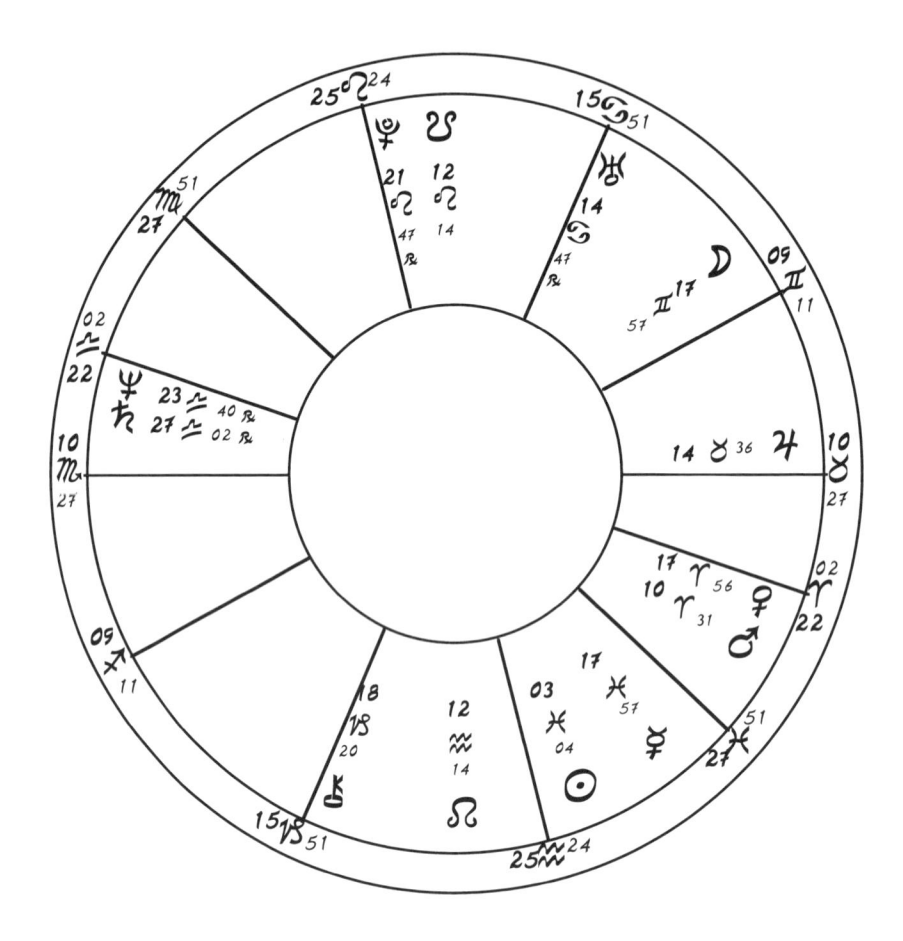

Example chart 3
Female, 21 February 1953, 11.45 pm GMT, London

Venus has a difficult time in this chart. It is in the sign of its detriment, and it is caught in a grand cross with the Saturn-Neptune conjunction in Libra, Chiron in Capricorn, and Uranus in Cancer. I would understand this as a reflection of great insecurity and fear of rejection (Venus opposite Saturn and square Chiron), which collides with idealised romantic dreams of perfect love and fusion (Venus opposite Neptune). A deep resistance

Part One: The Psychology of Defences and their Astrological Significators   113

against dependency and compromise (Venus square Uranus) will fight against the Venus-Neptune, and align itself with the Venus-Saturn and Venus-Chiron aspects, producing a defence system which probably makes you keep people at an emotional distance as much as possible. The Saturn-Neptune conjunction, in itself, reflects a conflict between two inimical principles, of separateness and fusion, so the same theme is suggested yet again. The entire configuration may be linked with a parental pattern of conditional love, or love which was insufficient to meet your needs as a water sign. Venus-Neptune is friends with the Sun in Pisces, and also with the Scorpio Ascendant. But it is likely to be blocked by the hard aspects of Venus to Saturn, Chiron, and Uranus.

Then the Moon joins in the fun. It reflects the same dichotomy – it is trine Saturn but also trine Neptune. And it squares Mercury in Pisces. Mercury-Moon squares can sometimes reflect the mind used as a defence against feelings. The Moon in Gemini aligns itself with Saturn and Uranus, and relates through words and facts rather than through feeling. Air in this chart is not really any more dominant than water, but it is easier to express and identify with, because of the painful Venus aspects. So the Geminian tendency to create distance, through detached observation and information, is mobilised against feeling overwhelmed by emotional needs which might lead you into being hurt or humiliated – as you might feel you were hurt or humiliated quite early in life. Of course a Scorpio Ascendant carries its own defences against emotional hurt, one of which is the utilisation of intuitive insight into others for the purposes of controlling relationships and ensuring that one can always hit back hard if one is rejected or humiliated.

At the moment this grand cross is taking very powerful transits. Uranus and Neptune are moving across it, activating the inherent conflict. Transiting Saturn and transiting Chiron, which are moving in opposition to each other in Pisces and Virgo respectively, are also currently using the Moon as a football.

Audience: I am feeling more and more unhappy with the way I relate. I know I have a problem. Right now I feel committed to expressing my own feelings.

Liz: Your basic nature is watery, so there must be some very good reasons why you are defending yourself against being a Piscean, and relating almost wholly from the Gemini Moon. There is probably a lot of pain involved in expressing your feelings, and with the grand cross activated, this might be an excellent time to explore the underlying issues. The Venus-Chiron, Venus-Neptune, Venus-Saturn and Venus-Uranus aspects seem to me to hold the key to what you experience as most threatening. Also, you may share a fear of the irrational with many others of your generation born under the Saturn-Neptune-Uranus configuration. In this planetary grouping, Saturn and Uranus tend to gang up against Neptune, which is your Sun-sign ruler. There are also inherent differences and conflicts in the Sun-Moon combination of Pisces and Gemini. But they do not have to polarise, and in fact it is a marvellous combination for anyone who is involved in working with others. The capacity to enter into others' feelings, and the ability to express in articulate ways what one senses and perceives, can also contribute a great deal to any creative work which is intended to reach a lot of people. These signs are mutable and therefore open and tolerant, inclusive in their outlook, and able to view life from many different perspectives. They don't have to fight as they are doing in you at the moment.

Audience: My mother was very invasive. I think I am very defended against that. I've sometimes thought that the simplest way to live is to observe other people's feelings, rather than feeling anything myself.

Liz: There is a lot of unhappiness and bitterness in that statement. I think it is terribly important for you to explore the bitterness. It sounds as though you despise yourself for needing other people, and are determined not to allow this need to put you in a vulnerable position, as you probably were with your mother. Yet you can't really stop being a Piscean despite your efforts, because you are still dependent on others to provide you with knowledge as a defence against yourself.

Audience: You've mentioned my family. I very much want my own family, but it never seems to happen. I make sure it doesn't happen.

Liz: Perhaps until you separate from your "family of origin", as it is called in family therapy, you won't feel emotionally able to cope with a family of your own. You haven't separated yet, on the psychological level. Physically you may have left them long ago. But when a person is dominated by defences against childhood experiences, rather than living his or her own life, then I think it is fair to say that such an individual has not yet separated from the family matrix.

Audience: Ouch.

Part One: The Psychology of Defences and their Astrological Significators 115

Liz: When the Sun is in the 4th house, one's sense of identity is bound up with the background into which one has been born. You haven't failed or done something wrong; you are reflecting the archetypal pattern of a 4th house Sun. Sooner or later, because the Sun reflects a powerful need for self-creation, one must, in a sense, start afresh. One has to become one's own progenitor, and this means psychologically separating from family and roots. This can be very painful for Pisces, which hates any sense of isolation or separateness. Psychologically I think you have not yet left your parents, or the emotional world which you inhabited as a child. You still relate to life in the same context. Until you are able to perceive yourself and others in a different way, this Sun in Pisces won't operate in the creative way that you want it to.

Audience: Do you feel that Pluto's passage through early Sagittarius will help?

Liz: Yes, I do. When transiting Pluto moves into Sagittarius it will square the Sun. This square will occur in early 1996, although Pluto actually dips into the first degree of Sagittarius at the beginning and end of 1995. Pluto casts strong ripples before it, as it moves into orb of an aspect to a natal planet. The next two years may prove very important in activating the drive to be your own person, free of the assumptions, expectations, and emotional inheritance of your background. This may be powerful enough to crack through the defences which prevent you from letting yourself be a vulnerable Pisces. At the same time, Uranus will be squaring natal Saturn, and then, a bit later, Neptune will square it. That also suggests the breaking down of defences and barriers.

Audience: This year, Saturn was conjunct my Sun. It was a terrible experience. I was constantly asking myself who I really am.

Liz: That's usual for Saturn over the Sun. Did you get any answers?

Audience: It's why I started studying astrology. To get an answer. I haven't really got it yet.

Liz: You will need a lot of patience. The transits over the grand cross aren't finished yet, and the transit of Pluto square the Sun should prove very decisive and illuminating. But in the end you are someone with the Sun in Pisces, and all that this implies in terms of receptivity to the greater unity of life. Although we are all, of course, the whole of our chart, our conscious sense of identity rests on the Sun. Without this central sense of "I", we may feel like ping pong balls, bouncing between planetary configurations which periodically claim they are our real selves and are then superseded by another configuration. One morning you are a desperately dependent Venus-Neptune, the next you are a cool, detached Venus-Uranus, and the next you are a fiery, energetic Mars in Aries square Uranus, who can conquer the world as long as nobody messes with you. The unifying principle in the chart is the Sun, and until you are able to live it without fear or shame, you will keep wondering who you are.

Audience: Fear of abandonment is a very strong fear for water. How does that fit into this chart?

Liz: Fear of abandonment is certainly a water issue, but it is especially threatening if the Moon or Venus aspects Saturn or Chiron. Venus-Saturn often receives conditional love in childhood – "I will love you as long as you behave in ways which are acceptable to me. If you don't, then I will reject you." There is sometimes a sense of deprivation, as if there were not enough love to go around, or love is shown in chilly, dutiful, or practical ways rather than tactile, spontaneous, emotionally warming ones. Venus-Chiron may experience unpleasant circumstances which necessitate temporary or permanent separation from loved ones, on either a physical or emotional level. These circumstances are often unfair, and not necessarily because parents have "failed". There may be financial difficulties, or illness, rather than a specific person acting in a cold or unloving way. The aspects are painful in any chart, but especially when water is strong, as it is here.

Audience: What about Pluto and abandonment? It somehow seems to be implicated.

Liz: Pluto may be implicated, but the feeling tone is different. Pluto may be so defensive that it plays the abandoner rather than the abandonee, on the principle that if one leaves first then the other person can't put one in the helpless, humiliating position of being manipulated or rejected. Sometimes childhood issues reflected by a strong Pluto are connected with experiences of abandonment due to great suffering on the part of the parent, a kind of "act of fate". Moon-Pluto seems to turn up a lot in the charts of children who have been adopted. Sometimes spite or vindictiveness colour the family emotional atmosphere, and power-struggles may involve the deliberate withholding of feeling. But Pluto's innate defensiveness may be at work in the child right

Part One: The Psychology of Defences and their Astrological Significators 117

from the outset, and feelings of emotional abandonment may reflect a power battle between parent and child. I would associate Moon-Pluto and Venus-Pluto contacts not necessarily with a fear of abandonment, but with a fear of being humiliated or destroyed through falling under someone else's emotional power.

Audience: But a small child would not express such defences and reject the parent first. Let's say a child has Moon in Scorpio square Pluto in Leo. There may be a real experience of abandonment at an early age, and maybe later, in adulthood, the person would try to manipulate relationships to avoid being abandoned again. Surely that child wouldn't do something to the mother which invoked a rejecting response.

Liz: I am not sure it is quite so simple. We begin our defensive patterns very early. And it is important to remember that any factor in one's own chart reflects one's own perceptions. Family patterns in a horoscope may coincide with qualities in the parents, or events in childhood. But they are really descriptions of how we perceive our parents and our childhood, and the hook is not always identical with the projection. Often a dynamic is set up between parent and child, through planetary contacts which trigger the defences in both. Venus-Saturn may describe a childhood experience of conditions attached to being loved, but the child may equally place conditions on the parent, and each may mistrust the other's expression of feeling. A child with Moon in Scorpio square Pluto may experience what I called an "act of fate", a situation over which no one has any control, and a sense of abandonment may be the result. There is no sense in which the child could be accused of "causing" such an experience. But the child also has his or her own nature, and may respond to that "act of fate" in intensely defensive ways which might be alien to a child with Moon in Sagittarius trine Uranus. Not all children interpret separation as abandonment. And sometimes the child's own intensity, instinctive and inherent, may trigger reactions in the mother which lead to an experience of rejection on both sides.

Audience: Surely that's the mother's problem.

Liz: It usually seems like the mother's problem, because we cannot imagine that we could ourselves do or be anything which merits rejection. Sometimes the opposite occurs, and we are convinced that it is wholly our own problem, and that we must be evil and unlovable; otherwise we would have been loved.

The problem is that no love is perfect, and every parent-child bond contains experiences of hurt. We may blame either the mother or ourselves, but these are extreme polarisations which only lead to an adulthood spent searching for an ideal partner who will love us perfectly. Then the real partner, when he or she fails, becomes wholly to blame. Melanie Klein called this "splitting".

Audience: In my case, my father went to war, where he was killed when I was a month old. I have the Moon square Pluto. I suppose that is an "act of fate".

Liz: Yes, that is a collective fate, which has intruded on the lives of individuals through no fault of their own. But Moon-Pluto describes the experience of the mother, not the father. Perhaps the repercussions on your mother of this tragic and unfair death, and her own loneliness and grief, are partly involved with your sense of abandonment. I would guess that she was very depressed, and perhaps even in a state of great despair, and this may be connected with your feeling of being abandoned by her. In the perfect world of our infantile fantasies, all mothers should always be unconditionally loving, regardless of their child's nature or the events which impinge on their lives from without. But the reality is that it isn't always the mother's problem. One can suffer a loss which leaves one quite incapable of responding to a baby's Scorpionic needs. Or one can have a child who triggers one's own defence system, in the worst possible way or at the worst possible moment. One can even have a child who enjoys the feeling of power which comes from triggering one's defence system.

If, for example, you have a lot of air in the chart, and a strong Moon-Uranus contact, and you have a child who has the Moon in Scorpio square Pluto, you may experience that child as very demanding. If you are suffering a loss or conflict of your own, you may simply find the child unbearable, and push him or her away. And the child will grow up feeling abandoned. Yes, abandonment has occurred. But it may be the result of bad chemistry and unlucky timing, rather than the "fault" of the mother. Very occasionally, Moon-Pluto reflects emotional or physical brutality on the part of a mother who has mobilised the defence of cruelty to protect herself against feelings of weakness and impotence. But more often, Moon-Pluto in a child's chart reflects the experience of a mother who is unhappy or depressed, and finds herself inexplicably reacting defensively to a child who seems to be too demanding, willful, or manipulative. And such a child usually has a long, long memory, and may never forgive the mother who failed to respond to Pluto's needs.

A strong Pluto in a child's chart may trigger deep reactions in the parent, because a mother who is a child herself may be terrified by so much unspoken intensity and mistrust. "Why is my baby looking at me like that?" says the mother to herself. We say this to Plutonian adults who fix us with the impenetrable Scorpionic stare. Plutonian babies stare too. Yes, it is the mother's "problem", if the world were perfect and everyone were fully conscious. Are you fully conscious? Do you think blaming one's mother for the rest of one's life is an intelligent way of dealing with one's own destructive Plutonian defences? Especially when the problem probably begins many generations back, and the mother is as much a victim as the child? It is a sad situation, but in terms of Pluto's compulsive defences, and the poison which these can unleash in adult relationships if left uncontained, it may be very important for a Moon-Pluto person to remember that the mother is, in all likelihood, neither evil nor guilty of any deliberate abandonment of her child. Moon-Pluto may need to rage for a while. But ultimately, one's destructive reactions are one's own responsibility.

A few weeks ago, in the seminar on synastry, we looked at the chart of Princess Diana. Diana's mother abandoned her for a time, when the parental marriage broke up. This abandonment was not desired by either mother or child. But the mother had been desperately unhappy and unable to cope. When she met a man who treated her well, she went off with him, and there was a nasty custody battle. You can read all about it in Andrew Morton's book. Initially – and perhaps later too – Diana was not capable of putting herself in her mother's position. I will not comment on the ways in which her perception of emotional hardness and lack of feeling in the mother may reflect something in Diana herself. There is a Moon-Uranus opposition in Diana's chart, as well as a Venus-Uranus square. These are her aspects, not her mother's. They describe Diana's reactions to her early experiences. They may also describe certain personality qualities of which Diana, as a Cancer with a grand trine in water, is deeply unconscious.

In the end, all we can do is understand our own emotional needs, which dictate how we interpret our experiences. If our interpretations feed our defences, and we use those interpretations to justify defensive behaviour of a highly destructive kind, we cannot really blame anyone else for the mess we are then likely to create. Defences exist to preserve life, and they can be our greatest strength as well as a source of creative gifts. If we refuse to own what we are made of, then it is likely that our defences will begin to run our lives and dominate our natures. Then the fault, dear Brutus, is not in our stars, but in ourselves, that we are underlings.

Chart sources

All charts referred to in the seminar, partial or complete, with the exception of the examples given by members of the group, are from Hans-Hinrich Taeger, *Internationales Horoskope Lexikon,* Verlag Hermann Bauer, Freiburg im Breisgau, 1992. It should be noted that the reliability of the data given in this collection varies, and is annotated carefully by Taeger according to the quality of the sources. The chart data for Richard Burton, for example, is classed by Taeger as belonging to Group 4, indicating that there are a number of conflicting birth times given and the data should therefore be treated with caution.

Bibliography

Campion, Nicholas, *The Great Year,* Arkana, 1994
Freud, Anna, *Ego and the Mechanisms of Defence,* Hogarth Press 1968
Hillman, James, *Suicide and the Soul,* Spring Publications, 1976
Jenkins, David, *Richard Burton: A Brother Remembered,* Arrow, 1994
Morton, Andrew, *Diana: Her True Story,* Michael O'Mara Books, 1993
Person, Ethel Spector, *Love and Fateful Encounters,* Bloomsbury, 1988
Renault, Mary, *The Alexander Trilogy: Fire From Heaven, The Persian Boy, Funeral Games,* Penguin, 1984

Part Two: Saturn and Chiron as Defence Mechanisms

This seminar was given on 13 November, 1994 at Regents College, London, as part of the Autumn Term of the seminar programme for the Centre for Psychological Astrology.

An overview of Saturn and Chiron

Today I would like to focus on the particular kinds of defences which are represented by Saturn and Chiron in the birth chart. I am examining these in a separate seminar because I feel they are in a different category from the general defence mechanisms we discussed in the seminar a fortnight ago. During that seminar, I talked about defences as a natural means of protecting what we value. We can look at any component in the horoscope, not only from the perspective of its character qualities or attributes, but also from the perspective of how it will defend itself against the loss of what it most needs and values. We can approach every zodiac sign in this way, and every planet, because each astrological symbol, which reflects a particular dimension of the psyche, has its own inherent characteristic methods of defence.

So do Saturn and Chiron, in the sense that they represent basic human urges. But they are different because they also represent areas where we have been hurt by life. The kinds of defences that these two planets reflect are not entirely straightforward. These defences are not mobilised simply to protect what we value. They invariably involve a good deal of suspicion and self-doubt. We have been hurt through our Saturn and Chiron placements, or, perhaps more accurately, we believe we have been injured, or subjectively experience hurt. These planets do not produce their defences solely in response to an immediate threat to what they need. The defence is a permanent structure because there is a deep-rooted belief that there will always be a threat, and one relates to life accordingly. Moreover, the defence is active all the time, because we are always on guard against being hurt again. The nature of the hurt varies from one individual to another, and we have to look at these planets in terms of their house placements, signs, aspects, and relationship to the rest of the chart. But their defences are like suits of armour. They are ongoing spawning grounds of anxiety in the personality, and for that reason they are commonly linked with difficult emotional and psychological issues.

Despite what I have just said, Saturn's and Chiron's defences should not be seen as inherently pathological, because the experience of being hurt is universal to all of us. Everyone has got these planets in the birth chart. There is no such thing as an individual who has never experienced hurt, and the pain of deprivation and wounding is an archetypal experience. It is part of being human. Even if the deprivation is as basic as discovering one's parents are not perfect, or the wounding is as diffuse as a recognition of mortality, nevertheless as human beings we carry, from childhood on, an experience of being injured by life.

On the most profound symbolic level, the experiences of both Saturn and Chiron reflect the pain of being expelled from Eden. The experience of birth is a wounding in itself. We are all thrown out of Paradise, and we must endure the process of separation in order to survive. Whatever we do in our lives, we can never wholly heal that wound. We cannot become immortal, nor climb back into the womb again. We are always, on some fundamental level, alone; and we will always feel that life's imperfections are unfair. Because they are rooted in experiences which are archetypal, the defences of Saturn and Chiron are not pathological. They are, if you like, part of the human condition. But they do mess us up.

When people come for an astrological consultation, they are often hurting, and usually it is because one or other of these two planets is in some way creating a stasis which is blocking the flow of life. Because of Saturn and Chiron, other planets may not be able to express their own needs and natural defences properly. Difficulties in other areas of life may often be traced back to the characteristic kinds of blockage that belong to Saturn and Chiron. For example, a person might feel that he or she has creative talents which for some reason can't be expressed. Or there may seem to be a constant rejection of these talents by the external world. We may find something like a hard Sun-Saturn aspect in the chart, and it becomes apparent after some investigation that there is something within the person which is sabotaging every effort at self-expression before it even gets born. This internal saboteur may be planted in the 4th house, or the 8th, or the 2nd, and the root of the dilemma may have nothing to do with creativity at all, except as a by-product; the creative block is really a way of ensuring that nothing of the person's real feelings are exposed, because rejection and humiliation must be avoided at all costs.

A lot of things that don't look like Saturn or Chiron issues can be traced back to these planets, whose defences may be so great that they stop the rest of the chart from functioning. Either of them can be so powerful that they effectively bring the flow of life to a halt. Such severe defences produce a kind of autism, or a very profound depression where the person is psychologically paralysed. Saturn and Chiron are the most psychologically complex of the planetary pantheon, and are probably the most difficult to deal with, primarily because they reflect aspects of ourselves that we generally dislike or are ashamed of. Both are connected with the experience of humiliation, and this is a word that I would like you to remember because you will find me referring to it throughout the day.

Is there anyone here who doesn't know what humiliation feels like? It is one of the most unpleasant feelings that we can experience. In many ways it is far worse than simple rejection, because there is an element of shame attached to humiliation, as well the crippling sense that we are somehow inadequate or less than what we ought to be – not because we are blameless victims, but because there is something deformed or misshapen inside.

When we try to get near the core of the psychological state connected with these planets, we may find a powerful sense of being maimed or crippled. That's why dream images occurring under Saturn or Chiron transits often portray a deformity of some kind, a handicapped, mutilated, or stunted figure, whether it is the dreamer or another person or animal. These images convey the feeling of being shamefully misshapen, along with the fear that, if other people see the deformity, they will be repelled and will reject us. This goes straight back to the mythic image of the angry God not wanting Adam and Eve once they have sinned. We are thrown out of Eden, and our parents do not want us. Closely allied with the feeling of humiliation is the feeling of being permanently flawed. In this place of shame we feel incurably unloved, unloving, and unlovable.

The defences of both Saturn and Chiron spring from this core. Today we need to explore the different kinds of defence systems that these planets reflect, and how they are likely to express, depending on their chart placements and aspects. Equally important is the question of how we might work with Saturn and Chiron defences and the wounds they protect. In some ways this is an area that opens up a fundamental conflict within astrology itself, and also within the therapeutic profession. To what extent can a person be healed of such wounds? To what extent does the astrologer broach these issues to a client? Saturn and Chiron focus us on our personal values as astrologers – how and why we work with astrology, and how, and on what level, we interpret Saturn and Chiron to the client.

Another area I hope to have time to explore today is the way Saturn's and Chiron's defence systems work in synastry. We often discover these planets within ourselves through our defensive reactions to other people. If we want to get a really good look at these planets at work, we need to look at any relationship in which another person's planets form strong aspects to our Saturn or Chiron. This is one of the most powerful ways in which our defences are constellated. Curiously, both planets seem to exercise a remarkable power of attraction in relationship. We do not ordinarily think of either as carrying any special sexual charisma. Yet virtually every important relationship I have examined with my clients over the years reveals Saturn or Chiron in tight cross-aspect with a personal planet in the synastry. We seem to need other people to trigger these planets in us and make us conscious of them. The reasons for this are fascinating and worth some careful investigation.

We can begin by looking at the nature of the hurt reflected by each of these planets. They are very similar in many ways, but there are also some very important differences. The differences lie primarily in how we attempt to interpret and cope with our wounds, and what creative resolutions might come out of our efforts to work with them. In this way they are radically different, although they may feel very similar in terms of the pain quotient.

Saturn

Denial and deprivation

When we experience Saturn, we often feel that something has been denied us. The moment we face this denial, we must deal with the problematic issue of whether we have really been denied the thing we wanted, or whether it is a subjective interpretation. We must also question whether the denial was the fault of oneself or of others, or whether it was the result of a bad chemical mix of inherent temperament and environment. Looking through Saturnian spectacles, we can always find evidence in our family background that someone did something wrong or failed us. But Saturn, like every other planet, reflects a mode of perception. We perceive the lack of something, regardless of whether it is available or not, and for one reason or another we cannot not recognise or receive it, even if is on offer. Something was missing from our early diet, and its lack has resulted in a deficiency of some kind. This sense of lack or deficiency is generally linked with the experience of the parents and family background. Neither parent has a stronger claim to being the "culprit"; Saturn is happy to blame, or play the part of, either one.

Saturn's experience is of being denied something, being limited, constrained, or stifled, or having something withheld that we need very badly. This denial or curtailment also feels like a punishment. It is as though our need makes us bad people, and the denial is a just retribution. Our need is the cause of our being kicked out of Eden, so we are tainted or humiliated by wanting something, and punished by having it denied. Let's take the example of Saturn in Gemini. Saturn will emphasise the deepest need of a sign, but at the same time conveys the sense that this need has been and will always be denied, because the need in itself is wrong or bad. What does Gemini need most?

Audience: Communication.

Liz: Yes, communication is the lifeblood of Gemini. Gemini must feel that there is somebody "out there" with whom to exchange thoughts and feelings. This sign must breathe. It must give out and take in, and give out and take in. It cannot exist in a vacuum; it is a social sign, even if society is a good book. A person with Saturn in Gemini may feel that this very fundamental ingredient of communication, of contact and exchange, was not on offer in childhood, or that the wrong sort was on offer. And deep down, consciously or unconsciously, Saturn in Gemini will usually believe that this is because there is something essentially wrong with wanting to share and communicate.

When one works in counselling with people who have Saturn in Gemini, one often hears this articulated. "My parents never talked to me," says Saturn in Gemini, or, "I was an only child and I was often very lonely and had no one to talk to," or, "Nobody in the family ever discussed anything relevant. They just sat around the dinner table talking about the weather," or, "No one was interested in me. No one listened to me". All these remarks express the sense that something very fundamental was denied. But on the heels of such comments one may also often hear, "I suppose my parents found me boring," or, "Maybe I just wasn't intelligent enough." This may be harder to admit, but it is a common accompaniment to the sense of denial. We believe that, if others can't understand us or aren't interested, the fault must lie in us.

Because we feel we have been denied some essential ingredient very early in life, we may also feel that we have never had the chance to grow properly. We are constricted in our growth; we are stunted, undersized, or deformed. Like someone who is missing protein in the diet and never reaches his or her full potential physical size and strength, we may feel dwarfed, restricted, awkward, shy, or inadequate about those spheres of life over which

Saturn presides in the birth chart. But we need to think hard and honestly about whether these special things really were denied, or whether our subjective experience of denial springs from their extreme importance to us. We cannot work creatively with Saturn's defences until we do this. It may be necessary to go beyond the sense of external lack. We may have to face the possibility that something so precious is never going to be adequately provided, because no other human being is identical to us and therefore cannot fulfil the exact specifications, no matter how hard they try. Even if others did provide this magical ingredient to a reasonable degree, we would probably still feel short-changed, because our internal standards and expectations are so high. Where Saturn is concerned, no family can get it right. There is no way that any parent could have furnished the precise ingredient that we required, and perhaps we need to recognise that the huge emphasis that we place on the area of life indicated by Saturn actually reflects a property of our own souls.

I am not suggesting that there is no parental issue involved with Saturn. Because psychological (and astrological) patterns run through families over generations, there is usually some external justification for Saturn's feelings of deprivation. But I have a question about the extent to which trying to place the responsibility for Saturn's wounds entirely on other people is in any way useful, helpful, or even truthful. It may be true subjectively. If something is desperately important to me, and I am not being given it, then I may easily feel that it is your fault because you didn't recognise how badly I needed it. Or I may assume you have deliberately withheld it. Therefore you have failed me.

Now that may make me feel temporarily better, but it will do nothing for my hurt in the long term, and I will remain as insecure and defensive as ever. I may even go around assuming that everyone with whom I come in contact will automatically fail me in this way, and then I can enjoy the indulgence of nursing a long-standing grievance. This is typical unconscious Saturnian behaviour. But if something is that deeply important to me, I must learn, one way or or another, to find it for myself. In the end, that is what we all have to do with Saturn. Some of us take longer than others to get the message. Saturn's defences are primarily focused on trying to get this missing ingredient, by fair means or foul, honestly or dishonestly, truthfully or falsely, manipulatively or overtly. We have to have it, but we may attempt to acquire it in questionable ways, because we feel so ashamed to admit that we lack it.

Something very important happens if we begin to take responsibility for Saturn. By this I don't mean intellectual recognition, I mean a genuine heartfelt realisation of the ways in which we set others up by asking them to supply what ultimately we must supply for ourselves. If we interpret the spheres of life that Saturn touches in an individual chart, not as something which has been denied us, but rather, as something which is desperately important to us, we can begin to see a way to work with our wounds which is far more constructive than blame. Then important questions may begin to occur to us. Why is it so difficult for Saturn in Gemini to feel that people are really listening? Is it really true that the whole world is so intent on its own business that no one has time to pay attention? Or might it have something to do with Saturn's own closed-mindedness, or Saturn's own reluctance to communicate in any language other than its own? Why is it so hard for Saturn in Leo to feel that people are really recognising one's specialness? Might it reflect Saturn's own reluctance to risk vulnerability through self-exposure? Why is it so difficult for Saturn in Taurus to feel safe and secure in the world? Is the world really such a tough place, or might one's own attitudes toward security be too inflexible or idealistic? Why does Saturn in Cancer find it so hard to feel wanted? Or might Saturn itself fail to recognise and accept other people's affection?

Audience: Perhaps we carry an inherent lack of self-worth, a conviction of not deserving the thing we want.

Liz: You seem to be saying that, from birth, we have feelings of inadequacy in this area, and that is why we can't digest the food that is given.

Audience: Perhaps. I think it is because we want it too much. The intensity of the wanting dams up all the energy, and also frightens other people off.

Liz: Then you are not describing an inherent sense of inferiority. You are describing an inherent intensity, which may precipitate rejection and a consequent reaction of *mea culpa*. That accords with my own interpretation.

Audience: The intensity becomes a threat to others. There was a programme on television the other day about American men going to Russia to get wives. And you could see the look of desperation on some of their faces. "I've got to have a wife. I've got find one." The poor Russian women, although they wanted husbands very badly, said, "No, thanks. I'll wait."

Liz: And I suppose the American men went home thinking how cold and unresponsive Russian women are. It makes me think of a wonderful line in one of Mary Stewart's novels: Isn't it extraordinary how so many people who complain all the time about being unloved, never stop to ask themselves whether they are in fact lovable? I would cap that with: Isn't it extraordinary how so many people who are desperately seeking love, never stop to ask themselves whether such global desperation is any kind of compliment to the recipient?

You are touching on a very important issue connected with Saturn. This came up at the end of our previous seminar on defences, and provoked a rather strong reaction in one or two participants. We tend to help along, if not actually create, our own rejection in childhood. There are such things as truly appalling parents, but fortunately they seem to be in the minority. In the main, there are ordinary human parents, who are trying to do the best they can but aren't very good at relating to certain areas of their child's personality. These areas may be perfectly healthy but can trigger a sense of lack, inferiority, or envy in the parent. Equally, the problematic areas may reflect something difficult and inaccessible in the child. We are not born blank slates upon which the world writes; we each have an individual horoscope which can contain problematic as well as attractive configurations.

We can be very good at provoking rejection, even when we are very small. No parent, however loving, stands a chance with our Saturn. If we are showing our Saturnian side, we are not likely to ask for something in a relaxed way that invokes a relaxed response. Saturn is more likely to convey a different message: "Look, I want it badly, but you're probably incapable of giving it. I am going to ask anyway, but I'm certain you'll cock it up, so don't even bother to go through the motions. We both know you'll fail." Saturn may also transmit other, equally difficult messages. It may say, "I want it so desperately that if you don't give it to me I'll die or be permanently injured, and then it will be your fault."

We transmit very complex unconscious signals to our parents, who, more often than not, are psychological children themselves, and really have no idea what it is they are confronting. Suddenly they feel like failures. This child who was perfectly easy and wonderful to love a moment ago suddenly changes, and one simply can't get it right. If the parent has the Sun, Moon, Venus, or Mars forming a conjunction or hard aspect to the child's Saturn, then that parent may feel paralysed and incompetent. The child is emanating a strong feeling of criticism and blame, or seems to shut the parent out, and the parent may find it extremely hard to give the child what he or she needs. It is all very well to whine on about how in an ideal world, parents should understand these things and respond with sensitivity and understanding. But how on earth can they, when there is nothing remotely resembling psychological education available in this enlightened society?

Audience: What if the parent has the same Saturn as the child?

Liz: This is quite common, because twenty-nine is often an age when people feel settled enough to have children. The Saturn return may trigger a desire to put down roots and create stability in one's life. In such cases there tends to be a sort of hall-of-mirrors effect. Both parent and child desperately want the same thing, but neither knows how to ask for it without being defensive. Both may want a display of affection and reassurance, but both may be convinced that the other one has got to show it first, because otherwise there is too much risk of rejection and humiliation. This happens all the time in adult relationships, and perhaps some of you recognise the scenario. Neither person feels safe, so neither person makes the first move. Then we are faced with a stalemate of two defence systems, behind which both people may deeply love each other, but cannot express it. And both are likely to come away feeling hurt and blaming each other.

Audience: Perhaps in the end we have to accept the fact that no one can give us what Saturn needs. We have to give it to ourselves.

Liz: This is my own view. It may seem harsh, but Saturn is a hard teacher. On the other hand, if one is willing to learn the lesson, one builds something indestructible inside. I think there is something about Saturn that, from the beginning of life, requires that we find this thing ourselves. Ultimately I think we get the right parents, not the wrong ones. Parental failings may be necessary for the unfoldment of individual character and destiny. I have no idea whether it is synchronous, or whether the soul chooses its family. Perhaps both viewpoints are correct. In a sense it doesn't matter. In the end, the thing that Saturn wants so badly, and guards so ferociously, is the alchemical gold, the indestructible essence of the individual. We would never seek it if we did not feel we lacked it, and we would never feel we lacked it if we did not already know, deep within, its real nature and importance.

Dane Rudhyar made this observation in one of his books. He said that Saturn is the real essence of the individuality, even more than the Sun. It is the one thing in us which can become absolutely our own, because we have to earn it. The Sun, with its bright sense of meaning and individual purpose, is a kind of free gift from the gods. Of course we must be willing to take on the burden of individuality to express the Sun, but if that is accepted, it will light the way without stinting. But with Saturn, nothing is free. Everything must be paid for, and dearly. The radiance of the Sun is invoked largely through intuition, through a recognition of uniqueness and inner purpose. It is like Parsifal's vision of the Grail, initially vouchsafed without effort. But Saturn requires work, and depends on time to unfold its rewards. There is no way we can have a self-reliant Saturn in infancy. By its nature, it will inevitably experience hurt, because there is not yet any ego to contain and direct it. Saturn in myth is the lord of time. And Saturn's fruits do not come into being until they are ripe. They must follow a particular process of maturation, and they must be consciously harvested or they will rot on the tree.

There is a great mystery about Saturn, that is concerned with the essence of individual identity and the capacity to survive as an independent being in the world. It is through Saturn's defences that we discover we can survive and remain up and walking regardless of what changes, crises, or losses occur in our lives. There is no way we can recognise this gift in infancy. It only develops through experience. So of course we feel a lack. We want someone else to give us our knowledge of individual survival, but no one can.

Saturn in Gemini may be surrounded by communicative people in childhood. The family may be talkative and spontaneous, but they might not be communicative in the way that Saturn in Gemini needs, because the child actually wants an adult form of communication which wouldn't be understood even if it were given. The child wants something from the outside that can only come from the inside. There is no way that we can avoid feeling that we have been denied the thing represented by Saturn. Certainly our parents can exacerbate the difficulty through ignorance or meanness, and in such cases therapeutic work can be very healing. But therapy doesn't cure Saturn. All it can do is give us a different perspective on those experiences which seem to confirm our belief that we are missing something and are inadequate in some way. That is a great deal, if one has been badly wounded. But many people involved in psychotherapy entertain the remarkable fantasy that they can be made into somebody else, somebody Saturn-less.

"Fake" compensation as an unconscious defence

Saturn's experience of deprivation tends to produce a characteristic range of defences. We are denied something we need, we feel restricted or limited, and consequently we feel awkward, undernourished, or inadequate in a particular area of the psyche. Unless and until we achieve some consciousness of Saturn's wound, what do we do to try to protect this vulnerable area? What do unconscious Saturnian defences look like?

Audience: We compensate.

Liz: Yes, that is one option. Compensation can have many forms. The most unconscious is a kind of "fake" compensation. We may pretend that we are very good at the thing we secretly feel we cannot do. This is a superficial kind of compensation, a sort of smokescreen which has little or no substance. It is a very common Saturn response, and probably we all do it at some time in our lives. If we fear being exposed as weak, crippled, or inadequate, we may pretend. Sometimes we pretend so well that we even fool ourselves, and are convinced, for a while, by our own sleight-of-psyche. But this kind of compensation is very fragile. It can have holes punched in it very easily, and sooner or later it usually does. Then we have got to come up with a more effective compensation mechanism. "Fake" compensation only works on a superficial level, when we don't know people very well.

For example, we might see Saturn in Gemini monopolising the conversation at a party, nattering away at great volume and speed because of the terror that, if silence ensues even momentarily, others will realise that one has nothing interesting or intelligent to say. Saturn in Gemini may also adopt a pseudo-intellectual stance, dropping literary names or erudite concepts which are only half-digested but are meant to impress or to make other people feel stupid, in order to conjure the illusion of intellectual superiority and confidence.

We may find Saturn in Cancer being intensely sentimental, dripping with apparent emotion, and full of Valentine's day cards, bouquets of flowers, and effusive compliments. This display of emotional excess may be meant to conceal powerful emotional inhibitions and a deep fear that one's real feelings will not be acceptable. Or we may find Saturn in Leo exhibiting intensely theatrical behaviour, strenuously broadcasting individualism in order to conceal a deep fear of being unimportant. We may find Saturn in Virgo behaving in an obsessively self-disciplined and orderly way in superficial matters, masking a deep fear of incompetence and inner chaos. These examples demonstrate the surface level of Saturn's compensation. Usually, even as we attempt it, we know perfectly well that if someone gets to know us better, we are going to be seen through. Sadly, some people are too frightened to move beyond even this superficial level of compensation, and therefore back off from any deep relationship in which the defence may be exposed for what it is.

Avoidance as a defence

If this "fake" compensation is exposed, Saturn will have to work to produce other, more effective defences. What might these be?

Audience: We could refuse to get involved at all.

Liz: Yes, Saturn can try to escape exposure of the vulnerable area by avoiding situations or people who might threaten it. Avoidance, like "fake" compensation, is a characteristic Saturnian defence. Saturn in Scorpio, for example, might simply avoid a deep relationship, refusing commitment and playing one person against the other while remaining emotionally defended and in control. Equally often, Saturn in Scorpio might choose partners who themselves have some kind of emotional or sexual block or difficulty, so that one's own never gets noticed. Saturn is very subtle. One of the things it does is gravitate toward people who are worse off than oneself. By finding someone else to complain about, one's feelings of inadequacy are deflected. Saturn says, "This is clearly the other person's problem, and any fool can see it." One's own issues are never even touched upon. We may be drawn to a partner who is sexually inhibited or emotionally restricted, so that the fear and withholding reflected by our Saturn in Scorpio, Cancer, or Pisces goes unchallenged, and we can go on appearing to be the loving, giving, emotionally open partner.

We may also avoid situations where anybody challenges us to express what we fear we cannot do. If Saturn is in an air sign and we feel we are going to be exposed as stupid or intellectually incompetent, we may choose to be around people who are our intellectual inferiors. We may find excuses not to complete our education, because we are terrified of putting our mental abilities to the test. We may avoid jobs which require us to lay our intellectual capacities on the line. With Saturn in a fire sign, we may avoid any situation which requires us to express original ideas or assert our own identity. With Saturn in an earth sign, we may avoid any position of responsibility which requires us to relate competently and sensibly to the mundane world. We may adopt a militantly anti-materialistic philosophy to mask the fact that we feel hopeless at handling material issues. We may set up situations in which we are apparently restricted by other people, or by the nature of the work we do, so that it looks as if life, not our own terror, has thwarted us.

Paradoxically, the variety of ways in which we pursue this peculiarly Saturnian kind of avoidance reflects incredible creativity and ingenuity. When we start thinking about the amazing brilliance the psyche displays in selecting and perpetuating these elaborate avoidance dances, we may well wonder what might be done with all that creative energy if it were used for something other than escaping Saturn's pain. Saturn is so exceptionally fertile at constructing subtle defences in every sphere of life. Until we can understand and recognise the element of avoidance in our behaviour, it can cause us a great deal of unhappiness for no apparent reason. Avoidance can begin to feel like a bad fate, until we see it for what it is. But from the moment we actually catch its slippery tail, and begin to get an inkling of what it is up to, all kinds of doors may begin to open which previously seemed permanently closed. Saturn can create situations of apparently unending frustration, which appear to be the fault of the outer world. The individual may then live with a dreary sense of being limited and denied happiness. But such situations often reflect an unconscious effort to avoid being free, because of the exposure of inadequacy freedom might bring.

One of the things Saturn may fear most is freedom, because freedom means that one might have to rely on one's own resources and express what one truly is. Then one's vulnerability might be exposed, and one might fail or be humiliated. Saturn may avoid situations where the possibility of freedom poses too great a challenge, and the person will often create or be drawn to an external reality in which he or she is imprisoned by someone or something "outside". Although this defence system may thwart one's life in very fundamental ways, it serves a purpose. It is a truism in psychology that many symptoms, both physical and emotional, have a payoff, a secondary gain. It is not a bad idea, when confronting Saturn's feelings of imprisonment and frustration, to ask, "What's in this for me? What is this gaol sentence helping me to avoid?" This can be particularly helpful if one is afflicted with the conviction, "I can't do anything about this. My wife/husband/lover/child/parent is imprisoning me. My job is oppressing me. Society is keeping me down. The government is thwarting me." Institutions and "establishment" structures can draw Saturn's projections as easily as individuals do.

We may come up with some surprising answers if we are straight with ourselves about the hidden benefits of our frustrating situation. One of the benefits will usually be the protection of something deeply vulnerable and frightened, and we may unconsciously believe imprisonment is better than humiliation, rejection, or failure. Being stifled or thwarted may not be as horrible a feeling as being exposed and humiliated, because when we are in

prison we can be righteously angry. But if we feel inadequate and ashamed, with whom can we be angry? We are stuck with ourselves.
What other defences might Saturn mobilise?

Projection as a defence

Audience: We can try to find somebody else to do Saturn's job for us. That might apply in both negative and positive ways.

Liz: Yes, Saturn can find surrogates. One of the most common Saturnian defences is the projection of Saturnian qualities, both dark and light. We may try to find someone else who will shield us from life and protect us from being hurt in that place where we feel so vulnerable. That is seeking the "good" Saturn outside, the ideal Saturnian parent-surrogate whose authority will keep outside threats under control. Or we may project onto someone else the fearful, controlling, restrictive thing that is imprisoning us and making us feel inadequate. That is seeking the "bad" Saturn outside, the negative Saturnian parent-surrogate whose authority stifles our individuality and crushes our spirit. One way or another, wherever Saturn is placed, we generally manage to rope other people into it.

Saturn tends to blame others a lot. It is one of the main Saturnian defence systems. It may also be full of self-pity. This is one of the least attractive dimensions of Saturn's nature. Catching the culprit can become a favourite Saturnian pastime. Or it may indulge in a frenzy of self-blame. "It's all my fault," says Saturn. "I'm a terrible person." That is simply another form of blame, but instead of someone or something outside catching the projection, one's entire personality, one's whole life, becomes the hook for Saturn's feelings of failure and deprivation. Total self-blame is as unproductive as finding a culprit outside, and just as suspect because the main issue is successfully avoided.

Because Saturn is linked with the parents as carriers of the archetype of law and authority, Saturnian parental issues often get projected on authority figures in society, such as employers, government officials, and "the establishment". Saturn may also be projected on anything which requires us to limit ourselves – in other words, the law and the legal system. There is a certain kind of Saturnian complaint which is monotonous in its regularity and is usually voiced against any law which triggers the individual's sense of personal inadequacy and frustration. The inevitable rules and restrictions which exist in every society, to preserve mutual respect and civilised behaviour, may stir Saturn's wound and evoke an angry and self-righteous response, cloaked in political language to deflect the perspicacious observer and also fool oneself.

The mythology of Saturn reflects the image of the tyrant. Saturn is the king of the gods, and although the very beautiful myths of the Golden Age describe his benignity and generosity, he is also the god who swallows his own children in order to retain power. We associate this dimension of Saturn with tyranny and the suppression of everything which is new, young, growing, and full of potential. When our secret fears make us crush the youthful potentials in ourselves, we may go about looking for a culprit in the outer world, a social or political structure which appears to be the oppressor and can provide a good hook for our projections.

Traditional or conservative views of life, respect for the rules, or recognition of the necessity of hierarchy may enrage us when we encounter them in other people, because we carry our oppression internally. There is a tyrant inside somewhere, setting rigid rules and imposing intolerable restrictions, because in this way the shameful aspects of our own personalities can be controlled, silenced, and kept locked away. It is very difficult to track that inner tyrant down, and courage as well as honesty is required. It is much easier to find a tyrant outside, because there always seem to be a lot of them about. Or so it would appear, at least to the imprisoned part of ourselves. We can always find one to attack. Some are more fashionable to blame than others, depending on the social climate of the time. Saturn's defence systems often involve not only social projections, but political projections as well.

Scapegoating as a defence

Scapegoating is a form of projection. Just as we may try to find a good Saturn outside who will protect our vulnerability and weakness, or blame a bad Saturn outside for causing our pain and inadequacy, we may also try to find an element in other people which we can blame for the ills of the world. We are then projecting Saturn's entire inner drama on outer objects. This allows us to avoid any sense of personal inferiority, because the failure appears in the external world. Our own feelings of inadequacy and deprivation become society's failure, while the culprit becomes an individual, group of individuals, or a racial or social collective which we can blame for the failure. This is a very popular Saturnian defence, because by mobilising it we entirely avoid individual consciousness of Saturn's problems. We can then be very pleased with our altruism, humanitarian vision, political correctness, and selfless commitment to improving the world.

Any sort of scapegoating of a social, racial, or religious group immediately reflects a deeper psychological problem, because there is no such thing as a uniform group. Any collective is made up of individuals who vary enormously in terms of their temperaments, strengths, and weaknesses. The moment we hear sweeping generalisations, such as, "All blacks are lazy," or "All Jews are Communists," or "All Irish are drunkards," or "All Italians are untrustworthy," we are in the presence of scapegoating. We are also in the presence of an individual, or group of individuals, who cannot bear to face their own deep feelings of inferiority and inadequacy, and who are trying to make themselves feel better by vilifying others. In the phenomenon of scapegoating we hear one of Saturn's ugliest and most ferociously defensive voices.

Unless we personally know all blacks, Jews, Irish, or Italians, we cannot speak of anything other than our own direct experience of a few individuals from these collectives. And personal experience is itself highly subjective, because each of us carries prejudices which reflect our own racial, national, and religious background. These prejudices can affect the way in which we perceive any direct contact with an individual from a different social, racial, national or religious group. We can speak of the national characteristics reflected by a country's birth chart, if this is available, but such a chart will describe the kind of government in power and the aspirations and conflicts of the national entity. This can be relevant and helpful, especially when comparing the charts of two countries hostile to each other. It can also be helpful in understanding why any individual might find particular national structures and ideals personally incompatible with his or her own temperament and goals.

If my Sun is trine the Sun in the chart of the United Kingdom, for example, I may find the British monarchy admirable and the British world image worthy of respect; but if my Sun is square the British Sun, I may deeply disapprove of the monarchy or disagree strongly with the country's image. But national charts do not tell us what the people are like as individuals. The chart of the United Kingdom will not tell me what my neighbours are like, or how individual British people will behave in individual relationships. It may reveal how they believe they "ought" to behave if they wish to uphold the national image; but they might or might not subscribe to that image. Everyone who lives within the boundaries of a national entity will be aware of, and to some extent circumscribed by, the characteristics of the nation.

At a seminar in Zürich some months ago, we discussed the Swiss national chart, which has the Sun in opposition to Saturn. Several members of the group expressed the feeling that they were restricted by certain rules of correct behaviour which they felt were part of the social and political structure of their country. But they themselves were not restricted individuals – except those who happened to have Sun opposite Saturn. The characteristics expressed by national charts do not describe individuals. When we generalise about groups, especially when we try to identify how and why they are inferior, we reveal inner conflicts and fears which we might prefer to avoid. Saturn usually feels better if it can find somebody else who can be viewed with contempt.

We may not necessarily be racial in our scapegoating. We may have contempt for uneducated people, for example, and identify with an academic elite. Or we may despise intellectuals, and identify with a working class milieu. We may be suspicious of people who are introverted and serious because we are socialites, or ridicule people who are sloppily dressed because we aspire to being fashionable. We may condemn those who worship God under a different name, or those whose sexual proclivities are not the same as our own. We may make sweeping statements about the opposite sex, never realising that the qualities we are mocking or condemning are patently obvious in our own unconscious behaviour. We may select, within any group of people, a type of individual whom we feel is in some way inferior or threatening to us; and if only they could be got rid of, the world would be a better place. I don't need to elaborate on where this can lead, if we remain unwilling to face our individual contributions to collective scapegoating. The road leads to apartheid, to Auschwitz, to Bosnia, and to other atrocities which raise the question of whether we always merit the dignity of being called human.

Contempt

Allied to scapegoating is another of Saturn's typical unconscious defence mechanisms: contempt. I think we should always be very suspicious of ourselves when we feel contemptuous. If we don't like someone, that is fair enough; it is a feeling response which reflects our own tastes and values. We cannot like everyone or find every person's company congenial, because each of us has an individual horoscope which may harmonise or collide with the horoscope of the other person.

But contempt is a very different phenomenon. Contempt reflects an element of scapegoating, because it defines a hierarchy of what is superior or inferior in another person. We may be bored by someone who is shallow, or irritated by someone who is emotionally manipulative or lacking in boundaries. If so, then we are probably wise to admit the incompatibility, remove ourselves, and cultivate more congenial companions – always remembering that others might feel equally derisive things about us. But to express contempt for another person is essentially a means of dismissing the other person as having no value. It allows us to avoid recognising our own inadequacies. When we feel contemptuous, we feel superior, and we may justify treatment which we would never dream of inflicting on someone whom we deemed simply incompatible with our own tastes.

Audience: But what about a criminal? Someone who has done terrible things? Don't we have the right to be contemptuous?

Liz: I don't think this is an issue of "rights". You have the "right" to feel what you please. I also have the "right" to question the expression of contempt as distinct from feelings of dislike, anger, or even repulsion. I am suspicious of contempt even when it is directed at a criminal. One might feel many things – shock, horror, anger, or a certainty that the person should be locked away behind bars for the protection of others. But one can feel all these things and still recognise that the criminal is a human like oneself, and subject to unknown pressures which, if we were in his or her place, might twist or break us too. Those whom society judges criminal are usually people who have the same destructive impulses as the rest of us, but who have not tried, or have not been able, to control them. Punishment may sometimes be appropriate; rehabilitation may be equally appropriate. But the decision to incarcerate, punish, or rehabilitate need not involve contempt.

I believe there is something in the Christian message about those without sin casting the first stone? Or has that now become politically incorrect? Contempt casts stones freely, without reflection. One can judge the suspect guilty of the crime, and justifiably send him or her to prison. But at the same time one can be realistic without being contemptuous. Rather than feeling superior, one might even feel gratitude that one has somehow managed to remain a relatively decent and honest person, in a world which could easily drive everybody mad sooner or later.

Pride and envy

When we experience contempt, we know that Saturn is at work. There is something going on beneath the surface of our superiority. Scapegoating and contempt are linked with the feelings of humiliation and inadequacy which so often lie at the core of Saturnian defences. Two other related defensive reactions to this inner discomfort are typical of Saturn: pride and envy.

Saturn often defends its vulnerability with pride. This is not the sort of pride in oneself which reflects confidence and self-esteem. That is solar, and a healthy expression of the ego's awareness of its unique qualities and gifts. Saturnian pride is of the cut-off-one's-nose-to-spite-one's-face variety. "No one is going to see me showing weakness," says Saturn. This is very different from, "I know I did that well, and I'm proud of myself." The Sun can say, "I'm worth something as a person. I may have flaws, but basically I am who I am and I don't wish to be anyone else." Saturn, in its unconscious form, cannot say this, because one feels exactly the opposite. Beneath the display of pride lie deep feelings of inadequacy. Saturnian pride may make us deny ourselves the help, support, and love of others. It may also make us refuse to offer others the help, support, and love they need. And it can make us use proud contempt as a defence against a sense of inferiority. We can spot Saturn's pride most easily in relationship dynamics, which we will be discussing later. We can also see Saturnian pride in scapegoating of the kind which involves a self-righteous attitude of "Of course I would never do such a thing/behave like that/look like that."

Envy is another fundamental Saturnian response. There is no one exempt from the experience of envy in one form or another, just as there is no one exempt from Saturn in the birth chart. Envy is not an inherently pathological response to feelings of lack or inferiority, because envy can be extremely creative. Through making envy conscious, we can discover what we want and value, because we see it in someone else and wish we had it. Then we can begin to glimpse the real strength and value of Saturn. Envy, recognised and constructively channelled, can spur us toward developing qualities and abilities which we might otherwise not have recognised as our own potentials. But if it is unconscious, Saturn's envy can work very destructively. It can surface as contempt. If we are secretly envious of another person, we may seek to humiliate or denigrate him or her, without recognising our real motives. Examples of this are as common as mud, in personal relationships, family dynamics, and professional rivalry. Envy may also lead to collective scapegoating. What we despise in others may in fact be what we unconsciously envy. But rather than admitting the envy, we may prefer to destroy the carriers of those qualities we feel we lack. Once they are gone, we can feel better about ourselves.

I would like to emphasise that all these undeniably awful but typically human defences are the expressions of an unconscious Saturn. The less we know about Saturn, the more frequently we will display one or another of its less appealing qualities. We do not sit down and consciously construct displays of scapegoating, contempt, pride, or envy. At least, most of us don't; there may be certain exceptions, such as Hitler, who knew exactly what he was doing when he began fomenting antisemitism among his people. But usually these defence mechanisms operate in the darkness, and often we have no idea what havoc we are wreaking on others. When we are confronted with our unconscious Saturnian defences, we may become peculiarly wriggly and evasive, or compulsively self-righteous. It is very hard, and usually painful, to stop and think about what we are doing. That is why I am talking about these negative dimensions of Saturnian defences first. We are not born conscious, but must work toward self-awareness, and Saturn is, for many people, the greatest challenge of all.

We have probably all experienced the irresistible inclination to have a dig at someone. We want to put the person down, or make them feel small. Or we may be the recipient of someone else's efforts to denigrate us. Parents may do this to their children if the parent's Saturn is triggered by powerful synastry, such as an opposition to the Sun or Moon in the child's chart. A parent may be unconsciously envious of his or her child, and for many reasons – among them youth, beauty, talent, intelligence, or a future full of potentials. Equally, a child whose Saturn opposes the parent's Sun, Moon, Venus, or Mars may be envious of that parent. Envy can occur between any two people of any age and either sex, if one feels the other has what he or she painfully lacks.

If we are the recipient of someone else's Saturnian envy, we may not realise what it is. We may feel deeply hurt and undermined by it, and we may begin to doubt ourselves. When we most need the other person's reassurance, support, and encouragement, the other's Saturn will refuse to give it. Saturn's envy may provoke an anal defence, and affection and support are withheld at the critical moment. Envy may create feelings of powerlessness along with inferiority, and powerlessness can lead to an assertion of control through withholding. Or we may suddenly catch ourselves withholding, and view the hurt we have inflicted with bewilderment. There is an edge of cruelty that can colour Saturn's unconscious defences. Just when our partner or child really needs a compliment or a pat on the back, we say, "Haven't you gained some weight?" or "You're looking really tired, haven't you been well?" or "Oh, yes, I saw your new book at the shop. I haven't got round to buying it yet. But surely the publisher could have chosen a better cover?"

Saturn can exhibit incredible subtlety when performing an envious attack. When confronted by a hurt and angry child, parent, colleague, partner or friend, Saturn replies, "What on earth are you talking about? I wasn't putting you down. You're too sensitive. You're reading things into what I said." I don't doubt that we have all been the recipients of this kind of thing. We also dole it out to each other, without recognising what we are doing. We may claim that we didn't mean it, that it is the other person's problem, that it was only a joke, that it was "objective" professional criticism. But then perhaps we ought to think twice about arriving in the astrologer's or therapist's consulting room with an unfaithful or runaway partner, an alienated colleague or friend, or an "ungrateful" child, and bleat about how badly we have been treated.

Contempt and scapegoating are the characteristic products of unconscious envy. Corrosive envy is usually the product of feelings of inferiority that we believe cannot be changed, and therefore those who trigger our inferiority make us feel humiliated and angry. If we feel inferior about something we know we can work at or improve, we don't tend to experience such destructive self-denigration. But at the core of Saturn's world is a sense of permanent damage, a feeling of being permanently maimed. It's very tempting to find someone or something to blame for such feelings. But we must face them and begin to understand them, before Saturn's destructive defences can shift and reveal their positive face.

Dissociation as a defence against Saturn's pain

There are one or two more issues I would like to mention here. One of them is dissociation, which is linked with the other defence mechanisms we have been looking at. Saturn's dissociation leaves us completely unconscious of feelings of shame, pain and inadequacy. Some of you may be sitting here saying to yourselves, "What on earth is she talking about? I have never felt envy, or shame, or inadequacy." We can dissociate completely from our wounds when we feel too threatened to cope. We simply do not acknowledge that such feelings exist. Then we can remain completely oblivious of all the various Saturnian emotional mechanisms, and they are wholly projected.

We may also confront Saturnian feelings of humiliation and inferiority and say to ourselves, "Why bother trying to work with this stuff? I'm a mess, I'm a wreck, I'm a total failure, and I'm going to stay like that." That is another form of Saturnian defence. We can indulge in all the dark feelings, to the exclusion of everything else; and this allows us to avoid working at them to turn Saturn's lead into Saturn's gold. Self-pity can be a very effective Saturnian defence. One tells oneself, "I've been terribly wounded in childhood. This went wrong, and that went wrong, and my parents were beastly, and I was treated horribly. Society is awful and no one understands me. I can't do anything about it. I am a failure and I can't help it. Somebody else is going to have to come and look after me."

Audience: And if one is an astrologer, one can also say, "And look at where my Saturn is anyway."

Liz: Yes, you are quite right. It's actually rather funny. You should hear it when psychologists do it, mobilising all their best jargon to justify the mess they are in. It is even better than when astrologers do it. When we hear other people giving voice to this peculiarly Saturnian form of self-pity, it tends to push buttons in us. We tend to lose our sympathy, even if ordinarily we respond to other people's pain. Saturnian self-victimisation doesn't often draw the response that it is meant to draw, and consequently it is a very self-defeating defence mechanism.

Audience: Why don't we feel compassion?

Liz: One reason might be because what we are hearing is not an expression of genuine feeling. It is a defence mechanism, and defences of this kind don't invoke empathy because there is an element of calculation, of contrivance, involved. We feel manipulated, or shut out. We may also sense a great deal of anger and aggression in displays of self-pity, as though we are being told, "It's all right for you, you've had an easy time of it, I'm the only one who has suffered." There is a faint odour of superiority in such an exhibition. We can't identify real pain, and consequently our sense of identification with the other person's hurt is not touched. I think this is why Saturn's self-pity often drives other people away. Somehow it doesn't "smell" right. Nothing is really being shared.

On a deeper level, this may be one of the reasons why we need relationships with people whose planets hit our Saturns. Such people don't fall for our performance, and we have to learn to be more honest. And in the end, if we can't fool other people, we have to take up the problem ourselves. There is a profound intelligence at work behind the way in which extreme Saturnian defence mechanisms fail us. If they succeeded, we would never have the opportunity to work creatively with our wounds.

Creative compensation

We have looked at Saturn's propensity for "fake" compensation. But there is a more creative form of compensation which can provide a key to working constructively with Saturn. This other kind of compensation is, in the end, what we must do with this planet, to get the best from it. Saturn's creative compensation is genuinely defensive; but it is a defence which yields extremely positive results. We actually have to start "from scratch", and work to develop the thing that makes us feel so inadequate and ashamed. We must do it authentically, and that may take a very long time. But if we doggedly persist, and learn to bear all the feelings of shame and inadequacy, we wind up with gifts and strengths which are truly our own, and which cannot be destroyed no matter what circumstances life inflicts on us. This is the precious thing we wanted and were denied when we were small, and we have learned to build it ourselves, stone by stone. It may sound rather harsh, but in the end no amount of therapy is going to do this for us. One of the purposes of therapeutic work in relation to Saturn's defences is to help us recognise where we are wounded, so that we can begin to understand how envy, avoidance, scapegoating, and all our other delightful Saturnian defences, have sprung from the same inner hurt. Working with a therapist or counsellor can help us learn to be honest with and about ourselves. Much of Saturn's pain is connected with loneliness, and the act of sharing this pain can make an enormous difference. But ultimately we still have to go off and work at the issues reflected by Saturn's sign, aspects, and house placement. We have to do it ourselves. No one else can do it for us.

No therapist can cure the discomfort that Saturn in Gemini feels in communicating. The person with Saturn in Gemini must work at learning to speak openly and directly with people. This is only possible if he or she recognises when Saturnian smokescreens such as scatter-gun chatter are being used. Learning to write clearly, to formulate ideas, to educate oneself, may all be necessary. If Saturn in Gemini reflects difficulties with early education, the person may need to pursue higher education later in life, facing all the difficulties such a task involves. The only way Saturn will cease to mobilise its defences in restrictive or destructive ways is if we actually grab hold of the problem and say to ourselves, "I'm terrified of looking like a fool. I'm vulnerable and frightened of failure. I may never be very good at this. I feel very inadequate. But I'm going to do it anyway."

If we experience a repeat of childhood failure or humiliation in the midst of this effort, we will probably discover that we are still alive and walking at the end of it. We can get up and try again. It may take many many years, but I don't think there is any other way to work with the defences created by this planet. Saturn's unconscious defence systems choke us. This one doesn't because it's conscious. It is still a defence. But defences are intrinsically healthy when they are balanced with the rest of the personality, and in the end we have no recourse except defence when dealing with Saturn because its nature is inherently defensive. That's what it is there for. Saturn provides us with the sense that there is something in us that can surmount obstacles and survive, that is totally and permanently our own because we have earned it ourselves. We have worked for it. We have not borrowed, begged, or stolen it. We have not been handed it free, and no one can take it away from us. Paradoxically, Saturn's defences are our great bastion against mortality, although it is this planet above all others which ceaselessly reminds us of that very same mortality through our flaws and failings.

Saturn is our finest and most honest defence against the human sense of transience, dissolution, and disintegration. We know that one day we are going to die, but if we can build a sense of real self-esteem and self-respect through making the best of what we have been given, we acquire something that allows us to face death with greater equanimity. The real horror of death is the feeling of never having lived, of never having been real. In order to develop this potential inner kernel of solidity, we must avail ourselves of Saturn's defence mechanisms. But from practical experience, so far as I can see, the only path which doesn't stifle, choke, injure, and ultimately frustrate us as well as those close to us is to actually work with rather than against our Saturn placement – however dreadfully vulnerable it may make us feel.

Audience: It is interesting because Saturn is often thought of as a teacher.

Liz: Yes, that is the deeper interpretation. But we may not fully understand that teaching is only effective if we do the homework. It may be that we are all bewitched by a Jupiter/Neptune sense of divinity, and secretly believe that we should be immortal. There does seem to be something in human beings which bitterly resents being mortal. Perhaps this is because we can recognise our mortality and its implications, unlike animals, who seem to live unquestioningly within the cycles of nature. Or perhaps it is because we recognise our innate divinity, and don't cope very well with the duality implied. We resent the fact that we have to pack it in. We resent dying, because we are conscious of our potentials in a way that makes us miserable about having to forego them, and angry about being flawed because we can envisage

Part Two: Saturn and Chiron as Defence Mechanisms 145

perfection.

There is a quality in the human spirit that fights against any feeling of limits. We might associate this with several astrological factors – Jupiter, Neptune, perhaps also the Sun and Mars. In this context Saturn is our great teacher. The limits that Saturn places on us are irrevocable. The difficulty is that they are inside, and are only incidentally reflected outside. We can convince ourselves that our limits are external. We can be mysteriously and unconsciously attracted to them, and place ourselves in situations which are limiting. Or we may take a situation which someone else, with a different Saturn placement, might not find limiting, and turn it into a prison through our own subjective response to it.

That is another thing which is very uncomfortable to realise about Saturn. If we talk to other people about how they feel about the same situation which we find so dreadfully restrictive and frustrating, they may say, "What on earth are you complaining about? I would give anything to be in your shoes." Our sense of what limits us is very subjective. It is not a universal objective truth which can be applied to everyone. One encounters this very strikingly if one works with many people over a long period of time. Someone who has suffered appalling hardship, or a terrible handicap of some kind, may face life with faith and confidence, while someone else, who seems to feel totally deprived and persecuted, may make a giant meal out of very little. Recently I heard the violinist, Itzhak Perlman, perform Sibelius' Violin Concerto in Birmingham. Perlman suffered from polio as a child, and had to walk out on stage using crutches. He moves with great difficulty. Yet he has poured his life and soul into becoming a superb musician, and there is magic in his playing. Perhaps we can link Saturn with his handicap. But I also link Saturn with the grim determination to make something of his talent – which requires a lot of physical discipline and effort – rather than sitting about complaining about how dreadfully life has treated him. It was a very salutary experience.

A person who has Jupiter in the same place that we have Saturn may be at a loss to understand what on earth is the matter with us, because to Jupiter the lack of something is a challenge, an opportunity, and a means of growing. To Saturn, it is crushing. The intense and interior nature of this planet tends to generate enormous defence systems, and until we begin to realise where these defences are operating, we can't do anything about them. We are at their mercy. Having experienced denial or deprivation early in life, by the time we have arrived at the age of thirty our Saturnian defences are firmly in place. By this time Saturn has gone around the chart once, and has done its job erecting effective bastions against hurt. We have got the basic system set up, with the alarms and the surveillance cameras fully operating.

The defences may be unconscious and very brittle, and they may have to be pulled down and rebuilt – perhaps when transiting Saturn opposes its own place for the second time, and transiting Uranus reaches the opposition to natal Uranus as well. These defences may also have cost us dearly, in terms of suppressing important personality qualities. But by the age of thirty, after we have experienced life through Saturn's transit of all twelve houses and all the natal planets and angles, we have worked out how to defend ourselves against possible threats in every sphere of life. And by that time we may also have begun to realise, albeit dimly, how much of ourselves we have stifled in order to achieve this.

Not everyone expresses Saturn's dark side to the same degree. In some horoscopes, Saturn is not so problematic. A person with Saturn in Capricorn in the 2nd house, trine the Sun in Taurus, may have an easier time of it, in certain ways, than someone with Saturn in Cancer in the 12th, square the Sun in Libra. Life is unfair in this way, unless one espouses a philosophy, such as reincarnation, which attributes cosmic justice to the horoscope under which we are born. But thinking in this way, however true it might be on the deeper level, often provides only illusory escape from immediate unhappiness, and can be a defence in itself. It makes more sense to work creatively with what one has, rather than explaining it away through something one did in one's last life. Some people have really difficult aspects to Saturn. Others have nicely trined and sextiled Saturns which don't give them a lot of obvious trouble. Saturn is still Saturn, and is defensive by nature; and everything I have been saying about it still applies, trines notwithstanding. However, for many people Saturn mobilises its defences so intensely that huge chunks of the personality are frozen up as a result.

It sometimes seems that an inner voice can be heard at about age thirty, which says, "Very good. You have built these walls very well. But you forgot to repair the shaky foundations on the east side of the house. If you don't deal with them now, the house will come down in spite of your efforts, and all that good work will have counted for nothing." Or it might say, "Very good. But you've built these walls so thoroughly and obsessively that you have blocked up all the windows and doors. Now how are you going to get out?" By the time Saturn makes its opposition at around age forty, we are really in trouble if we have ignored that voice. If Saturn's defence systems have become inflexible by then, Uranus opposition Uranus, which hits just a little earlier, and Neptune square Neptune, which hits at roughly the same time, will bring the voice back along with a big bag of explosives. Some people even enjoy the added pleasure of Pluto square Pluto. At this juncture, with so much outer planet activity, we need room for movement and growth. If Saturn's defence system is false or too rigid, the whole structure will come down. We euphemistically call this mid-life crisis.

The outer planets are not intrinsically destructive. But if our Saturnian defences have grown too tight, or are brittle or false, the influx of new ideas, feelings, and perceptions, which coincides with these major outer planet cycles, cannot be integrated into ego consciousness without something violently giving way. Instead of growth, there may be breakdown, although this is sometimes the best possible thing in the long term because, understood and worked with constructively, it can lead to breakthrough and a healthier defence system. But if we have ignored the message of the Saturn return, the bill tends to arrive at the time of the mid-life Saturn opposition, and usually interest has accumulated. At the time of the Saturn return we have a chance to have a good hard look at what we are suppressing and what we are not dealing with.

Audience: What about the generation with the Uranus-Saturn-Jupiter conjunction? That would be people born in 1940 and 1941.

Liz: Saturn is always Saturn, aspects notwithstanding, and it can display a remarkable capacity to dominate the planets it sits on. This domination may not last very long, of course, and sooner or later Jupiter and Uranus will gang up on Saturn and destroy the existing structures. But for a time there may be a total suppression of freedom and spontaneity. We can look at the collective expression of this conjunction, which occurred during the first years of the war, to get a sense of how it works. I am inclined to associate the Nazi regime with Saturn, as the birth chart for the Third Reich has Saturn conjunct the Sun firmly planted in the 10th house and dominating the chart. Hitler also had Saturn placed here. Saturn's mythic role as tyrant has many parallels in what we saw happening in Europe during 1940 and 1941. For a time the whole of Europe was overrun. But then the tide turned.

Audience: Can Saturn suppress even Uranus?

Liz: Yes, for a while. In the individual, one of two things is likely to happen. Saturn may stifle Uranus, and the person may be heavily defended against anything unconventional, chaotic, progressive, or anarchic. We can see this type of personality quite frequently. They tend to talk a lot about the good old days, and law and order, and traditional morals, and so on. Uranus is then usually projected on "undesirables" – hippies, gypsies, communists, single parents, homosexuals, "New Age" types, even astrologers. Alternatively, the person may identify with Uranus, and project Saturn. In this case there is often a constant struggle against Saturn in the outer world. Authorities of any kind are fair game for the projection of Saturn, and the person may consciously espouse an anarchistic or revolutionary political ideology. There may be a complete rejection of material values, and an overemphasis on an ideal world, an ideal society. We might remember that the vanguard for the "Flower Power" movement in America was primarily made up of musicians born under this Saturn-Uranus conjunction. Bob Dylan is a good example.

National collectives can also express this dichotomy. Every national chart has Saturn in it. From the nation's natal Saturn we can get a very good sense of how that particular country will defend itself as an independent entity. It is also the area of the nation's greatest fear and vulnerability. The chart of the USA provides an interesting example. Saturn is in Libra the 10th house in this chart, square the natal Sun and Jupiter in Cancer. Where would you say America's greatest vulnerability lies? As a national entity, this country is terrified of the world's bad opinion. The American government is excessively concerned with its own image in the eyes of other nations. It likes to be seen as the world's policeman, the world's bringer of law and order. This is appropriate for Saturn in Libra in the 10th. But the tyrannical element in Saturn – the tendency to try to stifle other ways of living and thinking – is also in evidence. However, it is usually projected onto other nations, which are then called "tyrannies" and have to be brought in line. America's involvement in the Vietnam War may be directly related to this.

Audience: You ought to have a look at a book called *Political Science* by Radley Newman. It's all about American foreign politics. No one likes us. I don't know why.

Liz: You know perfectly well why, after all we have been discussing about Saturn this morning. If you want to have a good laugh as well as a good cry, look at a few national charts. Nations behave like individuals. Countries have psyches which operate according to the same inner laws as the individual psyche. Saturn's system of defences, with all its subtleties and complex mechanisms, can apply to a collective in precisely the same way as it can to an individual personality.

Audience: Is our Saturn in the 10th as well?

Liz: If we use the 1801 chart for the United Kingdom, it's in the 11th. We can see this in action right now, in the distrust and suspicion we feel about entering the European Union. Britain is a very insular nation in terms of its "friendships" with other nations. It resists being part of any group. We can even see this defensiveness in our approach to other languages. The rest of Europe is, in the main, bilingual. Most French, Italians, Germans, Dutch, Swedish, and so on, speak more than one language. It is considered a handicap not to be able to communicate in more than one tongue. The Swiss are of course brilliant at this, being a nation in which four different languages are spoken. But when the British travel abroad, they cannot understand why the rest of the world doesn't speak English. Language is not only a 3rd house matter, for purposes of communication. It is also an 11th house matter, because it allows ideas and ideals to be shared across national boundaries, and unifies disparate collectives. Individual British may of course feel very differently, and be fluent in European languages, and look forward to a single currency. Individual Americans may be very opposed to America's international policing role. But national policy tends to follow the nation's Saturn in terms of where the country's defences lie in relation to other countries.

Audience: I'm wondering about what happens to young people between the ages of fourteen and twenty-nine, between the first Saturn opposition and its return. I've been watching young people in their teens and early twenties, and observing a few things. How much flexibility do you feel there is, in developing healthy Saturn defences rather than obsessive or rigid ones?

Liz: I think there is often a great deal of flexibility at this stage of life. Before the Saturn return, defences will be roughly in place, and childhood wounds will have taken their toll. But the more fearful and destructive Saturnian elements seem to be able to heal more quickly in youth. Positive experiences seem to get through and register more easily than they do later on, and good relationships in adolescence – with friends, teachers, mentors, lovers, a sympathetic therapist – may have the power to heal quite savage parental wounds. One can get a lot further more quickly, working therapeutically with individuals in this age group. The older one gets, the more entrenched the defences tend to become, and trying to work with them can feel like chipping away at stone. Positive experiences later in life may only be met with suspicion or disbelief, and are discounted because the cynicism runs so deep. But there are always exceptions. In the therapeutic process, one cannot really generalise. With people of any age group, every individual is different, and in any individual one particular problem might shift quite quickly while another might stubbornly resist years of work. Often these more stubborn issues are linked with Saturn, and it may take a long time, as well as the catalyst of powerful transits, to see any movement at all.

Saturn unaspected

Audience: What if Saturn is unaspected?

Liz: If Saturn is unaspected, the defence mechanisms are likely to be deeply unconscious. Sometimes this can reflect a problem in establishing healthy boundaries; the positive side of Saturn is not available for the ego's use. Sometimes it can suggest someone whose defences are incredibly powerful because they are very primitive. They are not mediated or tempered by the ego. When something is deeply unconscious, it tends to remain in a very primitive or archaic state. We "civilise" the planets in our chart through the mediation of consciousness. When this does not occur, we see a much more obviously archetypal, almost mythic, expression of the planet's qualities.

Have any of you seen a film by Werner Herzog, called *The Enigma of Kaspar Hauser?* This film was released many years ago. It tells the true story of a boy who had been kept in a locked room from babyhood. There was a complete mystery about who had imprisoned him, and why. He was found one day wandering about in the fields, unable to speak. He had to be taught to behave like a human, because he had experienced no human contact at all. He turned out to be highly intelligent, but initially he had no concept of human speech or socialised behaviour. This story is rather like the myths of children who have been raised by animals. But these legendary children, like Romulus and Remus in Roman myth, had the benefit of intelligent animal care, whereas Kaspar Hauser had nothing at all.

When a planet is unaspected, it is not easily accessible to other aspects of the personality. It tends to remain very primitive, like Kaspar Hauser. Its archetypal nature is not mediated. It hasn't had a chance to become sophisticated and adapted to life through being linked with other areas of the psyche. It isn't socialised. It sleeps in the basement, or expresses itself through deeply unconscious channels, until it is triggered – either by transit or progression, or by somebody else's planet through a synastry contact across two charts. Of course an unaspected natal planet will be nudged constantly by the transiting inner planets. It is not totally isolated. But it seems that only major transits, such as those from the slow-moving planets, have the power to really rouse it from unconsciousness. Then it tends to erupt into conscious awareness with great power, and it may take over one's life for a while, for good or ill or, sometimes, both.

I have known people with an unaspected Saturn who are very obsessively defended, but they have no understanding of how or why. The emotions attached to such defences do not seem to reach consciousness. The defences are expressed in one particular area of life, often in a highly ritualistic way, and form a sort of pocket of obsessive behaviour which makes no sense to the individual. Or they may be quite unaware of even being obsessive, and assume their behaviour is perfectly ordinary. A kind of dissociation occurs, and nothing changes until the Saturnian feelings and fears emerge into consciousness. Sooner or later they will, of course, because something will always trigger an unaspected Saturn when the right moment has arrived.

Audience: Can you chose to do that? If you are an astrologer, and you see an unaspected Saturn in your chart, can you say, "Right, I'm going to do something about that"?

Liz: You could try taking an ad in the *Evening Standard.* "Wanted: Catalyst with natal planet in 4° Cancer to conjunct my natal Saturn. Those with Saturn in this degree need not apply." But actually, the answer is no. All you can do is wait for the right time. Life will bring it to you. You can't really do anything about unaspected planets through an act of will, like standing in front of the mirror and shouting, "Come out, you bastard!" At the appropriate moment, transits will inevitably cluster round it. The likelihood is that an important relationship of some kind will form. That seems to be the main way in which unaspected planets get activated. We tend to become involved with someone who has a natal planet sitting on the unaspected point in our own chart. We can't plan that. Even an ad won't work, because strangely, relationships which look right on paper rarely feel the way we think they should feel in actuality.

Audience: How about choosing a situation less close to home? For example, if you had Saturn in the 11th, you might chose to join a group or commune, which might bring up the unaspected Saturn.

Liz: Yes, it probably would. But the manner in which it was brought up might not be very pleasant, because it would be compulsive rather than conscious, and the ego might not be ready to take it on. It's like forcing oneself to swallow unchewed food because it is supposed to be "healthy". The theory is right. But have you ever tried to do something important based on an intellectual decision, when it wasn't the right time? With the best will in the world, the 11th house Saturn might try to seek a group. But the group has disbanded, or one can't find them, or they are full and not taking on any new members, or the leader has died, or one keeps forgetting to ring, or one loses the bit of paper with the address. Somehow it just doesn't happen.

In principle you are right; we can put ourselves in the path of something, and make preparation. After all, we get experiences of every planet in the chart whenever the transiting Moon passes over, which is once a month. And of course there are the transiting Moon's squares and oppositions as well. Wherever Saturn is placed, it is often a good idea to expose oneself. I don't mean that literally. But it can be helpful to put ourselves in a position where our secret vulnerability, and all the defences we have erected around it, will be challenged. However, I am not enamoured of the idea of violent challenge. Over the years in which I have worked with people, I have found that gentle development is far more helpful and lasting than a forced acceleration through some kind of deliberate shock.

If a shock is truly needed, usually the psyche will arrange for one, and life will manifest it in one way or another. But I have never been very impressed by the "blow it out of the water" school of psychological techniques, especially with Saturn and Chiron problems. There can be great cruelty in these techniques, and I wonder sometimes about the motives of those who work with them. Everything living has its own natural pattern of growth, and the psyche is as much a living thing as the body, or a flower or tree. Things take time to heal and emerge from the dark. We do not stand over our roses, dowse them with boiling water, and demand that they bloom in January. What can we hope to gain by doing this with the extreme vulnerability reflected by Saturn? So if Saturn is in the 11th, by all means, try it out and join a group. But preferably, join a slow-moving therapeutic group run by qualified people, in which your fears and defences can be treated consciously and compassionately. And expect it to be difficult, because it will be. If the time is not right, you may want to leave, and you should be able to do so without feeling that you have failed.

Audience: Some of us were talking during the break about the relationship between humiliation and humility. Several of us have the Sun in aspect to Saturn.

Liz: Did you reach any interesting conclusions?

Audience: I have a square between the Sun and Saturn, and I've just had my Saturn return. It was not a pleasant experience. I was made very aware, as a woman, of the hierarchy which exists in society. I understand hierarchy as a Saturnian principle. Would humility help an understanding of the hierarchy? I experienced humiliation, but not humility.

Liz: Your point is extremely important, because hierarchy is certainly an attribute of Saturn's archetypal world. Hierarchy angers many people, especially when it is based, not on merit or effort, but on factors like inheritance, or unfair or unjust assumptions, many of which may reflect sexist or racist attitudes. But hierarchy, in its essence, is not built on false premises. It is a necessary dimension of earthly life, and humilty helps us to understand its necessity. If we look carefully at mythology and folklore, we will find that every quest requires that the protagonist, male or female, must prove himself or herself through submission to preset rules, or steps of training or learning. One doesn't simply grab for the treasure, or win a dead dragon in a lottery. There is a ritual procedure, usually involving elders or authorities, visible or invisible, which must be respected and followed.

The same applies to all initiation and mystery cults. One doesn't take the mescalin or the magic mushroom without preparation, any more than the practising Christian walks into a church and grabs the wafer and wine out of the priest's hands without the preliminary communal act of prayer and consecration. Otherwise the initiatory experience will be received by an untrained psyche, and at best will simply be forgotten afterward. At worst, one may be destroyed, because all things that have power have the power to bring to the surface what we might not yet be ready to face.

If we are humble enough to recognise and work through the stages, we are prepared, and then we keep what we have earned. This kind of hierarchy is the hierarchy of experience, and it reflects the most profound side of Saturn as teacher. The problem is that we may not always understand the significance and value of the steps. An individual collision with sexist attitudes may seem simply unfair and outrageous. But it may also provide a trigger for self-discovery, because there may be identical attitudes lurking within oneself, which one has not yet understood or come to terms with. We meet in the outer world what we carry in the inner.

Audience: I related humility to Innana's Descent. Each step down into the underworld required the removal of one of her garments of power.

Liz: It is an excellent mythic portrayal of this more profound kind of hierarchy. Humility is experienced when we allow Saturn's sense of lack to be acknowledged, and accept what must be learned or performed, without the ferocious pride which usually protects and defends us. It is pride which generates humiliation. Also, humiliation may be linked with secret feelings of inferiority. If we unconsciously feel inadequate, then someone who treats us as though we were inadequate can invoke a terrible sense of humiliation. Why should we feel humiliated, if the other person is clearly being malicious, stupid, ignorant, or projecting his or her own problem onto us? When we feel humiliated, we are secretly agreeing with those who are attempting to humiliate us. We cannot be humiliated unless Saturnian defensive pride is at stake.

During the break I was talking to someone about the Roman Saturnalia. The Romans were far cleverer than us in many respects, particularly in understanding the Saturnian side of the psyche. They set aside two weeks at the end of each year, under the governance of Saturn, to celebrate the overturning of pride. Our medieval Lord of Misrule is derived directly from the Roman Saturnalia. All those who were in positions of power and status were humbled by having to act as slaves. All the slaves were put in charge of their masters, and the whole of society's hierarchy was overturned during those two weeks. General chaos ensued. This celebration of Saturn recognised the importance of humility, as an alternative to humiliation. Of course it provided a safety valve for angry feelings, but it was more profound than that.

Saturn's humility is concerned with being able to be a real ass. Interestingly, the ass – the animal, not the American slang for the body part – is traditionally ruled by Saturn. In early Christian iconography one can find some very strange images of Christ in the form of an ass or donkey, hanging on the cross. This imagery is playing with the idea of the king being a holy fool. Medieval kings always had a fool, who was allowed to make an ass of them when no one else could do so without suffering instant punishment. The relationship of the king and his fool is a very mysterious one, because they are two halves of the same thing. The dialogue between Lear and his fool in Shakespeare's play is extraordinary; the king is truly a fool, and the fool is truly wise. The archetypal figure of the Fool of the Tarot reflects the same theme. Even earlier, we can find the imagery in Apuleius' *The Golden Ass*. This ancient Roman novel is concerned with initiation into the mysteries, and the neophyte is first turned into an ass.

There is great healing magic in being able to laugh at ourselves, just at the moment that we catch ourselves being really defensive and insufferably proud. This is where the Monty Python team exhibits such genius. They mercilessly send up the stuffiest, most ludicrous aspects of our defensive pride. I would suggest that you find a video of *The Life of Brian,* if you want clarification. A bit of genuine belly-laughter, particularly at oneself, can shift some of the most rigid Saturnian defences, where the most sophisticated astrological and therapeutic techniques may fail. Being able to be a fool can sometimes make the difference between humiliation and humility.

As you can see, some very profound issues emerge around our Saturnian defence systems. It is very difficult to make a real mess of something, and have egg all over one's face, and actually find oneself funny – particularly in front of other people. Some people seem to be able to do this without too much difficulty, while others find it incredibly painful. Yet there is a level on which we are all extremely funny, especially when we are stuck in our most unbending Saturnian postures. We are an absolute riot. This may be black humour, but Saturn's humour is inclined to be black, and rich in irony.

If we wish to make friends with Saturn, we must acquire a taste for irony. It is a special form of humour which can go a long way toward healing those characteristic self-inflicted wounds of Saturnian pride. Those of you who find this kind of humour cruel and awful might try thinking about it more deeply. We need to understand what it really represents, and what we are really doing when we create black humour in films, plays, and novels. We are sending up our most cherished sacred cows. Wherever we find sacred cows, we usually find Saturn. When we become so deadly serious and humourless about an issue that we daren't find anything silly or ironic in it, we will find Saturnian defences at work. Yet it is also Saturn which gives us the gift of irony, and the ability to appreciate the utter absurdity of life.

Saturn and taboos

Audience: What's the connection between taboos and Saturn?

Liz: Taboos in the anthropological sense are not really Saturnian. They are based on the necessity of tribal survival, and I would relate them much more to Pluto. The incest taboo, for example, doesn't originate in a moral issue. It emerges from the recognition that if families interbreed, they can produce defective children.

Audience: I really meant social taboos.

Liz: Yes, I would say these are Saturnian. For example, not so many years ago a woman was expected to be a virgin when she married, and those who were not could incur terrible social ostracism. They were "fallen" women. To many of us now this may seem idiotic at best, and deeply oppressive and destructive at worst. But once upon a time it seemed the only way to ensure that the firstborn child was really fathered by the official husband, and the social structure depended on this guarantee of family continuity. Saturnian taboos are often connected with fear of the renegade or chaotic element in society, which will disrupt the laws by which Saturn preserves the integrity of the social structure. Many of these social taboos have vanished from the world now, and will not be missed, although a hundred or even fifty years ago they were absolute and one broke them at one's peril. The more collective a group is, and the less individuals are conscious of their own individuality within that group, the more rigid the Saturnian taboos are likely to be. Some of them are extremely destructive, and spring from Saturnian pride, fear, or attempts to protect an image of some kind, or the power or position of a particular group or family unit.

Many taboos are concerned with sexuality, which is a realm in which Saturn's defences don't always function very effectively. They tend to get swept aside by Plutonian compulsions and passions, or Neptunian loss of boundaries. Some Saturnian sexual taboos exist because this is a sphere of life in which we are extremely vulnerable and open to humiliation. We cannot disguise our inadequacies very well in the intimacy of the bedroom. Sexual taboos may exist to maintain control. Control is, of course, a Saturnian defence mechanism.

Some taboos, as I have said, do not seem to be Saturnian, or are only partly Saturnian in nature, and these arise from the necessity of survival. Some taboos arise from the religious instinct, or the fear of chthonic powers. One doesn't dig open the graves of the ancestors, for example, and throw the bones around. It is taboo. Fear of supernatural forces lies behind many taboos. That may be partly Saturnian, but I would also associate it with Pluto, or perhaps Neptune. But we don't have much of this kind of taboo in Western societies any more, since we have less respect for the supernatural these days. Instead, we have things like Political Correctness, which is also a form of taboo, and typically Saturnian in nature. Or our government decides that homosexuals mustn't hold hands in public. That's a Saturnian taboo.

Really odd taboos can turn up in quite absurd places. A film is registered as "Parental Guidance" because somebody says "Shit!" in it. Another film is passed as suitable for twelve-year-olds, in which fifteen people are shown murdered and dismembered, and that is deemed acceptable for young people because nobody is using any four-letter words. We have some very strange ideas about what is taboo at the moment. Saturnian taboos exist for the purpose of controlling and suppressing anything that threatens the established order, because the established order, positive as well as negative, is one of Saturn's chief forms of defence. That is why Saturn is associated with social structures, hierarchies, and rules. Some Saturnian taboos are deeply necessary and serve a positive function, because they are concerned with moral issues which involve respect for the boundaries, lives, and property of others. Without these taboos, without which the law alone is insufficient, society disintegrates. We are seeing some of this occurring at the moment.

Audience: There seems to be a taboo about death and discussing death. Would you say that was Saturnian or Plutonian?

Liz: There would seem to be elements of both involved. The fear of mentioning death overtly, without euphemisms, is quite a recent phenomenon, and along with certain other psychological issues it would appear to be a peculiarity of modern times. Fear of death is of course not modern, and combines our archetypal Plutonian terror of chthonic powers with Saturn's struggle to defend itself against the helplessness of mortality. But the kind of embarrassment currently displayed when the subject is mentioned has been evident since Victorian times. One has only to wander through Highgate Cemetery, and look at the messages carved on the Victorian tombstones. We are told that Samuel Johnson "went to sleep", or Mary Smith is "in the arms of God", rather than that these people actually died. Many taboos have lingered from the Victorian era, which was riddled with Saturnian don't-mention-it's. As many of you probably know, the legs of furniture were clothed in fabric, rather than being allowed to show naked wood, and one had to say "limbs" rather than "legs".

One of the issues reflected in this proliferation of Saturnian taboos in the 19th century, apart from Queen Victoria's particular neuroses, is the rise of science and technology. Since the discovery of Uranus at the end of the 18th century, we have become more and more certain that we can control the powers of nature, and in the process we have disconnected from religious feeling of a more sincere and internal kind. In losing that religious feeling, we may have gained control over certain aspects of the material world; but we have lost our humility and our appreciation of the nonrational world. Consequently we have become arrogant.

Saturn is connected with the ego's sense of potency, which can be both healthy and dangerous. On a collective level I think we have experienced a loss of contact with many aspects of life which previously were part of humanity's world-view. In the last two hundred years these have been excluded from our world-view, and we have established a different set of priorities which are focused on control. The difficulty is that, when we defend ourselves against dimensions of life which are real and powerful, we remain aware of them on the unconscious level, and are secretly frightened of them. Extremely rational people are often the most superstitious souls one can encounter, when they think no one is looking. Saturn's taboos against the invisible powers have not cured our fear of those powers, but the fear has been driven underground and is expressed indirectly rather than in a healthy, open way. So we avoid discussing death, because we want to believe that medicine will eventually find a cure for it, and we cannot accept it as the inevitable culmination of life and a mystery to which we must all ultimately submit.

To some extent, the Enlightenment, and its espousal of the materialistic world-view, were a legitimate and necessary defence against superstition and the control of the Church. Defence mechanisms of a collective kind occur throughout history, as new world-views emerge which must defend themselves against old ones. The Church was itself a defence against the pagan overemphasis on physical reality and the powers of nature. The early Church, along with other mystery cults which were proliferating at the same time (such as Mithraism and Orphism), established the belief that the human spirit existed as an immortal entity independent of the body's mortality. This belief gave intrinsic value to the life of the spirit after death, which meant that an individual human life was not insignificant or a mere plaything of aloof and disinterested gods. But this world-view, arising as a defence against the depression of fatalism which infected the Hellenistic epoch, became too entrenched, as all Saturnian defence mechanisms do over time. First the Renaissance, and then the Enlightenment, rose up as defences against the oppressive control of the Church through superstition and guilt. Having achieved this, the new world-view itself became too entrenched, and now we have lost touch with the natural cycles of life, of which death is a fundamental part.

We create taboos against things that we want to believe we have some control over, but of which we are still secretly deeply afraid. Sooner or later the taboos are challenged and broken, as many Victorian taboos about sexuality have been challenged and broken in the last few decades. When Saturn's defence systems become too entrenched, they start to become suffocating, and then a new collective defence arises which in its turn creates new taboos. This process is enacted in the myth of Saturn becoming king of the gods through overthrowing his father, and then suffering the indignity of his son Jupiter overthrowing him in turn.

The new king starts off as a revolutionary, but he is also defending himself and his people against oppression and extinction, and so he is secretly Saturnian in nature from the outset. He becomes a king, sets new laws, becomes increasingly oppressive as he seeks to enforce those laws and defend himself against disorder, and eventually becomes a Saturnian tyrant just like the one he got rid of. Then a new revolutionary arises, takes over, sets new laws, becomes a tyrant, and so on. Taboos are linked with the values of the ruling tyrant, and are usually strongest when the forces of rebellion are just beginning to make quiet noises in the basement. Taboos protect the authority of a given structure, and they are meant to control anything which might threaten that structure.

Saturn as a symbol of natural law

Audience: Can you say something about Saturn's relationship with nature?

Liz: In myth Saturn is a god of agriculture, and a symbol of the law of the seasons and of time. He seems to represent natural law, rather than nature in the prolific sense. The fertility of nature was usually imaged as a goddess, and in Saturn's world his sister-wife Rhea took this role. Later, Demeter, the sister of Zeus, became goddess of nature. Saturn decides the natural term of everything that lives. Everything has its life cycle; everything is circumscribed by the limits of time. All living things follow fixed stages, from seed to adolescence to maturity to disintegration to death, just as the seasons do. When these mortal limits have been reached, all life must obey the law. Nothing lives beyond its allotted span. One cannot suddenly freeze time.

Saturn himself attempted to do this, to avoid the inevitable cycle which brought the end of his kingship, so he failed to follow his own law, and suffered the consequences. Saturn's scythe is the instrument of harvest, with which human beings reap the rewards of obedience to the cycles of nature. But of course it is also the scythe of death, and the image of the "Grim Reaper" which has come down to us from medieval times is really a poorly disguised version of the pagan Saturn.

Saturn's natural law is that all things have their time. The world of nature is the most vivid example of this irrevocable law, because everything is cyclical. Nothing is permanent except the life-force itself, and the laws which govern it. In Hesiod's *Cosmogony,* Saturn presided over the Golden Age, in which human beings lived in harmony with natural cycles, rather than controlling or fighting them. Therefore, although they were mortal, they did not suffer illness or fear. They simply went to sleep when their time was up. The cultivation of the earth as a Saturnian art is perceived as devoid of violence or aggression. Discipline and hard work are necessary, and obedience. But obedience to natural law is not the same as the ruthless exploitation of nature.

Obedience to natural law can be double-edged, as Saturn is. On the one hand, Saturnian respect for the laws of material life can result in a deep serenity and acceptance of the world as it is. One does not fritter away time and energy dreaming of what might be, or raging against what cannot be altered. But this kind of obedience can also be a defence against change. It is an interesting issue, which Arnold Toynbee discusses at length in his *Study of History.* He suggests that there is a type of social defence system, which he calls archaic utopianism. This involves a fantasy of going back to the purely natural. One throws away all the artificial accoutrements of so-called civilisation, without discrimination or selection, and returns to the cycles of nature and the tilling of the land. Archaic utopianism is an escape from the reality of the world in which one exists, which may be imperfect and negative in many ways, but which also has much to offer if one can meet its challenges realistically.

Hesiod's Golden Age has become the great myth of escape for many cultures. Whenever things go wrong, we tend to look back over our shoulders and talk about Saturn's Golden Age, even if we don't recognise what we are really talking about. Whatever government is in power, things were always better when the last one was in power. It was always better twenty years ago, before Ecstasy and Crack, or sixty years ago, before the War, or a hundred years ago, when the working classes knew their place and we still had an Empire.

That's very Saturnian. The fantasy is that, in those good old days, everyone obeyed the law. That is the real core of our backward-looking dream. We confront chaos, and we are afraid, and we talk about a time when everything was orderly. Whether such a time ever existed is of course questionable, unless you literally believe in Eden. I have met old Italians who still talk about the Mussolini era as the Golden Age, when the trains ran on time and there was less crime. They forget about how the peasant farmers starved, and people mysteriously disappeared if their political sympathies were questionable. The struggle for survival has always existed, along with its inevitable chaotic edges. But we have a fantasy about Saturn's Golden Age. Perhaps we are groping toward some deep sense that we have not yet found an inner law by which we can live in harmony with our own natures.

Audience: In the Saturnian process, you are suggesting that healing comes from producing something substantial in the outside world. In psychotherapy, you have to dig inside.

Liz: "Outside" doesn't necessarily mean concrete or physical. This depends on where Saturn is placed in the birth chart. But wherever Saturn is placed, we have to make something real out of it, which is reflected in outer life. "Real" may mean a strong sense of boundaries, for example, which can allow us to respect someone else's differentness and insist that our own is respected as well. That is not a concrete object, but it requires action, and involves other people in the real world. We may have to work in psychotherapy to discover that we have a problem with our boundaries. But I don't think it is sufficient to work with Saturn solely on the level of interpreting its meaning. The insight must be acted on, and built into our lives.

If Saturn is in the 4th house, for example, or the 8th, the issues may be very personal, and not for public consumption. They are not "outside" in the worldly sense. But Saturn will still require the person to build something real, even if this is on the level of learning to accept emotional boundaries or recognise one's essential aloneness. A 4th house Saturn may need to build a life which is not dependent on roots and family background. This may initially require insight and inner exploration, because there is usually a lot of childhood hurt and loneliness, but sooner or later one will have to act on that insight, and perhaps accept separation from the family or country of origin, or make peace with a failed parental relationship.

Audience: What I really meant was that, in my view, Saturn represents an essentially masculine approach, whereas psychotherapy is a more feminine approach. Would you say that is correct or not?

Liz: I'm not very happy about such black-and-white categorisations. Firstly, there are many different kinds of psychotherapy. If you work with positivist psychotherapy, for example, you will find that it is action-orientated. There is no poking about in the psychic dustbin. Such an approach may be perfectly valid for those people who need help in learning to make decisions and act on them. What you might call masculine types of psychotherapy are currently available, which are right and appropriate for certain individuals of both sexes at certain times. At the other extreme, there are deeply interior and virtually mystical forms of psychotherapy, which appear to have very little to do with external life. These may also be perfectly valid for certain people of both sexes at certain times. We have a great range of approaches under the label of psychotherapy, because the psyche isn't just "inside" or "feminine".

Equally, I think Saturn is quite happy to be either male or female. Producing things, or taking action in the world, is not necessarily masculine. If that were the case, men would have babies. The materialisation of the invisible world into the world of form is not an exclusively male or female act, archetypally or individually. The way in which people make things manifest may vary, depending on the sign in which Saturn is placed. So may the sphere of life in which manifestation occurs. But Saturn is a bisexual or asexual planet. In myth he is a male figure, but he is also connected with the she-goat Amalthea, and with the earth-goddess Rhea, as well as with his mother Gaia, by whom he was given his scythe. All these mythic figures are part of Saturn's nature.

It may be that all the planets are bisexual or asexual, with differing proportions of male and female components. We can get into a lot of trouble, and badly distort our understanding of astrology, let alone human beings, if we try to define things strictly according to whether they are masculine or feminine. I am not convinced these terms are very useful at all in interpreting astrological symbolism, except in very loose ways. Venus was a war-goddess, and the great macho solar hero Hercules spent a number of years dressed as a woman, serving Queen Omphale. Apollo and Zeus both had boy lovers, and the moon-goddess Artemis was a violent and savage huntress. No deity in myth is exclusively one sex or the other.

Defence mechanisms are neither masculine nor feminine. They partake of both. They can be expressed through both and by both. The balance of dynamic and receptive, or inner and outer, depends very much on the individual. In the same context, Saturn is neither mother nor father. It is Parent in the most profound sense, as the giver of law. It is not the lunar mother, nor is it the solar father. It is that which sets limits, and parents of either sex, by their nature, set limits. They both protect us and define the boundaries within which we must develop. Either parent, or both, can be represented by Saturn in the chart of a child.

Chiron

Wounding and spoiling

When we consider Chiron from the perspective of defences, we are once again looking at an area of life, or of the personality, in which we experience feelings of being wounded or damaged. But there is a different quality to Chiron. With Saturn, we feel something has been denied us, something withheld that we badly need. This lack or sense of deprivation makes us feel inadequate, and eventually forces us to develop self-sufficiency. With Chiron, there is a sense of something unfair hurting or humiliating us, something that we didn't merit. We have been irrevocably spoiled or damaged. I don't mean spoiled in the sense that a child is "spoiled" by too much fussing and attention. I mean the word in the sense of spoiled goods – the innocence and original state of perfection have been taken away. There is an irredeemable flaw. Something has crippled us, and because of that injury we must take a different path in life, one which often we feel we would not have chosen if we had been left "intact".

Saturn is connected with feelings of deficiency on a personal level. We say to ourselves, "It's *my* fault that I was deprived. There must be something wrong with me." Or we project our feelings onto particular people or institutions: "It's my mother's fault, she didn't give me enough affection," or, "It's the government's fault, otherwise I would be able to get a job." With Chiron the feeling of "It's my fault," or "It's their fault," is not really sustainable, even if one tries very hard to find somebody to blame. There is more of a sense that life is bloody unfair.

One of the big differences between Saturn and Chiron is that Chiron generates enormous rage, of a kind which reflects impotence in the face of a cruel or disinterested cosmos. Savage rage of this kind is not something I associate with Saturn. Resentment and envy are Saturnian, and so is the sort of slow corrosive cynicism which blights trust. But Chiron says, "Life has dealt me a terrible blow, and, by God, I'm going to hurt the rest of you." There is a quality of primitive violence in Chiron, the rage of a wounded animal, that arises from a recognition that something utterly unfair has happened which is totally unjustifiable. We might recall the myth about Chiron's wounding. It is unintentional and unmerited, but it results in an incurable and agonising wound. This wound afflicts the horse part of the centaur, the animal side of him. Many of you who keep pets will know that an animal in extreme pain will bite, kick, or claw anyone who comes near, even if one is trying to help.

Some people experience the feelings of Chiron through an accident or illness of some kind, which has either physically crippled them or rendered them incapable in some way. For example, one can't have children because of an infection, or one can't walk properly because of a congenital birth defect such as a club foot, or one has always wanted to be a dancer but one cracks one's ankle and has to give it up. These kinds of circumstances are often linked with Chiron. So are the random experiences which bring us face to face with destructive elements in other people. The neighbour who for no reason poisons one's cat, or the gang of youths who mugs one's grandmother for the sheer hell of it, bring us face to face with the savage side of Chiron.

But Chiron's revelations of the savagery of life aren't always on the physical level. Sometimes they manifest on the emotional level. Chiron may be expressed through a feeling of physical ugliness which has no basis other than that one doesn't "fit" the prevailing collective standard of beauty. It may be evident in the feeling of being outcast that sometimes accompanies being a member of a racial or religious minority group. The unfairness may be social or racial. We all get a wild card dealt to us, and this is where Chiron turns up. It is the joker, the bad card in the spread, which overturns all our best-laid plans and forces us to accept a handicap of some kind.

Chiron's wounding is usually much bigger than the sins of one's parents. Although initially one's feelings of being badly treated may focus on parental failings, with even a little bit of reflection the realisation occurs that there is a larger, more complex issue at work behind such personal experiences of suffering. It's not simply that the parents have been brutish or insensitive. Even if they have, it generally becomes clear that they have behaved in this way because they too are victims of life. Chiron may lead us to the discovery that the whole of society is full of injustice, and that wounding may be the product of human nature and the times in which one lives. The more we explore Chiron's wounds, the more we are forced to recognise the inevitable.

A good analogy might be the experience of being born in London in the middle of the Blitz. One can't blame one's parents if the house is blown apart; and if one's father has gone off to fight, and doesn't come home again, one can't blame him for that either. Something much bigger has swept everyone into a collective nightmare, and one's personal suffering is part of a greater suffering. One might be the victim of racial or religious persecution, or one's family may have been immigrants who were the victims of it. One might have lost a child to an IRA bomb, or lost a partner in an air disaster. One might have been living in Hungary when the Russians came in; or one's parents may have survived Auschwitz but cannot forget, and one is forever reminded by the tatoos on their arms. These kinds of things are wounds that arise from collective atrocities, collective unfairness, collective blindness. This is the sort of wounding that we discover at the heart of Chiron's defences.

Bitterness and cynicism

For these reasons Chiron is much more difficult for us to deal with than Saturn, because where are we going to find a culprit? How can we do anything about circumstances or conditions which are so much bigger than we are? We can blame the whole of society, or we can blame God (or the lack thereof), which Chiron will sometimes do as a means of defence. Chiron can develop a very negative philosophy of life. I know all of you are waiting to hear about Chiron's healing potentials. But we cannot heal unless we understand the nature of our wound. One of the dangers with Chiron is that we may unconsciously carry a profound sense of injury and victimisation. Unless we look at such feelings, lots of nice talk about healing is ultimately irrelevant and ineffectual. And one of the defences we may develop, to protect ourselves from a similar injury happening again, is a bitter, black vision of life. Chiron the Wounded Healer is a beautiful and positive archetypal image. But before he can exhibit such potentials, he will usually spend some time in the black despair of cynicism, or the unconscious savagery of a wounded animal. Chiron can lead us to carry an unsuspected cargo of psychic poison.

Chiron shares a sense of wounding with Saturn, but the nature of the wound is different. It doesn't seem to reflect something that one wanted from one's parents and didn't get, or some ingredient necessary for the ego's confidence that was denied or suppressed in childhood. As I have said, Chiron is concerned with much larger issues. When we start trying to track these issues back to their source, what happens is that we must begin to ask philosophical or religious questions of a profound and difficult kind, and we may be left with a feeling of hopelessness. How can we heal a problem that is not personal, that arises out of the collective in which we live and will probably never be solved in our lifetimes? One of Chiron's difficulties is that we may be facing things we cannot heal. To some extent, healing is not possible with Saturn, in the sense that we cannot create a different childhood. We can't ever get that gift in the natural, innocent way in which another child might have received it, and consequently we can never take it for granted as one of life's bonuses. But we can acquire Saturn's "treasure hard to attain" if we are prepared to work for it.

In that sense Saturn is healable. We will never have what we want without effort. In Saturn's world there are no free lunches. But we may discover that hard-won self-respect is not a bad substitute for the loss of naive confidence.

With Chiron, I don't think we ever get the kind of healing we have in mind. We get something else instead, but we cannot make the wound go away. There is something about this planet that seems to represent a deeply disturbing element in life. This element may be part of a greater cosmic intelligence, but it is not part of Western religious and spiritual ideals, and it is often a great challenge to the astrologer's ideal framework. Many people who are drawn into astrology and psychotherapy have a secret belief that, sooner or later, if the right key can be found, everything can be healed. Everything can be transformed. It may be that we need to believe this, and we need to work as though it were true. But then we run up against Chiron. Astrologers in particular may experience considerable difficulty in taking Chiron on board.

There are quite a few publications out now on Chiron. The best is Melanie Reinhart's *Chiron and the Healing Journey,* which you should all read to get a fuller background on the planet. But when I compare most of these books with the way I have seen Chiron operate in birth charts and by transit, I have found that there are serious discrepancies between the given astrological interpretation and the actuality. The literature is sometimes so terribly innocent. It is all about the Wounded Healer, the operative word being 'Healer', while 'Wounded' is in very small type. But the hidden clause in our contract with Chiron is that the wound is permanent. Chiron is the *healer,* not the *healed.*

The myth of Chiron

Before we look at the ways in which we might deal with this most unnerving of astrological symbols, I shall risk boring those of you who already know the story of Chiron by outlining the mythic material.

To begin with, the name Chiron in Greek is actually spelled Cheiron, which means "the one who has hands", or "the one who knows how to use his hands". From the same root we derive the word "cheiromancy", which is the art of palm-reading. Chiron begins life as a wild creature, a hunter, like others of his race. The centaurs live on the fringes, in the forests and mountains, off the beaten tracks of human kind. They eat only raw meat. Apollodorus called them "savages, without social organisation, of unpredictable behaviour". An attempt was made in later myth to divide the centaurs into "good" (such as Chiron and

Pholus) and "bad" (such as Nessus). This split should tell us something about the nature of our astrological Chiron, who embodies both. The centaurs are the children of Cronus (Saturn), who manages to rape a nymph by turning himself into a horse. The products of this union are the result of an act of violent sexual union with an unwilling participant.

Some centaurs are amenable to human friendship, provided they don't get drunk, because when they get drunk they become incredibly destructive. This occurs in myth when Theseus attends the marriage of his friend Pirithoös, king of the Lapiths. The centaurs, who have been invited but are forbidden to touch the wine, manage to steal a jug or two, and go mad. They proceed not only to rape the bride, but also to burn down the king's house. The famous battle of the Lapiths and centaurs is portrayed in many classical friezes. It is an image of human "civilisation" battling against the chthonic forces. Everything is laid to waste, and most of the centaurs are killed; and Chiron, who is their king, is driven from his home on Mount Pelion into the wild and unreachable recesses of the mountain forests, only to return to plague astrologers since the planet's discovery in 1977.

Chiron is one of the "good" centaurs who is willing to form relationships with, and teach, human beings. Because myths do not give us a chronology of which episode happens before which other episode, we meet Chiron in many diverse and unrelated stories, generally as a wise teacher, instructing such figures as Asklepios in the arts of healing. He is also a prophet. He is already an archetypal teacher and healer before he is wounded – a good, noble creature, in control of his darker centaur heritage, struck down by life's appalling unfairness.

What happens is that Herakles, the quintessential solar hero, engages in a battle with the "bad" centaurs, and shoots an arrow at one of them, which accidentally strikes Chiron – who has had no part in the fight – in the knee. In another version of the story, Herakles has been off doing his Labours and has just killed the Hydra. He has taken the arrows which he has used to kill this monster and replaced them, full of the Hydra's poisonous blood, in his quiver. One of these accidentally scrapes the centaur's thigh. In both versions, it is pure bad luck. It is one of the few myths in which such a piece of bad luck occurs. No god has initiated it. No *hubris* has invoked it. Neither Chiron nor Herakles has done anything deliberately wrong; neither character is bad or evil. Yet despite Chiron's wisdom in the healing arts, he cannot do anything with his own wound, and retires howling in agony to his cave. Yet he cannot die, because he is immortal. He is condemned to eternal suffering. Prometheus later offers to accept immortality in his stead, and Zeus approves this arrangement;

so Chiron is released from his pain at last, but only through death.

This is not a pretty myth. It is also not a myth which we can neatly fit into our own fantasies of how the cosmos ought to work. We like to think that Chiron becomes a wise healer because of his wound, and thus the wounding serves a constructive purpose. In fact he is wounded *despite* his goodness and wisdom, and nothing except death can release him. There is nothing romantic or glamorous about this story. It is a very stark vision of a particular dimension of life which I think we must be willing to face if we want to work with Chiron constructively. The most important thing in this story is the utterly random, undeserved nature of the wound. There is no reason for it. I think this is very hard to swallow. There is logic, if not fairness, in the myth if we see Herakles' battle with the "bad" centaurs as a primal conflict for which Chiron, although innocent, must suffer. He too is a centaur, although he does not participate in the fight. In this sense we suffer for the destructive acts of our fellows because we too are human, and goodness and knowledge will not protect us. If we take the second version of the story, which involves Herakles' fight with the Hydra, there is also logic, if not fairness, in that Chiron once again suffers because of a battle which does not concern him, but with which he is linked because of his relationship with Herakles.

The key to both versions of the story is Herakles. In both, the solar hero, like the conscious ego in each individual, or the conscious values and structures of a civilised society, fights a chthonic foe. Chiron too is chthonic. Although he has risen above his wild nature, and is the friend of Herakles, he is also kin to that which Herakles struggles against. Something in us is irrevocably injured when we consciously attempt to do battle with the destructive powers within ourselves and within life. The evil which we see around us would be our own evil, if we had not struggled so hard, like Chiron, to contain our savagery; and it seems so unfair when, despite that struggle, we suffer more than the recognisable villains. Chiron's pain arises from the archetypal battle between light and darkness; somebody must pay, and often it is not the guilty.

The astrological Chiron's feelings of woundedness are rooted in a deep sense of injustice and victimisation. "Why me?" cries Chiron. "I didn't ask for this battle. Why am I being punished for it?" This cry must have been on the lips of thousands of nice, decent Germans during the last war; it is on the lips of thousands of Bosnians; it is on the lips of the Irish; and it is on the lips of all of us who are witness to carnage of which we have never approved and to which we have never contributed, but in which we must share because we are in the wrong place at the wrong time and are part of a collective which is still prone to destructiveness. To put it very succinctly, Chiron makes us aware of collective guilt. That is why we don't have the luxury of blame.

It is possibly worth reflecting on the fact that Chiron, as a heavenly body, is generally considered to be either a cooled-down comet core, caught in our solar system by gravitational pull, or an asteroid or meteorite which has been trapped in the same way. It is an "outsider", on the fringe as the centaurs were in myth, not part of the civilised society of the other planets. It does not fit into our neat system of planetary rulerships, nor does its orbit behave with any regularity. Like Pluto, Chiron makes an elliptical path around the Sun.

The planet Chiron appears to have wandered into our system. Our Western sense of cosmic justice rests on the Greek idea of a harmonious and orderly cosmos. This means that God is orderly and ultimately just. In this essentially Pythagorean universe, cosmic law never deviates. It never cocks up on us; it can always be trusted, and consequently society can be modelled after it. Nothing "wanders in" or doesn't "fit". Even in a post-religious world, we have replaced the Greek vision of cosmos with the scientific vision of cosmos, which likewise trusts implicitly in undeviating scientific laws. Likewise we trust a socio-political vision which attributes all antisocial elements to basic laws of "have" and "have not", rather than facing the unpredictable elements of individual character.

Chiron is an alien. It doesn't belong. It doesn't follow the same pattern as the other planets in our system. We don't know how it got there, and this physical "differentness" echoes its astrological symbolism. Chiron doesn't fit into our sense of cosmic order. It flies in the face of our concepts of cosmic justice, in which everything is ultimately governed by the law of reason. Astrologers keep trying to make it fit into the grand plan by assigning it as co-ruler of one of the signs – Sagittarius or Virgo being the usual candidates. But it is possible that Chiron doesn't "rule" any sign.

Even if we believe that only reincarnation, or an inscrutable Will of God, can explain the injustices in life, we nevertheless accept the idea that somewhere, on some level, a just and orderly plan is being enacted. But Chiron says to us, "I may be just in my own terms, but not in yours." Our most cherished ideals often will not accommodate this component of life. We can therefore understand why one of Chiron's characteristic defences is a great rage against life, an animal rage against wounding. On the most profound level it may be seen as a religious rage, a rage against the cosmic powers. It is not rage at a particular person, in the way one can hate one's mother because she represents a negative Saturn. Whom are we going to hate for Chiron's wounds, except the gods? Whom can we blame, except Adam and Eve? With Chiron, we can never really find a place to begin, if we are looking for a "cause" for our hurts.

Audience: I find myself reacting with rage to what you are saying.

Liz: Of course you are. You wouldn't be the first person to do so.

Audience: On the other hand, I'm proving exactly what you're saying. I have the Sun conjunct Chiron.

Audience: You said we can't find a place to begin with Chiron's wound. Doesn't the journey lie in trying to find out where to begin?

Liz: When I say we don't know where to start, I mean that we don't have an immediate object to hand that we can comfortably blame. I don't mean that there is nothing to reflect upon. Chiron's wounding is concerned with collective imperfection, and the inevitable consequences of trying to civilise ourselves. We can't start as we might with Saturn, in the sense of looking back to childhood and deciding that our mothers did this or our fathers did that. If we do attempt to begin with an object to blame, we wind up in a morass, because the thread runs back and back, and eventually we wind up on a universal level. We need to begin in the place of our pain and examine the ways in which it may be connected with an issue of universal human suffering.

The route that Chiron forces us to take is one of deep reflection. Unlike Saturn, which requires doing something active to build what we have been denied, Chiron requires us to first disengage from our belief that life ought to fit a certain model. It is our world-view that is challenged by Chiron, so the place to begin is with the holes and fissures in our belief system – the places where we are masking our perplexity and doubt with platitudes or conventional formulae. If we believe that everything operates on the principles of Santa Claus and the Tooth Fairy, or that the cosmos is really just a big version of Disneyland, then we are going to have a lot of trouble with Chiron. No planet is better equipped to show us where we still believe in good chaps on white horses and bad ones on black, even though we may think we are spiritually sophisticated and inclusive in our thinking.

There is a place to begin, but it isn't what has been done to us by somebody else. It is where we are expecting life to conform to our own rules. Of course we can't do this kind of reflecting in childhood, which is when Chiron hurts the most. A child cannot sit down and say, "Well, according to

Plato's *Republic,* the problem lies in our lack of education about the eternal realities." We can only begin the process of reflection in adulthood, which is why, by the time we come around to our first Saturn return, a fair amount of poison has probably already accumulated. The same may be said about Saturn, of course; a child with Saturn in Leo cannot say, "I am not getting sufficient recognition from my parents for my individuality, so I will have to start learning to give it to myself." Yet we do know instinctively where we have to build wth Saturn, even if we initially do the building defensively. Usually that process starts quite early, around the time of the first Saturn square.

Chiron's poisoned wound

Audience: The Chiron process sounds a bit Neptunian.

Liz: In what sense do you mean?

Audience: With Neptune, we expect something to be one way, and it always turns out differently.

Liz: In that sense, yes, they are similar. Neptune expects Eden, winds up with incarnation, and then spends a lifetime trying to spit out the apple. Chiron starts off with a cosmology that is fair, and winds up having to cope with a universe that doesn't fit the model. Both planets can generate deep disillusionment. But Neptune's disillusionment and rage at Paradise lost don't usually lead to corrosive bitterness as a defence. More often they lead to self-victimisation. With Chiron, disillusionment can produce poison. This is one of Chiron's characteristic defences. How do you think it might show itself in an individual?

Audience: Physically?

Liz: Yes, Chiron is often linked with physical problems, of both an organic and functional nature. Bitterness and disillusionment can express themselves somatically – perhaps in really lethal diseases like cancer, but perhaps more frequently in a general lowering of resistance, leading to a predisposition to infections. Abscesses and boils, which are often linked with Pluto, may also reflect Chiron's inability to throw off infection. This is a kind of somatised depression, a retaining of poison and an insufficient ability to fight off the nasties which enter the system from outside. It is as though the body is saying, "What's the point? Life is horrible anyway, so I just won't bother to fight." I have seen a number of examples of Chiron's relationship with toxic conditions. Any of you who have undergone any sort of dietary procedure to clear toxins will know that one of the most immediate emotional effects is rage.

Audience: How does that work?

Liz: If one goes on a strenuous diet to clear toxins from the system, enormous rage can be released. With many people, the first thing that happens is that they get very, very angry, as if the toxins are in some way a physical reflection of emotional poisons that one hasn't got rid of. As the rage comes out, so do the toxins. One of the fastest ways of uncovering unsuspected rage is to deny the body its usual food, which we use to comfort ourselves physically. One of the things we tend to do with Chiron's wounds is that we try to silence the rage by numbing it, with any substance which will take away the pain. The moment we take away the comfort, the rage begins to emerge.

Audience: Could Chiron be linked with alcoholism?

Liz: Yes. Addictions of various kinds are usually associated with Neptune, but in certain cases it seems that Chiron can play a big part. There are different reasons for addiction, and often two or three threads will be woven together to generate the compulsion. The Neptune-based addictions reflect the sense of finding the world too stony and cold; Neptunian problems suggest a longing to go back to the primal experience of fusion, whether it is fusion with mother or fusion with God. Neptune resists incarnation, not because one has been poisoned by bitter experience, but because Eden is so beautiful and perfect that nothing in the earthly world can compare. Individuals who suffer from Neptunian addiction problems may be unconsciously attempting to reconnect with an ineffable unity which one feels one has lost. Of course no individual is purely Neptune, and addiction always involves a complex combination of factors. But often one can see clearly the longing for redemption which lies beneath attachment to the addictive substance. Neptunian addictions turn alcohol or drugs into talismans, magical substitutes for the primal source.

Chiron addictions serve as pain-killers. They are a means of stifling pain and rage. Redemption is not the dominant psychological motive, since Chiron has no sense of an *a priori* unity which one has lost. But there may be an intense and intolerable awareness of life's injustice, and too great an appreciation of the immense vulnerability of human existence. The magical substance is taken not because one longs to go home, but because one feels one might otherwise kill somebody. The emotional tone of the addiction is very different from that of Neptune, although the two may work together. One may be quite unconscious of this suppressed rage. But something inside says, "Stifle the anger quickly, or it will escape and cause damage and destruction. Stuff your mouth with something. Inject something. Numb the pain before you have to acknowledge it. Do anything you can to silence it." The moment the pain-killer is taken away, a terrible rage may begin to emerge. All the poison starts to come out – a black bitterness towards life because it is so unfair.

Chiron's poison must come out if any healing is to take place. This doesn't mean one has to go about beating people up. But we need to be conscious of the poison and find some vehicle through which to express it – perhaps in a therapeutic situation, or through painting, writing, or some other creative form which can honour as well as contain the suffering. One of the things that often goes wrong with our encounters with Chiron is that the divine half of the centaur can be very embarrassed about the rage that the horse half feels.

Let's look again at the myth. The place of Chiron's wound is not in the human or divine part, it's in the animal part. Have you ever had an animal that has been wounded – perhaps a dog that has had its paw run over? The animal doesn't sit and philosophise, does it? It will attack anybody that comes near it, if there is any strength left to do so. Chiron's rage is felt on the instinctual level. The other half of the centaur is busy saying, "What is the meaning of this?" But how can we begin to distill meaning from our wounds, or place them in the perspective of a larger pattern, unless we know they are there, and can appreciate how much they hurt? Chiron's wounds are linked to bigger collective issues. But they also feel personal, and our sense of grievance against collective wrongs is fuelled by those areas of our individual lives in which we have been injured by the backlash of the bigger problem. I am not suggesting that it is impossible to be genuinely and selflessly concerned with collective suffering. But we select particular areas of global injustice to get angry about, because these particular areas are linked with our personal experience of Chiron's wounding.

Chiron and Pluto

Audience: What about Pluto? What is the difference between the rage of Pluto and the rage of Chiron?

Liz: Pluto's core is utterly different. Pluto is concerned with survival, the instinctive effort to preserve the life of the species. We share this instinct with all the kingdoms of nature; everything living seeks to survive, including frogs, fig trees, and bacteria. The survival instinct is mobilised in an individual when he or she feels life is under threat – psychological as well as physical life. We draw on those survival mechanisms which we share with our generation group, reflected by the sign in which Pluto is placed. We also draw on basic human survival mechanisms of an emotional as well as a bodily kind, which look savage in the context of civilised ideals because they may involve destroying the thing which is life-threatening. Pluto may utilise power and covert manipulation as a defence. The bottom line is not adherence to an ideal, but rather, the preservation of life.

Audience: So Pluto is more ruthless.

Liz: It is more realistic. Pluto becomes poisonous when the individual feels he or she has been overpowered. Plutonian rage arises from power battles which are fought for survival. The darker expressions of Pluto reflect the feeling that someone else is controlling one's life, and therefore one is not in charge of one's own survival any longer. Plutonian issues are nothing like those of Chiron, although the two may join forces if they are linked in the birth chart. Pluto can behave in a paranoid fashion, because of an overdeveloped sense of life-threatening factors in the environment. Chiron is not paranoid in this sense; its defences are mobilised against repeated hurt and humiliation caused by the unexpectedly unfair nature of life's turns of fortune. Pluto is collective in the sense that we all have a survival instinct in us, and our Plutonian responses are not individual. They may erupt in individual areas of life, according to Pluto's house placement and aspects to personal planets. But the mechanism is universal – kill or be killed. Either we are in power, or we are overpowered. Bitterness, of the kind I associate with Chiron, is not a characteristic of Pluto, because bitterness results from crushed ideals.

Audience: Doesn't Pluto have a primitive sense of justice?

Liz: Yes, and the operative word is "primitive". It is the justice of nature, not the justice of a human concept of cosmic order. Pluto's justice says, "That animal bit me, and he's clearly after my piece of territory. I'm going to kill him, or else he'll kill me." Pluto's justice is also concerned with the overstepping of nature's limits. If the ego stretches beyond fundamental human limits, or denies basic needs, Pluto's survival instinct is mobilised, because too great an inflation on the part of consciousness can endanger the survival of the organism.

Chiron's morality

Chiron, in contrast, is a moralist. The divine half of the centaur thinks. And it is because of our morality that we are wounded. When we impose morality on the instinctual dimension of human nature, something inevitably suffers – civilisation requires a wounding of that which is natural. It is an insoluble dilemma. If Chiron were merely a horse, the horse would either fight back or die. If it fought back, there would be no guilt about killing the enemy; if it died, well, that is the way nature works. But there is deity in the centaur, as well as animal. That is why it is such a complex creature. The centaur's spiritual nature reflects a morality which questions mere brute animal survival. In myth he does not engage in the fight, nor strike back at the hero who has injured him. He suffers because of his morality. If we didn't have this innate morality, Chiron's wound would not be so difficult, nor would it be incurable. Through Chiron we are trapped, because the very thing which makes us noble is also the very thing which dooms us to the wound.

Audience: I was wondering how this would be expressed in children, before they are able to formulate a morality.

Liz: Children exhibit a very powerful and innate sense of cosmic justice. I have never been impressed by the theory that a child doesn't know right from wrong until a certain age. The parental background may play havoc with a child's sense of justice, and the instinctive feeling for rightness may not be in accord with conventional morality; but I believe it is inherent. Children are very quick to say, "That's not fair!" when something happens which is clearly unjust. Naturally this is in response to something which hurts the individual child, not to some distant African tribe or warring faction in ex-Yugoslavia. But although a child's world may be small, the instinct for fairness is not small. Children often seem to have a more developed sense of fairness than many adults. Yet they can also be incredibly cruel, in the way animals are. I don't mean individual examples of deliberate sadism, but the kind of unreflecting cruelty which is evidenced naturally by children on the playground. Many children suffer the experience of bullying or scapegoating, or they become bullies themselves, in subtle if not obvious ways. In the animal kingdom, we do not perceive it as bullying or scapegoating. When a member of an animal pack or herd displays signs of weakness or sickness, the other animals may turn on it and destroy it. This preserves the strength of the group unit, because a sickly animal may slow down the flight from a predator, or prevent the rest from reaching a source of food or water. Children seem to express both sides of Chiron in a natural, unreflective, but very clear way. When their sense of justice is outraged by an experience of deep hurt, it is Chiron's voice that we hear crying, "That isn't fair!"

It is very interesting to see how parents respond to children's perceptions of life's unfairness. For example, the sense of injustice about death, and the painful questions which a child might ask, can be stifled by parents who won't talk about it. The parents say, "Oh, your little sister's gone to heaven." That's not a sufficient answer, when a child begins to ask Chiron-type questions. The child may know perfectly well that this lovely little girl has suffered extreme physical pain, that she is not old like Grandma and therefore *should not* be dying, that the parents have been worried sick for months, and that there is a terrible grief and rage in everyone which may never go away. But no one will respond to Chiron's questions, so the wound is left untended, and festers. Many families, even the most loving, may be in collusion in avoiding the terrible dilemma of life's unfairness. In our present culture, we get very little help with Chiron.

Audience: Can you say something about interpreting an experience according to the way it is perceived, rather that the way it actually was? Is that the case with Chiron?

Liz: It's the case with all experience, which is interpreted according to how we perceive it. Justice is a deeply subjective thing, although when the collective of which we are a part agrees in defining what is just or unjust, we begin to feel it is objective and absolute. According to Chiron's house, sign, and aspects, we will perceive certain events as unfair, to a degree which is deeply and perhaps irrevocably wounding. This doesn't mean that the event is only unjust according to the individual's selective perception. But the fraught business of defining spiritual absolutes such as justice and injustice takes us onto very thin ice. We can come up with a workable social definition, and a valid personal definition which may form the backbone of our individual philosophy of life;

but we cannot know whether these definitions are absolute in a cosmic sense. An individual will feel an experience as brutally unfair and deeply wounding if Chiron is involved with the experience, which occurs if Chiron is linked to that domain of life through its horoscope placement.

The subjective nature of Saturn is also true of Chiron. It is why, when we look out at life and identify with scapegoats in society, we all choose quite different scapegoats to get upset about. Some people identify with animals, or a particular species of animal such as the whale, and they are shocked and deeply wounded by the cruelty which is inflicted on these creatures. Such people's rage and sense of injustice are directed at those whom they perceive as the perpetrators of the cruelty, whether it is farmers or laboratories which experiment on animals. Other people feel that it is women who are the true victims in life. Still others identify with a particular racial group which they feel is being unfairly treated. There is an enormous amount of unjust suffering in the world. It is doubtful that we can compare the different kinds of suffering and decide that one is less relevant than another. But we do not, and perhaps cannot, recognise or react to the whole of the world's pain. We resonate with those who carry the same wounds we do, and who reflect our own individual ideals of justice.

Chiron's chart placement can tell us a lot about our most deeply held ideals of justice and fairness. Where we are most idealistic, life is likely to wound us most. Chiron's house and sign reflect some of our noblest visions of what life could be like. Then, when we experience injustice in this sphere, it is horrifying. Our personal wounds are inextricably bound up with our individual sense of what justice ought to be.

Each of us has very different definitions of justice, and perceives very different areas where we recognise injustice. This can cause dreadful arguments between people. Try watching the evening news on television with your partner and a few friends. One person may get incredibly heated up about a 14-year-old who has raped someone and got off without a gaol sentence. For three weeks that is all the person can talk about, because this event has hit his or her own wound on some level. Maybe Chiron is in Scorpio, or opposition Venus. But another person may react with great venom to something the government has done. An MP has received a bribe for lobbying a particular cause in Parliament, or there is a cover-up about arms sales to Iraq. That individual may go on for three weeks about corruption in government, because untrustworthy authority touches his or her individual wound. Chiron might be in Capricorn, or in the 10th house. We perceive different spheres where we consider the grossest injustices in life to be perpetrated. They are probably all unjust. But they are weighted according to the individual's ideals and wounds.

Chiron and Saturn

Audience: What if Saturn and Chiron are more or less conjunct?

Liz: "More or less" conjunct? Well, one is more or less likely to develop a double dose of defensiveness, because the collective issues of Chiron are also deeply personal issues linked with the family background.

Audience: But we need to approach them differently.

Liz: Yes, but the approaches are not mutually exclusive. We can work with both at the same time. With Chiron it is important to try to detach from the personal identification that we tend to bring to any experience of unfair wounding. Chiron can be very good at generating self-pity and feelings of victimisation. The moment we begin to recognise that maybe life isn't pointing a malevolent finger directly at us, identification with the victim tends to lose its power. The more detachment we have in our perception of where the roots of Chiron's pain lie, the more able we are to face the pain and, in the end, accept it. In what sign and house is this conjunction placed?

Audience: They're conjunct in the 4th house in Pisces.

Liz: Let's begin by considering the sign, because it is in Piscean ways that hurts, and the defensiveness which arises from those hurts, will occur. What kind of wounding does this describe? Pisces is a water sign, so we can expect issues which are involved with feelings and relationship. What does Pisces want?

Audience: Love.

Liz: Everyone wants love. But we want it in different ways. Pisces needs a great deal of emotional intimacy – a kind of fusion-state with others, in which one is no longer separate and alone. So to be hurt in a Piscean way means being thrown out of Eden, forced into being separate, and one is left with terrible feelings of isolation. Early in life, the sense of belonging, of being an emotional part of the lives of others, has been injured or denied. The need for emotional intimacy has been restricted or rejected in some way. The result is likely to be extreme loneliness, and the defences may involve protecting one's emotional vulnerability through mistrust and the inhibition of feelings, at the same time that there is a powerful insistence on bonding with others through covert and emotionally manipulative means.

Saturn in Pisces suggests that there may have been problems with emotional sharing within the family. It is in the 4th, which emphasises parental issues. The emotional suffering may be particularly related to your relationship with your father, from whom you might have have wanted, and felt, a great degree of closeness; but this closeness may have been impossible to sustain. On the personal level, Saturn points firmly at early parental relationships as the source of emotional hurt which might create powerful defences later in life. But Chiron's involvement suggests that something bigger underlies the parental issues. It is not just your father who is implicated. It may also be connected with your father's background, and with social, economic, or racial issues which stretch a long way back. Whatever happened to generate a sense of failure or hurt in this early relationship, it is possible that your father himself was deeply and unfairly wounded by life, in ways which may point to a collective dilemma. The factors underlying hurt in the personal relationship are much bigger than a parental failure to relate. Is this making sense to you?

Audience: It makes perfectly good sense. But what I am finding difficult to reconcile is that Saturn, as you stated, requires active effort. With Chiron, one must accept what one cannot change. They seem to me mutually exclusive.

Liz: They aren't. You can work to build a better relationship with your father, and with others, so that you are able to be more open and honest in expressing emotional needs. You can learn to ask for what you want in direct ways, and recognise when other people are offering love even if it is not quite in the style you might prefer. But you will have to accept the limits placed on all human beings' capacity to love, and not expect perfect and unconditional loving all the time. You cannot expect a state of unending emotional fusion. Nor can you expect some kind of idealised "happy families" scenario, in which perfect understanding and emotional empathy exist between all family members. It is a question of valuing and nourishing your family relationships and family background, while accepting the fact that ultimately all human beings must learn to exist alone. The kind of fusion-state which you might once have longed for with the family, and which you may still secretly hope to find, may only be available to you through spiritual or creative paths which give you access to a deeper underlying unity. If you go about moping because you didn't have a perfect childhood or a perfect father, you will only waste energy and time in self-pity, and perhaps damage existing relationships, rather than opening the doors to the deeper levels of Piscean expression.

The same applies to your relationship with a lover or spouse. Whatever you do to be emotionally open and loving, your partner may not always respond to it. This might be because your partner is a human being and not an all-loving deity. Saturn in Pisces in the 4th says, "Try to move beyond the emotional limitations of your childhood, and learn to express and receive love generously, despite the fact that you were given a bad example early in life." Chiron in Pisces in the 4th says, "But even if you overcome your emotional inhibitions, don't count on others overcoming theirs. Despite all the effort in the world, people will still manage to hurt each other. There are endemic problems in human nature, and in society, which make people treat each other badly, and your father was probably a sad example of this." Saturn works best with active effort. Chiron places a limit on what you can hope for from that effort.

Audience: Chiron seems to tie in so much with families and family groups that go back over many generations.

Liz: Yes, it does, even if it is not in the 4th house. Chiron stands at the interface where personal family matters become collective matters through our inclusion in a family group or "tribe". Chiron is placed between Saturn and the outer planets, and links immediate parental issues with the collective dilemmas of one's epoch. The centaurs themselves are referred to in myth as a "tribe". The nuclear family is a paradigm of society as a whole, and the great collective currents which are at work in the fabric of society are transmitted to us through the medium of parents, grandparents, and on back to the national and racial "pool" from which the family has emerged. When we begin to explore the ways in which hurts pass down over the generations, we can feel enormous compassion for people whom we may have been busy blaming earlier. Rather than sitting on a stockpile of rage because we feel personally hard done by, we can see how world events such as wars, famine, poverty, and social disorder have produced defensive reactions which limit people's capacity to give love and treat each other fairly. Anger toward the parents starts to look pretty puerile in the face of such human tragedies. Entire generations, such as those born under the Uranus-Neptune opposition during the First World War, begin to appear more clearly as sacrificial victims, in the sense that the individuals involved – including our parents, grandparents, or great-parents – were almost wholly circumscribed by the social roles, pressures, values, and upheavals of their time. Our perspective moves from, "They hurt me!" to a profound awareness of how hard it sometimes is to be human.

On the other side of Chiron's rage is great compassion, born of understanding. That is perhaps one of the most powerful dimensions of Chiron's healing. Rage is Chiron's initial and instinctive defence against injury, but many people never move beyond that initial stage to what lies beyond. We rage because we cannot control life; we are impotent and helpless in the face of forces which are so much greater than ourselves. That is why physical violence is so often linked with feelings of impotence. When we see a perpetrator of violence, such as the husband who batters his wife and children, we will often find that he resorts to violence because he feels emasculated by life, and his rage is a means of compensation. The emasculation may have little to do with his family, and may reflect broader social and economic factors. Or it may be linked with his own parental problems, which have been passed down through many generations.

Chiron's violence

Chiron can be violent. Sometimes the violence is physical, but more often it is emotional. When physical violence is involved, we will often find Mars in hard aspect to Chiron, backed up by other configurations such as Mars-Pluto, Mars-Saturn and/or Mars-Uranus. Chiron's violence, whether physical or emotional, is the compensation for a sense of victimisation. The feeling of release we experience in being able to hurt somebody else gives us the illusion that we have regained control, that we are not wholly victims, because we can make somebody else a victim. The animal face of Chiron says, "The only way I can stop myself feeling utterly helpless, defenceless, and impotent in the face of life's unfairness is to strike back."

Audience: I feel that Chiron wounds without knowing what it is doing.

Liz: I think you are right; there is usually no calculation or premeditation in Chiron's infliction of pain on others. In the main, we wound others without knowing we are doing it. Chiron, like Saturn, tends to operate unconsciously. Most people do not go about perpetrating malice on each other in a deliberate fashion. There are exceptions, and in clinical language we call them psychopaths or sociopaths.

There are also some individuals who are well aware that they are inflicting hurt on a particular individual, but who justify it because their emotional responses have distorted not only their perceptions but their ethics as well. But in the main, we inflict hurts unconsciously. When we react from our Chiron or our Saturn, we can hurt people quite badly, but we usually have no idea what we have done, or why we have done it. Sometimes the injured party will let us know, but often in ways which make us reject the pronouncement, because it is all mixed up with the other person's desire to hurt us as well. It is very difficult to get any objective perspective on what Chiron is up to.

Audience: On the collective level we seem to inflict hurts unconsciously as well.

Liz: On a collective level we invariably hurt people who have less than we do, simply by having more. The only place we can exist without this kind of inadvertent injury is in Thomas More's Utopia. But in the real world, whatever we have – not just materially, but intellectually, artistically, emotionally, and spiritually as well – there will be someone else who has less and is hurt by one's very existence. Human beings may be equal in value, but they are not equal in terms of what life hands out to them.

We also sometimes have to fight as a collective, to preserve something precious, such as our liberty. We may fight a war against a tyrant such as Hitler, and there may be no escape from the conflict; tyrants are not known for their sense of fair play. Yet this conflict, however right it may be on the moral as well as the survival level, inevitably destroys not only innocent civilians, but also a great many young soldiers on both sides who have no idea why they are fighting to begin with, and who never wished anyone any ill. But they all get killed, and sometimes, as in the case of Saddam Hussein, the tyrant survives despite all the sacrifices. Sometimes we must fight, yet in such wars we all lose.

In the end, who are we going to blame? We would like to blame Hitler, yet Hitler depended on the support of an entire nation to wield the power he did. We would like to blame the Nazi inclinations of the Germans, yet Nazi sentiments were alive and well in every European nation, and still are today. And who knows what any of us is capable of as a collective, if our nation were on its knees as Germany was between the World Wars? The Germans needed a messiah, as all suffering and oppressed people do, and they chose the wrong one. Can we be certain we would have picked the right one? Are we really showing any better judgement now? It is because of these impossible questions that Chiron can be such a difficult planet. Only a hopelessly naive fool looks at history and says, "Oh well, this catastrophe is perfectly explicable because so-and-so was to blame."

Audience: I'm feeling pain and rage right now. I have Saturn and Chiron in trine. When you were talking about Chiron in Pisces, I thought, "What is the use of therapy?" and now I feel pain. And I was thinking about the centaur's desire to rid himself of the pain, and how it is a gesture of humanity to discover ways of healing other people when one can't heal oneself.

Liz: I understand, and I can see that you might interpret what I am saying as a statement that there is no point in trying. But that is not it at all. Therapy is of no use to heal Chiron's wounds if one expects therapy to remove the reality of human nature, or to somehow cancel out the past. Therapy will not grant you permanent emotional fusion with others, or create an ideal world in which everyone loves everyone unconditionally. But if you are prepared to accept the limits of human nature, without losing faith in the power of love and compassion, then therapy can be enormously creative in working with Chiron's wounds.

Some signs have a harder time than others with Chiron issues. Although I am not yet convinced that Chiron "rules" any particular sign of the zodiac, I think Chiron in the water signs is very difficult to deal with, because of the emotional level of the wounding. There is also a great potential for deep and heartfelt compassion when Chiron is placed in water, and this can help to compensate for the darker dimensions of the placement. But the capacity to detach and view things from an impersonal perspective, which is one of Chiron's strengths, is not a natural aptitude of the element of water.

Perhaps it takes a bit longer to find the kind of detachment so necessary to work with Chiron. And Chiron, as you may imagine, doesn't have many friends amongst the planetary pantheon. Jupiter can sometimes be a friend, in fair weather. But Saturn is an even better one, because Saturn is a realist. In many ways Saturn, and Capricorn, Saturn's sign, cope better with the issue of life's unfairness than most of the other signs and planets. Neptune and Pisces can have a very hard time with Chiron, for reasons which should be obvious. Bearing in mind that Chiron in myth is Saturn's child, it is not surprising that there is an affinity between them. The issues I have been talking about are likely to be deeply disturbing and painful to Pisces. But the trine from Saturn to your Chiron suggests that realism can help you to deal with the pain you are feeling.

In some ways we can work with Saturn to help cope with Chiron. Not only does Saturnian realism and toughness allow us to keep our expectations of life within sensible limits, but the sense of authenticity and substance which Saturn provides can offer us a greater capacity to make peace with what we cannot change. Through Saturn's efforts, we may discover that we do have some potency, at least as individuals, albeit within a narrow sphere. Therefore we are empowered to act and take responsibility for our actions, even if we also have to accept things over which we have no personal control. Without Saturn's grounding, Chiron can feel quite overwhelming.

Chiron's quest for understanding

Audience: Finding some meaning in all that waste seems to me to be the key to Chiron. Maybe using our vulnerability to help others is a way to discover meaning.

Liz: Yes, I think that is where Chiron ultimately takes us. Chiron's defence mechanisms can be very savage, and in this form they do not heal anything at all. They only perpetuate injury, from one generation to the next. But recognition of the pain which lies behind Chiron's rage and violence can put us on the road to some sort of understanding. We need to recognise that Chiron's pain is not personal. When we can move beyond the cry of "Why me?" and can say, "It's really rough being human, and a lot of people besides me are hurt for no reason," we have begun our journey. Then we may begin to feel a sense of meaningless waste, which is what you have expressed just now. This is what Chiron's pain is really about, beneath the primitive animal defences.

The feeling of meaningless waste is inescapable if one does a lot of charts or counselling work. It is also inescapable in the medical profession. Often people cross one's path for whom no one, whether astrologer, therapist, physician, or priest, will ever be able to do very much; and it is a dreadful waste. We can see waste everywhere, in every war, every aeroplane crash, every natural disaster. But this waste has particular poignancy when suffering individuals come to us for help and we know that help is simply not possible, except to a very limited degree. When we begin to acknowledge the waste, and feel pain because of it, then Chiron begins to produce other kinds of defences, some of which are very creative.

Chiron's most creative line of defence is understanding. That is Chiron's gift in myth, and that is what begins to emerge in people who can recognise what their anger and bitterness are really about. The quest for understanding is what brings a lot of us into astrology as well as psychology. Some people believe that "the Quest" in the archetypal sense is a quest for spiritual realisation. But a great many people do not think in those terms, which may seem rather abstract. Instead, they urgently wish to understand why human beings suffer, and what can be done to alleviate the suffering. Like the centaur, they seek answers here on earth, not in heaven. Chiron forces us to ask questions for which we cannot find a reasonable answer. So we try to acquire knowledge, and the knowledge is of a very special kind.

Chiron in myth, as in the astrological chart, initially seeks knowledge of the laws of nature and of the human condition. Whether this is reflected in the healing arts, scientific knowledge, or a combination of the two, Chiron is concerned with understanding the basic principles through which organic life operates. The mythic Chiron is a lover of knowledge, and works to penetrate the secrets of nature and the physical body. We should remember that Chiron is a teacher and healer *before* he is wounded by Herakles. But we may surmise that his desire to learn and teach springs in part from his loneliness and exclusion from both purely bestial and purely human existence. He is already wounded, because he is different. He is a beast who thinks, and therefore he cannot condone the savagery of his centaur tribe; but he is also half bestial, and he cannot aspire to a human shape or a human destiny. He teaches others who are more acceptable to the collective, such as Asklepios, to whom he imparts the arts of healing. Yet knowledge alone cannot protect him from life's vicissitudes. Something more is required before his suffering can end: an acceptance of mortality.

Chiron's pattern is echoed by many people involved in astrological study. They throw everything they can into learning how to read charts, in the hope of understanding life. In the end they know all about planets, signs, and aspects; but people go on suffering, and the astrologer may not be spared when the nasty Pluto or Neptune transit comes along. There is a crisis of disillusionment which lies in wait for that thing in us which believes knowledge alone will provide protection against life.

The same thing happens to people who go into training as counsellors and therapists, and are full of high ideals. I think it happens to everyone who pursues Chiron's archetypal journey. It is a stage in the unfoldment of this planet's pattern. We carry a sublime belief that we can heal everybody with whom we work. Every patient is "curable". But cured of what? Life?

Themselves? Some people don't get better. Sometimes they fail to get better because we have made a blunder; but usually we can recognise this, later if not sooner. Sometimes they fail to get better because they should be working with somebody else; and this too usually becomes apparent after a while. But sometimes they just aren't going to get better. Some of them never can get better, no matter what they do or with whom they work. Some of them may die. Some of them may kill themselves. Some of them go away saying, "Thank you very much, that was terribly helpful," and then they make the same mess all over again. Despite the idealistic spirit which says, "I'm going to go and heal the world, because now I understand psychology," we are still faced with this element of meaningless waste. It is at that point that we are confronted with the limits of knowledge. Many astrologers can't or won't acknowledge these limitations. They will persist in looking for some definitive method or technique which will give them the ultimate knowledge. But there are limits to knowledge, as the mythic Chiron discovered; and beyond those limits, where do we go?

Audience: Wisdom.

Liz: All right, we go to wisdom. But what does wisdom mean?

Audience: It's a combination of knowledge and compassion.

Liz: That is a lovely way of putting it. I would add a third ingredient: humility. We assume that our knowledge, once we have acquired it, can fix things. If something is "true", we believe it can magically alter what we find difficult in life. But of course it can't. Knowledge can do many things, but it cannot guarantee that we will be able to control the uncontrollable. I am not sure whether the conviction that knowledge can enable us to fix everything is part of our modern culture, or whether it is part of human nature. At present we are given this message by a scientific establishment which, to say the least, could be accused of great arrogance. But I suspect that there always has been and always will be something in us that refuses to accept what we cannot change. That is our Promethean spirit, and without it we would still be huddling in caves eating half-cooked mammoth.

Audience: I must say that I believe it is a very creative thing to have to struggle with finding solutions.

Liz: So do I, and we must do this with Chiron to get the best from it. We have to struggle to seek answers to unanswerable questions. But we also have to accept the limits, not only of one's own individual knowledge, but also of collective knowledge. We have to accept the limits of human feeling. In this sphere too, we have great expectations, and assume that love could fix everything if only we had enough of it. We cherish an ideal of unconditional love, and we believe that if only we could achieve it, no one would ever be wounded again. Human nature is limited on the emotional level, just as it is on intellectual and physical levels.

Chiron reveals limits in all kinds of areas, and we must come to terms with them, just as a healer has to come to terms with the fact that he or she can't heal everyone. This is not only because some people can't be healed, but also because there are only twenty-four hours in a day, and when is the healer going to sleep and eat? And when is the healer going to get healed himself or herself? So the healer must turn some people away. There are limits even to one's compassion.

After rage, Chiron's next line of defence is knowledge. It is a very positive and creative defence, and it needs to be pursued in the same way that Saturn's urge to crystallise and consolidate should be pursued rather than avoided. With Saturn too, we have to accept the fact that there are limits, because when we seek what Saturn wants, we will probably not get any help. We are limited because we must build it for ourselves. No one is going to give it away for free. And there are limits placed on what Chiron's knowledge can offer. Beyond that looms the issue of acceptance, and the compassion that is born out of acceptance. Acceptance is not resignation; it requires conscious understanding and cooperation, rather than mere passive giving up.

Chiron and the helping professions

Audience: It's the pinch of salt, isn't it? Accepting life with a pinch of salt. I think the counselling professions have a problem with this, because pride is involved.

Liz: I think so too. Power is often the unconscious underbelly of altruism, and acceptance of limits means a diminishing of power. Chiron is clearly linked with the helping professions, whether through psychotherapy, astrology, or orthodox or fringe medicine. As I said before, I think many of us go into these fields because we are feeling Chiron's pinch. Underneath our altruism, or whatever we wish to call it, we are hurting, and not just from Saturnian wounds, which don't necessarily require inner reflection or service to others. One can heal many of Saturn's characteristic wounds by simply getting on with it. Saturn doesn't always have to be psychoanalysed, particularly when it is placed in earthy signs and houses. One may need to get out there and build. Saturn requires some consciousness that there is a wound; otherwise we may revert to its less attractive defences, such as scapegoating, and then we never learn to develop its alchemical gold. But having got to the stage of recognising one's feelings of inferiority and envy, therapy may not always be the best route for Saturn problems.

Chiron, in contrast, requires a great deal of honest reflection. Those who wish to be practitioners in the helping professions have to come to terms with this planet. Think of what a newly qualified doctor feels like, the first time that a patient dies. Are any of you medical practitioners? No? Do we have any trained therapists here? Ah yes, quite a few. Do you remember what it was like when you first encountered a therapeutic "failure"?

Audience: Yes.

Liz: What effect did it have on you?

Audience: Well, I came in through social work, which forces you to recognise that some people can be helped a bit, and a lot of people not at all. I had to deal with so many desperate people, with few resources and very little time. I keep feeling that if only we had better resources – maybe a more committed government – many more people could be healed. And even in the worst cases, something can change.

Liz: So you blame the government. That is a perennially popular scapegoat for Chiron's ills. I quite agree that, in an ideal world, more facilities would be available to provide the kind of help people need. But whether, and how, they avail themselves of that help remains an open question. A great deal depends on how we define healing. I have no quarrel with the conviction that something can change even in an apparently hopeless situation. Something can transform if there is genuine acceptance, both of oneself and of the world as it is. But if you define healing as the achievement of a particular ideal, whether of perfection or of normality, then I have some deep questions about the validity of such an assumption.

There is something in Christian terminology which is known as grace.

The phenomenon is not limited to Christians, although some would like to think it is. This experience does not appear to belong to any particular planet or astrological configuration. When we are dealing with the apparently insoluble problems presented by Chiron, we can hope for grace, which we may or may not receive, and which may occur on many different levels, not necessarily in the form of actual healing. If we do experience it, I doubt that it is due to any power on the part of the healer, or any particular formula of prayer used by the believer, since God seems to answer to many different names. Grace is something for which we have no explanation. We cannot assume that we can invoke it through any conscious act. If there are preconditions for grace, then acceptance is probably one of them. But we don't know what the others are. In myth, grace visits Chiron when Prometheus intervenes and the centaur is granted the boon of death.

We may never find an answer to the question, "Is healing possible?" when we ask it about an individual situation. Healing by an act of will often seems to fail when Chiron is involved. But extraordinary things can happen to people who have been deeply damaged, for which we have no explanation. I don't think this is really the province of astrology. It seems to belong to that mysterious X-factor which expresses through the chart, and encompasses many things which the chart does not contain.

Chiron and the Moon's Nodes

Audience: This morning you said that Chiron doesn't have many friends among the other planets. What about the Moon's Nodes?

Liz: The Nodes are not planets, and I would not view them in the same way. They represent the intersection of the solar and lunar orbits, and therefore reflect the relationship between Sun and Moon. The Sun is concerned with self-realisation and meaning; it is the essence of individual destiny. The Moon is concerned with personal experience on a physical and emotional level. The point where these two cross is the nodal axis, which is expressed through a particular pair of houses in the birth chart, and therefore through a particular arena of life.

The nodal axis seems to represent the point where we exteriorise this combination of inner meaning with outer experience. Usually our vehicles for this meeting of essence and event are relationships of one kind or another, which is the central characteristic I associate with the Moon's Nodes. Planets connected with the Nodes by aspect, especially the conjunction, tend to be deeply bound up with our experiences in relationship. In whatever house the Nodes are placed, we seem to need some sort of encounter through which we can integrate our sense of meaning with our experience of everyday life. We attract relationships which reflect planets connected with the Nodes, and these relationships further our development in accord with the houses in which the Nodal axis is placed.

When Chiron is connected with the Nodes, one is likely to be drawn to people who are wounded and need help in some way, or from whom one is seeking help oneself. Or the relationship itself is complicated and brings suffering, not necessarily because either person is at fault, but because circumstances generate unavoidable and sometimes insurmountable difficulties. Chiron-Node configurations suggest that Chiron's process of moving from resentment to understanding and eventually to wisdom is set in motion primarily through relationships, which may feel "fated" because the emotional experience is combined with a deep sense of meaning and destiny.

Chiron and Asklepios

Audience: In myth, Asklepios is the son of Chiron.

Liz: Is he? I haven't encountered that variation. Asklepios has more than one myth about his parentage, but usually he is considered to be the son of Apollo. Chiron is his teacher.

Audience: Do you think Chiron can be linked with the ancient Asklepian cult of healing?

Liz: Since Chiron teaches Asklepios the arts of healing, they are clearly linked. However, in terms of archaeological evidence, the great Asklepian healing centres, such as those at Pergamum, Kos, and Epidauros, do not seem to have had temples or shrines to Chiron. Usually Asklepios is paired with Apollo at these centres, and often a temple or shrine dedicated to Apollo can be found within the sacred precincts of the Asklepion, since Apollo was also understood to be a god of healing as well as Asklepios' father. At the great Asklepion at Epidaurus, for example, there is a strange circular building called a tholus, whose function, although clearly religious or sacred, is not yet understood by archaeologists. Within this structure were found two paintings, one of which shows a figure playing a lyre. This figure seems to be Apollo, who is always associated with the instrument.

Asklepios is the prototype of the doctor as well as the psychotherapist, and interestingly, in certain versions of the myth, he is also a teacher of astrology. By Roman times he was celebrated as the deity or demigod who imparted astrological wisdom as well as the arts of healing. For this reason he figures in the Hermetic texts of the first centuries CE, in which Hermes Trismegistus may be found teaching astrological wisdom to Asklepios, who in turn passes it on to his disciples. In some respects Asklepios is a fully humanised Chiron, developed to the next stage, and freed of both his animal nature and his poison. But I would like to call your attention to one of the most important features of the myth of Asklepios. He was struck down by Zeus, because he attempted to raise the dead. His arrogance or *hubris,* in terms of his ability to heal, became excessive. He brought a dead soul back to life, and Zeus hurled a thunderbolt at him. This is very relevant to what we have been talking about. Chiron accepts mortality as the price he must pay for his release from suffering. Asklepios, who is not wounded as Chiron is, is too arrogant, and is struck down because he cannot accept mortality. Unlike Chiron, and perhaps like many doctors and therapists, he cannot countenance limits.

Audience: At the theatre at Epidaurus, they still perform the Greek tragic plays. Do you think the Greeks understood the nature of Chiron's unhealable wound?

Liz: Based on the content of Greek tragedy, I would say yes. The Greeks had less illusions than we do about the unfair nature of life, and their tragedies tend to reflect the unjust behaviour of the gods as well as invoking profound emotional experiences of awe and pity. Awe in the face of the gods, and pity for the human condition, are the two emotions that one is expected to experience when confronted with the fall of the tragic hero or heroine. Greek tragedy contains a profound respect for what cannot be changed. There is no attempt to rationalise or explain away injustice; the gods are simply unfair sometimes. But they are the gods, and one doesn't mess with them.

The Greeks don't appear to have had a problem acknowledging life's unfairness. Unlike modern drama, which often tries to sew everything up and tell us who the bad guys and good guys are (in case we miss the point), Greek tragedies present us with an incredibly complex moral overview. The Greek tragic hero or heroine is clearly at fault because of *hubris.* But the *hubris* may also be admirable, because it can reflect the most noble forms of human courage, aspiration, and initiative. The gods may be perceived as petty and spiteful at times. Yet their laws are absolute because they are the gods, and their mystery and majesty remain.

We should also remember that the Greeks presented their tragedies side by side with comedies, and the comedies were really gross. Satyrs and drunken dwarfs ran around the stage wearing grotesque masks and huge leather phalluses, and the general atmosphere was crude, obscene, and disrespectful toward humans and gods alike. They were even worse than Benny Hill. One of these satyr plays always followed immediately after Sophocles' *Oedipus Rex,* or Aeschylos' *Oresteia.* The idea of doing this now would appall us. But to the Greeks, both were essential, because the comedy put the tragedy in perspective. They seem to be saying, "Well, human life is tragic and unfair, but it's also a great joke." This double perception of life can be extremely healing, because it dignifies our suffering but at the same time forces us to distance ourselves from it and find it laughable. I mentioned earlier that Saturn's humour can be black and ironic. So can Chiron's. Black humour contains an intrinsic paradox, like the juxtaposition of a satyr play with *Oedpius Rex.*

The discovery of Chiron

Audience: When Chiron was discovered, were there any collective events which could be linked with it?

Liz: A lot of people ask this question. It's very hard to get a "fix" on it, because we are still so close. We can see the collective events surrounding the discovery of the three outer planets, because with hindsight we can discern a pattern. Many generations have passed since Uranus and Neptune were discovered, and Pluto has had over half a century to be digested. I don't think we have Pluto clearly in focus yet. And Chiron was only spotted in 1977.

Some people have linked it with breakthroughs in medicine and physics. It may be related to these spheres, and certainly the symbolism would fit. But it is very difficult to get a bird's-eye view of the collective imperatives of our own era, because we are part of them, and assume them to be the only reality. Apart from medicine and physics, Chiron may also be connected with the "information superhighway" which is now beginning to radically change our attitudes toward learning and communication. Chiron's symbolism is linked with knowledge and education, since in myth he is a teacher as well as a healer. Science and education have both transformed beyond recognition through the advent of computer technology. Sometimes we tend to think of Chiron in an overly mystical way, but knowledge is not always "esoteric".

But the discovery of a new planet does not really represent a specific event. We associate events with the discoveries of Uranus, Neptune, and Pluto, but we should also be looking at the changes in mass consciousness which precipitated those events. A new planet emerging into the light of day describes a new level of awareness, the breaking through of previously unknown ideas and feelings which, on a mass level, may invoke responses which generate particular historical events.

Seen in this context, what new realisations have dawned on us during the last twenty years? My own view is that we are just beginning to honestly face our collective wound: the limitations of human nature, and the damage which we have done to ourselves and to the planet. We have run out of scapegoats, and are being forced to grow up as a collective. After two world wars, we are still capable of extreme barbarity, and our superior medical and scientific knowledge has not protected us from AIDS or from our increasing capacity for self-destruction. We are desperately seeking answers, with a frenzy that guarantees we will not find them in the places we are looking. We have been suffering from a collective depression for two decades, and are only on the edge of understanding what it really means. That, I believe, is what the discovery of Chiron has brought us. It remains to be seen whether we can work with this understanding in constructive ways.

Audience: Is Chiron associated with Mercury?

Liz: What did you have in mind? Can you see similarities?

Audience: They both travel, and go into the underworld to seek information.

Liz: I find it difficult to see any real similarities between them. Chiron isn't a traveller; he tends to stick close to his cave. It's everyone else who travels to see him. And he doesn't go to the underworld to collect information; he goes to die. Mercury, on the other hand, is the divine psychopomp. He is a sort of tour guide for souls ready to reincarnate and souls ready to disincarnate. His reasons for being in the underworld are quite different.

Also, Mercury doesn't *seek* information. He *is* information. He symbolises the principle of comprehension, which is why he is sometimes credited in myth with teaching the alphabet to human beings. The network of roads over which he presides in myth is like the network of connections between disparate segments of life experience, which allows us to make sense of what we experience. Hermes-Mercury is what Chiron knows.

Audience: You said earlier that, although Chiron has knowledge, knowledge in itself is insufficient to heal the wound. There are other factors needed.

Liz: Yes, Mercury's information alone cannot heal. As astrologers, we should know this, not only about our clients, but also about ourselves. An intellectual appreciation of the difficulties of a particular aspect may help; but the work is not done with the mind alone. Some people may find a psychological approach to astrology difficult, because it can reveal personality dynamics which may be transformed only by a long period of inner work.

Mercury is one of a group of mythic figures who are called culture-bringers. Among these are the Egyptian Thoth, who teaches the alphabet; Prometheus, who teaches navigation, architecture, and astrology; Triptolemus, who teaches agriculture; and Athene, who teaches crafts such as weaving. These culture-bringers exist in every nation's mythology, and symbolise the human capacity to use intuition and inspiration to harness nature and order the material environment. In this sense Chiron in his pre-wounded state may be seen as a culture-bringer, because he teaches herbal lore and healing arts. All these figures have something to teach. But at that point the resemblance between Mercury and Chiron ends.

Chiron and Saturn in aspect

Audience: What if Saturn and Chiron are in difficult aspect, in view of what you said about them being friends? Would it make it impossible to harmonise them, or just take longer?

Liz: Both planets are essentially defensive in nature, so each will try to dominate the other in order to establish control. Usually one will win, at least for a while. If we identify with Saturn, we are likely to attribute our hurts to personal issues, and we may then strive to overcome our feelings of inadequacy through hard work, self-sufficiency, and control of ourselves and others. Saturn's defences may preclude any acknowledgement of the unchangeable. Then Chiron becomes an unacceptable image of victimisation and alienation, and the person may project this on others, perceiving them as pathetic, helpless, and inferior. On the other hand, if we identify with Chiron, we may attribute our hurts to global issues about which we can do nothing, and we may assume the stance of the impotent victim. We may smoulder about our injuries without realising that we have inner resources of strength and determination which could help us to make something contructive out of what we construe as a handicap. Chiron's defences may preclude any acceptance of personal responsibility. We may project Saturn on others, and feel that we are being oppressed or unjustly treated by authorities or by those who are too hard and self-centred to care about our woes.

Although they can be friends because they both deal with the tougher dimensions of life experience, these planets will usually engage in a power battle if they are in conflict in the chart. They may do this even if they are in harmonious aspect, or unrelated to each other by aspect. If a person's energy is focused on defensive maneuvres, there may be a particularly strong tendency to view life as fundamentally unfriendly. Saturn's propensity to seek scapegoats can find a good hook in Chiron, and Chiron's propensity to blame life and human nature can find a good hook in Saturn. Even though both are connected with feelings of being wounded, Saturn's way of dealing with wounds is to make something happen which restores a sense of self-control and self-respect, while Chiron, if it can get beyond primitive rage, attempts to seek relief through understanding, detachment, and acceptance.

For any person with Saturn and Chiron in aspect, life is a serious business, and has to be approached carefully and with weapons in place. There is too much consciousness of life's toughness, and too great an investment in survival. Such an individual can't go through life saying, "Let's go to a party and forget about it." One might try; but the morning after, the ground opens up under one's feet again. This combination in a birth chart precludes superficiality, even if one tries terribly hard to adopt a shallow or unreflective attitude. Although the nature of the defences is different for each planet, both have a sense of being threatened and a feeling of being different and excluded. Loneliness and mistrust are experiences which belong to both, and both can reflect a deep lack of confidence. From an early age the individual knows instinctively that he or she is not going to get away with pretending that life is just fun and games.

Any aspect between them therefore suggests a potential for great depth and insight. Something very solid and strong can form inside, because the individual will have to cope with certain experiences that are conducive to reflection and self-exploration. There is nothing quite as effective as pain and feelings of inadequacy to make a person begin to ask important questions.

There are other aspects besides Saturn-Chiron which can do this, but they almost always involve either Saturn or Chiron. Many people don't have to deal with these more complex levels of life. They are not likely to enroll on a seminar like this. They are also not likely to come to a psychologically inclined astrologer for a chart, because they can't see any reason to. They don't have "problems", and if they do, multi-vitamin tablets seem to take care of everything. But when Saturn and Chiron are in contact, an awareness of the heaviness of life usually begins in early childhood. There is usually agreement between Saturn and Chiron about the fact that life can be extremely painful, even if they disagree about the nature and potential resolution of the pain.

Chiron's relationship with Sagittarius

Audience: So Jupiter-Chiron always wants to philosophise its way out of things.

Liz: Jupiter gets on very well with the divine side of Chiron, the teacher and healer. Jupiter can join forces with this dimension of Chiron, and it can be a tremendously inspired and creative combination. Knowledge and intuition combine, and may produce a deeply optimistic and hopeful approach to the problem of suffering, as well as an instinctive feeling for meaningful patterns at work in life. This combination can be linked with inspired teaching and the power to enlighten others. But Jupiter doesn't like spending time with the wounded horse, and resents hearing about the fact that there is still poison in the wound.

Audience: It's strange, considering that Jupiter is the ruler of the horse.

Liz: Of uninjured horses, perhaps. I assume you are relating Jupiter to the horse because of the planet's rulership of Sagittarius. In myth, the horse was the creature of the Greek Poseidon Hippios, who later became the Roman Neptune. Many astrologers think that Chiron is co-ruler of Sagittarius, which seems neat and easy, since he is a centaur. But the constellation of Sagittarius was not originally associated with Chiron. The name Sagittarius comes from the Greek word for "bow-stretcher" or "archer". According to Richard Hinckley Allen, in his book, *Star Names: Their Lore and Meaning,* the constellation of the Archer preceded the Greek centaur Chiron. By Roman times it was sometimes associated with Chiron, but in earlier Greek myth it was simply the

Centaur. In India 3000 years ago the constellation was known as the Horseman, while the Babylonians called it the Giant King of War.

Even in Greco-Roman iconography, Chiron is always portrayed with a child on his back. He is never shown as an ordinary centaur, nor as an archer. One can always distinguish whether a particular sculpture, fresco, or mosaic represents Chiron because of the child. This image reflects his role as the teacher of young princes, because he carries them on his back. The association of Sagittarius with Chiron is tenuous, and I am not sure whether we will get very far astrologically by assuming that the two are the same.

As I said earlier, I am not inclined, at this stage, to assign Chiron to any zodiacal sign. In addition, we need to consider what we know of the character of Sagittarius. The Archer is not usually preoccupied with the problem of human suffering, except as an abstract concept to be explored in terms of its meaning and relevance on a universal level. Sagittarius can make a very quick exit when it comes face to face with a suppurating wound. This zodiacal sign has many gifts and wonderful qualities, but the capacity to be directly and personally involved with human pain and misery is not usually one of them. You all realise, of course, that no individual is purely Sagittarian, so I am not casting aspersions on individuals with the Sun or any other planet in this sign. Individual Sagittarians may be wholeheartedly committed to the alleviation of suffering; but the emotional identification required for such work is usually connected with something else in the horoscope. In short, Jupiter does not particularly enjoy hanging about nursing a wounded horse.

Audience: What about Chiron in synastry?

Liz: In my experience it exercises a powerful fascination in synastry. So does Saturn. We may be deeply attracted to a person whose Chiron lands on our personal planets, and we may also be attracted to one whose personal planets land on our Chiron. This should not be surprising, as compassion and awareness of another person's pain and vulnerability may form an important part of any strong attraction. Equally, the wounded part of us may reach out to someone who has the capacity, through his or her Sun, Moon, or Venus, to recognise our own suffering. We tend to feel more confident with someone when we know he or she is flawed and hurt just as we are. If we can't perceive vulnerability in another person, we may find it impossible to express our own.

A mutual recognition of each other's wounds may be as important as sexual or intellectual compatibility. Without Chiron or Saturn contacts in synastry, a relationship may never progress beyond superficialities. But two problems can arise with these Chiron contacts across charts. Firstly, if the Chiron individual is full of rage and bitterness, then the partner whose Sun or Moon acts as a trigger may be the recipient of great anger and unconscious cruelty. Chiron's defensiveness may prove very destructive in synastry, if the Chiron individual is unconscious of what is happening inside. Secondly, a person may be Chiron-prone in relationships, and that can be very difficult and discouraging. One may get involved over and over again in relationships in which one's Chiron is triggered. As Ian Fleming once wrote: Once is chance, twice is coincidence, but three times is enemy action. There are Saturn-prone people as well, who experience a repeating pattern of partners whose planets trigger their Saturn in difficult ways. When we don't deal with our Saturn and Chiron issues voluntarily, it seems that the psyche will force us to, through the agency of another person.

Chiron as outlaw

We have some example charts to look at, but before we move on to them, there are one or two more points I would like to cover about Chiron's characteristic defence mechanisms. One of the things that Chiron may do, to defend itself against experiencing a repetition of the original bitter disappointment, is to identify with the outlaw or outsider. We may elect to play this role because, when other people reject us, it doesn't hurt so much. There is an element of glamour in the archetypal figure of the outsider, as James Dean and Clint Eastwood have demonstrated so well. "Ordinary" people can then be despised for their ordinariness; only the truly gifted and special are outsiders. If we believe that we have chosen our isolation, then we can take pride in it, rather than feeling ashamed, inadequate, and humiliated. This can help to keep the pain at bay, and it is a characteristic Chiron defence mechanism, which may be emphasised by Chiron in the 10th or 11th houses, or perhaps Chiron in Capricorn or Aquarius. Behind the defence, of course, there may be unbearable loneliness; but pride helps to conceal this from other people. Chiron may display as much pride as Saturn, and for similar reasons.

Psychosomatic illness may also be a favourite Chiron defence. One may somatise one's sense of resentment and victimisation by becoming a physical invalid or a hypochondriac, and then one has a perfect justification for exhibiting rage against life. I am referring to those ailments which are medical mysteries, apparently functional and without any apparent organic basis. Not all illnesses are functional, and not all are Chiron-centred. Chiron may also be connected with sudden accidents, and with illnesses which are truly organic, although the psychological component in such cases always needs to be considered. But when an illness is functional and is linked with Chiron, natally or by transit or progression, there may be an undertow of rage and a strong desire to punish other people as well as punishing oneself. This is also a way of projecting Chiron and finding the healer in someone else, who can then be enlisted to look after us.

Chiron and suicide

Audience: Would you say that Chiron is related to suicide?

Liz: It can be. But there are many different kinds of suicide, and many different reasons for committing it. Sometimes it is an act of rage. Public suicides, such as jumping off a high building into the middle of a busy road, certainly suggest an element of rage and a desire to punish other people. If we really just want to get out, there are many quiet, peaceful ways of doing it, with a minimum of mess for other people to clean up.

Chiron's particular blend of suffering and rage may lead a person to hurl himself or herself under a train during the rush hour; the driver has a breakdown, all the passengers become hysterical, and some poor British Rail employee is left with the unenviable job of scraping the bits off the track. One has made a big statement, which bears the hallmark, not merely of simple personal despair, but also of a corrosive black bitterness against humanity and against life. The quiet overdose, which one takes because one has had enough, reflects a very different motive.

Audience: Suicide can be Jupiterian or Neptunian as well.

Liz: Yes, that is the point I am making. There is a violent element in Chiron, which I have spoken about already. These violent feelings seem to reflect a particular stage in the process which the planet symbolises. Violence is one of Chiron's most primitive defences, and it may be directed toward oneself as easily as toward others.

Audience: Can you make a connection between Chiron and trying to prove moral rightness through suicide?

Liz: You are describing the stuff of martyrs, political or religious. It is possible that Chiron might be involved with this, but in the main, I am inclined to see Chiron's style of suicide as an instinctive explosion of rage against life and other people. I would associate the martyr much more with Jupiter-Neptune combinations; there is a tremendous psychological inflation involved in demonstrating one's moral superiority through death. This may be combined with darker currents, perhaps with Chiron's rage, or perhaps with Pluto's bid for absolute control. Suicide may be a Plutonian way of saying, "I really do have power, and I can prove it by demonstrating the power to end my own life." Every human action is motivated by a complex combination of factors, and suicide is rarely a simple, one-motive affair.

Chiron can be extremely bad-tempered. We can see this most clearly when it is involved in synastry contacts. If Chiron's button is pushed before one has had a chance to recognise and work with the pain, a very irascible, irritable, snappish quality may erupt. Many people use this as a defence. Afterward, they may justify it with such statements as, "Sorry, I was just tired," or, "I've always had a bit of a temper." But it is not as simple as that. These people snap at bus conductors, ticket collectors, and waiters, whether they are tired or not. They snap at their partners and children as a matter of course. Lately we have coined the term "road rage", when they display verbal and even physical abuse toward other drivers for no ostensible reason. It is as though all their pain is expressed through a chronic animal snarl.

This defence succeeds in keeping everybody away, so no one can get close enough to say, "Are you in pain?" The pain goes unacknowledged and unadmitted, because there is always something to be angry about. As I said earlier, if one has a planet on one's partner's Chiron, one may get a lot of this in the relationship. Whatever one says or does, it hits the wrong way, and out comes a kick from the back end of the horse. The kick is meant to stop anyone getting too close to the feelings lying underneath.

Audience: I can see a lot of parallels with the Grail King and Parsifal. Do you see that as relevant?

Liz: There are parallels. The incurable wound in the thigh, and the quest for meaning, are common to both. There is, however, no animal element in the Grail Legend; all the characters in the story are human. Wagner's Parzival is rather different from the original figure of Parsifal in Wolfram von Eschenbach, and it is worth noting that Wagner had Chiron in Pisces square the Sun in Gemini. In the opera, the character of the wicked sorcerer, Klingsor, is peculiarly Wagnerian. He is wicked because he has been castrated. This impotent, raging embodiment of evil, who wounds the Grail King but fails to destroy Parzival's compassion, has echoes in the centaur's dark savagery, and also suggests the beast who has been wounded in the thigh. This is also where the Grail King's wound occurs, and one can certainly read sexual symbolism into it – Wagner clearly did. Klingsor and the Grail King are two halves of the same whole. It might also be possible to understand Chiron's wound as a sexual wound, a reflection of impotence in the face of life's unfairness, or impotence as a result of insoluble conflicts.

We cannot help but feel compassion for the Grail King, and in doing so, we become Parsifal seeking the Grail. But it is sometimes very difficult to feel compassion for Chiron. We don't relate well to its wounded bestiality. Saturn also has a way of alienating others, and we may find it hard to see beyond Saturn's defences, even though the person may be suffering behind them. This is because Saturn can give off distinctly anal vapours which make us feel put down, and we don't stay around long enough to find out why. The same often happens with Chiron. We may fail to appreciate Chiron's suffering because we get hit by the anger and react accordingly. Until the person can acknowledge what the pain is really about, he or she may drive other people away – partly to protect the wound, and partly because there is so much anger. These elements are missing from the Grail story, except perhaps in Wagner's Klingsor. But Chiron's eventual acceptance of mortality may also reflect the fate of the Grail King, who is finally able to die when Parsifal asks the right question. The injured King is redeemed, but he isn't curable. In this sense the Grail King is the wounded Chiron, and Parsifal's journey is an image of the path through which we can redeem our suffering.

We might be wise to remember that, with Saturn and Chiron, we are always liable to backslide. Because we manage to achieve major insights at a certain point in life, this doesn't mean that the old defence mechanisms are gone. They tend to be mobilised again when the old hurt is triggered. We may become wiser and quicker at recognising these defences, and more capable of expressing them in balanced ways, but they are indestructible because they are essentially life-protecting mechanisms. Chiron's anger doesn't vanish once we have become reflective. It may always be there, and we may to struggle with it repeatedly at different times in life. And there may even be times when that anger is appropriate and necessary in order to survive, physically or psychologically.

Barriers and Boundaries 202

Example charts and group discussion

Example chart 1

Shall we look at our first example from the group? What issues did you want us to explore?

Audience: Chiron's placement. I live in a community, and I am wondering whether it is the best thing for me, or whether it is causing me too much hurt. It's really like home on the spiritual level. But not on the personal level.

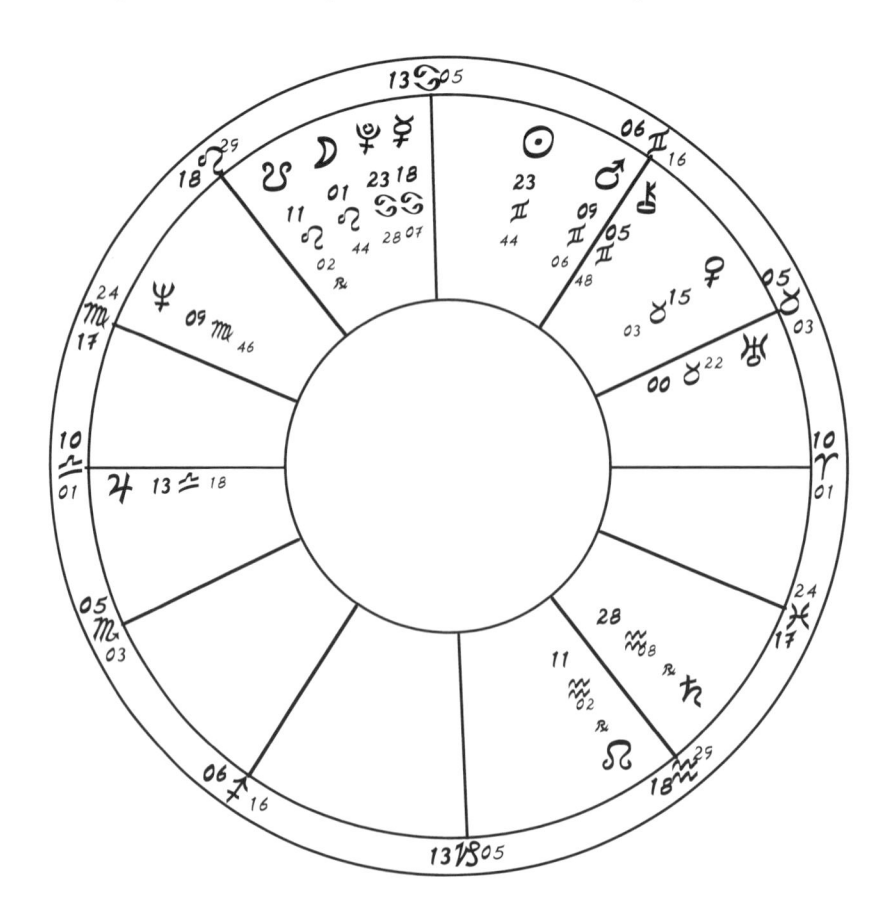

Example chart 1
Female, 15 June 1934, 2.25 pm BST, London

Liz: Chiron is on the cusp of the 9th house in Gemini, conjunct Mars. The 9th, as we know, is related to religious and spiritual matters. Chiron is also trine Jupiter, sextile the Moon, and square Neptune and Saturn.

Audience: Transiting Neptune is sesquiquadrate that natal Chiron at the moment.

Liz: Yes, and soon it will make a sesquiquadrate to its own natal place. Over the next couple of years it will set off the natal Chiron-Neptune square, most strongly when it opposes the Chiron-Neptune midpoint at 22°46' Cancer. So the issues described by this configuration are rather hot right now, and will continue to be so for some time to come. What might Chiron signify in the 9th?

Audience: It would be much more comfortable with the healer-teacher side, but the wounded horse might be a problem.

Liz: Yes, that is a good way of putting it. Jupiter is very powerful in this chart; it is conjunct the Ascendant, and the Sun is in Jupiter's house, along with Chiron. This emphasis on the spiritual seeker is underlined by the Chiron-Jupiter trine. The quest for meaning is likely to be a dominant life-theme. But the tendency to spiritualise or philosophise in order to escape suffering may sometimes be too strong. What is Chiron's wound, when it's in the 9th?

Audience: God.

Liz: Yes, exactly. With the Sun in the 9th, as well as the Mars-Chiron conjunction, formulating and living your life according to a strongly felt set of moral and spiritual convictions is essential for any sense of fulfillment. But there is something that has hurt you deeply in terms of your faith and spiritual convictions, which probably goes back a long way. Could I ask you about the religious background of your family?

Audience: I was married to a priest. My husband's family background was also a clerical one.

Liz: What about your family of origin and their religious perspective? Was there an issue about the quality of their faith, or the way in which faith was expressed or communicated?

Audience: My mother was a fundamentalist, and I became a scientist and theologist. I couldn't suspend my rational faculties, and she couldn't see beyond her dogma.

Liz: It seems that your wound lies in the way religious truths were communicated. Your Geminian nature, with its emphasis on reason and flexibility, couldn't accept the rigidity of the world-view you were given in childhood. It must have made you mistrust religion. Yet with the Sun in the 9th, you couldn't reject God either. It would have been simple if you could have dismissed the whole thing and become an atheist or an agnostic. But you can't. You probably can't dismiss the Christian ethos either. To find a faith which sustains your heart but also honours your intellect has probably taken you into some very dark and painful places.

It would be easy to blame your mother, who is represented in the chart by Mercury conjunct Pluto in the 10th as well as by the Moon in the 10th square Uranus. Clearly the two of you had a difficult relationship, not least because there may be similar elements in both of you, which are frightened of chaos and inclined to create rigid structures as a protection. Also, the 10th house Pluto might indicate that your mother's spiritual rigidity reflected deep-rooted emotional problems, perhaps a fiercely suppressed sexuality about which she suffered enormous guilt. But Chiron's placement suggests that this is an "ancestral" problem, which goes back far beyond your mother. It is probably embedded in your husband's family as well.

Audience: My question is whether or not this wound is curable.

Liz: That is the inevitable question. Behind it is the whole dilemma of your understanding of and belief in God.

Audience: And the place of suffering.

Liz: And the purpose of it. Behind the question of whether something can be cured are vast 9th house questions around which your entire sense of meaning and faith revolves. Unfortunately, I can't you an answer. But I think that the aspects from other planets to Chiron may give us some insight into what your confusion is about.

Earlier, we were looking at Jupiter and its relationship with Chiron.

Jupiter loves Chiron's wisdom, but doesn't want to look at the poisoned wound too closely. Jupiter's great assets are its faith in life's goodness, and its intuitive sense that we are meant to learn from our experiences. When it aspects Chiron by trine, Jupiter will say to Chiron, "Look, I know there are horrible inequalities in life, but there is always a meaning behind them. They are part of a larger purpose. You may not know what the purpose is just yet, but it is a benign purpose. One way or another, everything will come right in the end." That trine will work for you in both positive and negative ways. Its gift is indestructible faith. Its handicap is that you may be unable or unwilling to face or accept certain unpleasant issues that confront you. Neptune square Chiron on one side, and Saturn square it on the other, may shed some light on what these issues are. Would anyone like to try an interpretation of Neptune square Chiron?

Audience: Neptune is square Mars as well. Wouldn't there be a sense of impotence in dealing with pain?

Liz: Yes, probably, and this feeling of impotence may be very difficult to deal with. Mars conjunct Chiron suggests a powerful will, and a strong need to make things happen. By being active in the promulgation of your beliefs, you can defend yourself against the loss of faith. Your feelings of potency on a personal level are probably connected with the power to heal and enlighten others. You have to carry the message. This is a crusading spirit, fuelled, in part, by deep inner doubts. With this conjunction in the 9th, you can't sit passively and watch other people suffer or wander in darkness. You have to move in and take action.

Neptune is exactly the reverse. There is great resignation and passivity in Neptune. Neptune's solution to the problem of suffering is to avoid incarnating in the first place; or, if one must, one gets out as quickly as possible, in one form or another, literally or metaphorically. Because Neptune is in the 11th, you may project its passivity out into the world, and see its embodiments in suffering humanity "out there". Neptune's longing for dissolution may be a great problem for you, because it is one of the major reasons why people sometimes don't get better, no matter how hard you or they try. One of the things you may find very difficult is the mysterious element in people that doesn't want to be healed. They seem to be unhealable, not because the approach is wrong or the faith isn't there, but because something in them prefers oblivion.

Neptune's victimisation is different from Chiron's. Neptune is not an outlaw, or an injured animal, or a wise teacher struggling to understand life's unfairness. Neptune doesn't want to be in a mortal body in the first place. Nothing in this life can compensate for the sweet bliss of fusion with the source. I think this is very hard for you to understand when you meet it in other people. It may also be hard for you to understand when you meet it in yourself. You will see it in others because you have Neptune in the 11th, and this house deals with "society" and our perceptions of humanity *en masse*. You are probably acutely sensitive to the suffering victims in the world. Mars-Chiron wants to go charging out, banners flying, and redeem them all. But there is something about your own experience of victimisation that may merit closer examination. Where have you been a passive victim, and what in you has been unable or unwilling to find the strength to fight for your independence as an individual? These may be highly personal issues, which are being projected on society.

Audience: Wouldn't Neptune in the 11th mean a need to be involved with the collective?

Liz: Yes, and I am not suggesting that your concern for humanity is "false" because it may contain personal elements. I don't doubt that your compassion is real. But if we are unconscious of personal longings, hurts, and needs, then our judgement of the external world becomes distorted, and we wind up with Neptune's classic blindness, confusion, and self-deception. When I first asked you about the religious background of your family, your immediate response was to tell me about your husband's background. I had to ask a second time. Then you said that your mother was a fundamentalist. You have said nothing at all about your father, yet with the Sun in the 9th, there would seem to be some religious issue around him as well. There appears to be a reluctance to look too closely at what is closest to you. I wonder whether there might be elements in your family background that are very painful, and which may have bearing on what you are now experiencing. Community life has a remarkable way of constellating family patterns, because it is, after all, a kind of family; and you yourself have said that it feels like "home".

Audience: Well, I have got through my second Saturn return, and during that period I came to terms with a lot of things concerning my mother. I had to go through this recent Saturn experience before I could return to reality and start examining what I really feel.

Liz: Saturn has a way of building inner strength and authenticity, and often we need that before we can take Chiron on. And the two planets are in square in your birth chart, so whenever one is triggered, so is the other. Perhaps the Saturn return has allowed you to lay foundations to deal with the transits occurring over the next months. Transiting Chiron is at the beginning of Virgo now, opposing transiting Saturn, and both of them are squaring natal Chiron right now. Transiting Saturn is in fact in 4° Pisces today. You are clearly facing a lot of uncomfortable issues at the moment.

There are other transits which may help us to get a clearer picture of what is developing. Uranus will soon move into Aquarius and will make an opposition to the Moon in Leo, which will last for some time. This highlights issues surrounding the mother, as well as an awakening of the Leo qualities of self-validation and self-centredness which you may have difficulty in expressing. I suspect that you have been too immersed in the Herculean task of redeeming suffering that belongs to your family, projected out onto humanity as a whole.

During this last Saturn return you may well have come to terms with your parental issues on one level. But there is another level where deeper and more universal elements may be involved. Are your parents still alive?

Audience: My mother died 18 months ago. My father is still alive.

Liz: How did your mother die?

Audience: Very suddenly.

Liz: That was during the first stage of the Saturn return. When a transiting planet retrogrades over a natal planet, the second and third stages of the transit often represent further developments of a single theme. Transiting Pluto was exactly trine your natal Pluto at that time as well, going retrograde, and transiting Uranus was opposing it, also going retrograde. These transits seem to reflect not only the suddenness of the death, but the ending of very old family patterns inherited through the mother's line. This process of ending something may have begun much earlier than your mother's death, when these transiting planets made their aspects to the Moon for the first time. Around the time that Uranus makes its opposition to your natal Moon, Pluto will move into Sagittarius and trine it. So there is an enormous amount of present and future activity around these 10th house planets. It would seem that the emotional issues between you and your mother are still in an unfinished state.

The Moon in the 10th house often reflects a deep emotional identification with the mother, even if on the intellectual level the two of you were at odds.

Pluto in the 10th suggests that one perceives Plutonian qualities in the mother, whose life in some way appears to embody this archetypal energy. Although your mother's religious attitudes may have precluded any open discussion of her emotional conflicts, you must have sensed them, because with Mercury conjunct Pluto in Cancer you are probably extremely sensitive to hidden emotional undercurrents. Depression and deep frustration in the mother are often reflected by a 10th house Pluto, and Pluto is also conjunct your Moon, which underlines its connection with the mother.

Pluto is a survivor, but it can also describe someone who has struggled to maintain power and has failed. The depression and despair may reflect a mother who gave up on life, and perhaps on her marriage, a long time ago. Although the issues you are concerned about are much bigger than your personal mother, your mother is also much bigger than your actual mother, if you see what I mean. This oppressed, despairing, passionate, and frustrated woman is not only your mother. She is an archetypal figure, and your perceptions of womanhood may be strongly coloured by it in negative ways. Perhaps this is what you are beginning to free yourself of.

Audience: How would you interpret transiting Pluto opposing natal Chiron?

Liz: That's quite a long way away. It has to square Saturn first, and that square is already within orb. Saturn in the 5th in Aquarius suggests that your definitions of love are bound up with service to the collective, and it may be difficult for you to be spontaneous and self-expressive in showing your feelings. Saturn in the 5th often tries to do things for loved ones, rather than risk possible hurt and humiliation through showing emotions openly. There may also be a great reluctance to appear "special" or "different" in any way, because this might mean exclusion from the group. Transiting Pluto squaring Saturn may break down some of these Saturnian defences. When Pluto moves into Sagittarius and opposes Chiron, there may be a necessity for changes in your spiritual perspective, which are already gestating now. Transiting Pluto will also oppose Mars. You may encounter situations in which powerlessness, or an inability to act, brings about some very profound soul-searching, and certain elements in the framework of your beliefs and goals may need to change. You may outgrow them, or you may be forced to shift them through circumstances not within your control.

Mars-Chiron aspects

Mars-Chiron is a complex conjunction. It is very strong willed, and one can achieve an enormous amount, whatever one's goals might be. These goals may be intellectual and spiritual, because the conjunction is in the 9th in Gemini. They might be material if the conjunction were in an earthy house or sign. But whatever the nature of the goals, Mars-Chiron is unstoppable. Because of Chiron's deep sense of inadequacy and injury, one may feel driven to prove oneself over and over again. With Mars-Chiron, one way of coping with the problem of suffering is to grind ahead like a Panzer tank, refusing to give up or compromise. So there may also be a problem with your own stubbornness and intractability, your own brand of fundamentalism, as it were, which may be making it harder for you to let go of what needs to be left behind.

I would question the extent to which certain past experiences of pain and passivity are bound up with the intensity of the spiritual commitment that you have made. You may believe that you have to suffer, because that is the only way you can heal others.

Audience: Yes, I suppose that is true.

Liz: But the issue of your personal will, and even your personal pride, may be lurking beneath that ideal of self-sacrifice. Being able to heal others, even in the midst of your own unhappiness, is a vindication, not only of your beliefs, but of your personal potency. If you fail to heal someone, what does that imply? What does it say about the God in which you believe, and about your interpretation of God's will? Chiron will fight to defend itself against Neptune's weakness and victimisation, and it will enlist Mars' crusading spirit to help it. This defence is tantamount to saying, "If I will it, then it must happen." This can be a tremendously creative and constructive quality. Anyone with a Mars-Chiron conjunction possesses a great asset. But it lacks the ability of knowing when to bend. I believe this ability is sometimes called humility.

Audience: All this may be connected with my personal view of the real world. I suppose I see it as a place where one has to struggle.

Liz: Yes, Mars-Chiron in the 9th would probably predispose you to perceiving life as a battleground where one must fight to defend oneself against injury. What you assume to be God's will may reflect deeply personal attitudes, because of early feelings of being controlled and manipulated. This might apply particularly on the intellectual level. Gemini can easily feel stifled and oppressed, if the mental atmosphere in the family is dogmatic and lifeless. It can be as painful for the Gemini child as physical restraint might be for the Aries. The conflict of world-views which existed in your childhood may have produced a power battle, and the repercussions of this battle raise the inevitable questions: "Which God is the right God? Whose side is He on?" This kind of highly personal struggle can cloud the broader issue of human suffering, and confuse you in terms of its purpose and meaning. I think these are questions that have to be asked. I have no idea what the answers are, but I would suggest that you ask the questions.

Audience: If Mars and Chiron were in opposition, would the sense of self-will be just as strong?

Liz: Yes, and perhaps even more so, because the sense of injury and defeat may be more pervasive. An aspect between two planets is rather like locking two people in a room and forcing them into a marriage ceremony. It doesn't matter whether the aspect is an opposition or a conjunction; they are bound for life, for richer or poorer, in sickness and in health, until death parts them. When Mars and Chiron are bound in this way, enormous strength of will is usually one of the results, because the personal will reflected by Mars is perpetually fighting against the threat of injury and humiliation. If one keeps exercising a particular muscle, it will become extremely strong. With the conjunction, and also with the trine and sextile, feelings of woundedness are creatively utilised to build up the will as a powerful defence. But with the opposition, one tends to feel powerless a good deal of the time. The fear of impotence can be enormous, and sometimes depression and feelings of victimisation undermine Mars' ability to act. There is usually a lot more self-doubt with the hard aspects.

Audience: Yes, I believe my Mars-Chiron has soldiered on without respite. The simile of the tank is very appropriate. But underneath, something is crying, "Help, help!"

Liz: That is Neptune's cry, and it seems to be projected outside you. Even with a courteous and refined Libra ascendant, and Jupiter rising in Libra and the Sun in Gemini, Mars-Chiron will still behave like a tank. When this potent force is pointed in the direction of positive effort, it can achieve an enormous amount. But perhaps you need to learn how to say, "I give up. I can't redeem the world. I can't redeem my mother. It isn't my problem."

Audience: Is this a boundary issue?

Liz: Yes, in the sense that you may fail to recognise your own limits. It may also be a boundary issue in that Mars-Chiron is trying to compensate for Neptune's passivity and neediness. Your perennial heroic struggle may mask the fact that you are more dominated by your need of others than you realise.

Audience: Does the presence of Mars increase Chiron's anger?

Liz: I think there is a lot of anger in this aspect, rooted in a sense of personal impotence. But it may feel like righteous anger against evil in the world.

Audience: There is great creative and intellectual frustration around this Saturn in the 5th in Aquarius. I was thinking about what you were saying earlier, about Saturn reflecting something which has been denied. This Saturn is like a child who wants to be given the right to invent the meaning of life by himself. But the answers were already given, and couldn't be questioned.

Liz: Yes, and the answers came from a wounded family. They were probably answers coloured by considerable emotional and sexual frustration, and by a lot of parental misery and anger. I think you have described this Saturn placement very well. Saturn tends to feel unlovable when it is in the 5th. In this house in Aquarius, it seems to say, "I'm not really very interesting as an individual, and I don't have much to offer. It's terribly selfish to want to create the universe oneself. But if I contribute something to the group, and am seen as a "good" person, then I will be acceptable and loved and worthwhile."

It certainly seems that you weren't allowed to invent the meaning of life yourself. I would guess that you weren't even allowed to be a child. Probably you were expected to be selfless and eternally attuned to others' needs. It could be that you were supposed to look after your mother in her misery, and throughout your childhood it probably never occurred to you that God might also allow you to play.

Audience: He has lately!

Liz: There may also be issues around Saturn in Aquarius which have bearing on your conflict about the community in which you are living. A sense of fellowship matters terribly to Aquarius. One needs to feel part of a larger whole, and this sense of belonging, for the element of air, can be achieved only if there is free and open expression of ideas, and mutual respect for each others' thinking. Saturn in the 5th may necessitate your developing your own original ideas, but its sign placement ensures that you need to share these ideas in a group environment in order to feel you are being useful and worthwhile. With Saturn placed in Aquarius, this need is likely to be very intense, yet inevitably the early environment would not have been able to fulfill your inner requirements. Despite all the religious emphasis of your family background, there seems to have been no real sense of community. Very religious people often talk a great deal about community and service to others, but sadly they are often the least able to practise what they preach, because they frequently cannot tolerate a world-view different from their own. As is typical with Saturn, the thing that matters most to you is the thing you didn't get, at least not in the manner in which you needed it. This may make you rather desperate in seeking an Aquarian "family", even if the particular setup you have chosen is not really right for you.

Audience: This has been extremely helpful. I have a lot to think about.

Liz: So do the rest of us. Thank you for offering the chart. Shall we move on to another example? What issues did you want us to look at?

Example chart 2

Audience: I have great difficulty in group situations. I assume this is connected with my Saturn.

Liz: Probably. Let's have a look at what Saturn is doing in the chart. It's in 28° Scorpio in the 11th, opposition Mercury, square Mars, and square a Jupiter-Pluto conjunction. It is therefore part of a grand cross. It's also trine Uranus, and semisextile Neptune.

Audience: If Saturn in the 11th reflects difficulty in group situations, why has he offered his chart for the group to discuss?

Liz: Maybe it's a defence. How do you feel in this group situation?

Part Two: Saturn and Chiron as Defence Mechanisms   213

Audience: I hate being part of a group. Asking for my chart to be put up on the board isn't being part of the group. It's being special. I'm the centre of attention.

Audience: He always sits at the back.

Audience: That's for protection. I can get to the door more easily.

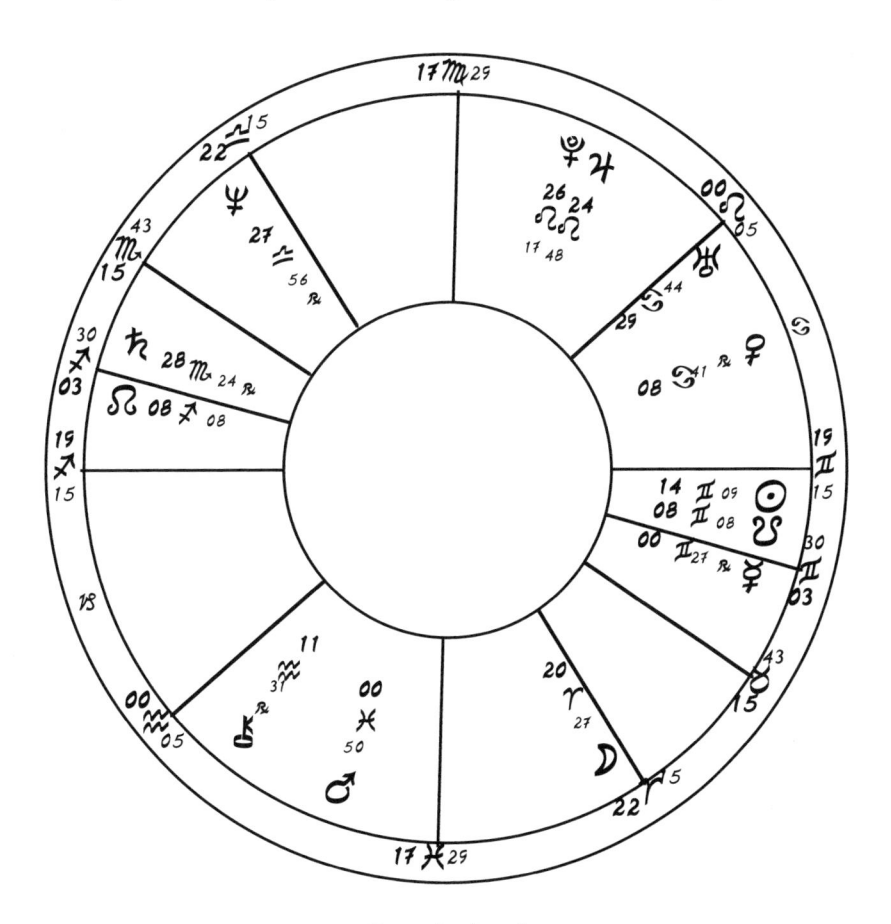

Example chart 2
Male, 4 June 1956, 9.30 pm BST, London

Liz: I think we are hearing Saturn in Scorpio square Pluto speaking. Don't worry, you aren't paranoid; they really are out to get you. We would expect this 11th house Saturn to exhibit its defences in group situations. But what are these defences, and what is their basis? What needs and fears might its placement in Scorpio suggest?

Audience: Scorpio needs intensely.

Liz: Yes, it needs intensely, and it also needs intensity. All three water signs need close emotional contact, but Scorpio is more discriminating that the other two. Scorpio wants very deep contact with very special people, on a truthful and unsentimental level. A child with Saturn in Scorpio requires authentic, straight, and honest emotional exchange, with no hypocrisy, manipulation, lying, or superficiality. Children with Saturn placed here would much rather have the naked truth about a parental breakup or a death, which they can cope with surprisingly well. What wounds them is the kind of cotton-wool evasiveness with which many parents shroud their emotional conflicts and crises. When such children are lied to, the response is to assume that the parents are perpetrating a deliberate act of betrayal. A child cannot recognise that the parents may be terrified of this kind of emotional truthfulness. It is probable that your family couldn't meet your standards, in terms of the quality of emotional exchange you wanted.

Audience: Yes, that is true. But the emotional directness and intensity you describe are things I have an absolute horror of. I have always thought that Saturn was defending me from emotional closeness, rather than seeking it.

Liz: You are right; Saturn's defences will ensure that you never let anyone get too close. But that is because emotional closeness matters so much. One always defends oneself against being hurt in a sphere in which one is intensely vulnerable. It is because your desire for emotional intensity was betrayed so early that Saturn now guards the gate and ensures that no one will ever humiliate or betray you again. I have found that, with Saturn in Scorpio, the feeling of betrayal can run very deep indeed. Forgiveness is merely an abstract concept. The intensity of your defence is in direct proportion to the intensity of your need. I would guess that you are determined never to put yourself in a vulnerable position again, and consequently even those you love deeply are likely to be barred entry. They are not allowed to see what you really feel. And if they try, they are probably put through incredible tests over a long period of time. Only the truly heroic will hang around long enough to get through all the tests, because I think you require constant proofs of emotional loyalty. Partners may find your behaviour at best inexplicable and at worst cruel, if they don't understand how frightened you are of being controlled and humiliated. Scorpio's pride is very great. The least indication of dishonesty, manipulation, or betrayal is experienced on an incredibly intense level. We don't protect ourselves so strenuously from something unless we have been badly hurt by it. Otherwise, why would we bother?

Audience: It's true. These things are a matter of life and death to me, and the 8th house Pluto thrown in as well really makes it an issue of survival. I suppose you are right, I wouldn't have this sort of attitude towards things that didn't matter. All you say about holding people at a distance, by the way, is entirely correct. I'm sure you won't be surprised to hear that most of my family think I'm heartless and unfeeling.

Liz: No, I'm not surprised to hear it. Part of the difficulty is that your particular emotional needs were probably quite alien to what your family understood as love. You must have experienced this as a rejection, a statement that there is something wrong with your way of loving and needing. But there are also warring factions within you. It wasn't just your family who didn't cope well with your Scorpio Saturn; it is also you yourself. The opposition between Neptune in the 10th and the Moon on the cusp of the 4th suggests that the quality of your emotional relationship with your mother was radically different from the particular nature and needs of Saturn in Scorpio. Scorpio wants intensity, but it doesn't want fusion. This sign possesses a very powerful sense of privacy, and while it can be possessive, it is not emotionally invasive. But Neptune is. Scorpio wants relationships to be deep, but love must also include respect for each person's boundaries. Fusion implies powerlessness, which is anathema to Scorpio.

The Moon-Neptune opposition suggests that you may perceive your mother as very invasive and needy. But this opposition describes something about your own feelings as well. Your mother may have wanted you to be her redeemer, and your need of her made you take on the role willingly. This mother-child fusion may have also precluded a solid relationship with your father, making you feel undefended against the maternal flood. You were probably swamped by boundless, oceanic needs – yours and hers – that made it very difficult for you to distinguish who was feeling what. That can be overwhelming, especially to someone with Saturn in Scorpio, Sun in Gemini, Moon in independent Aries, and a freedom-loving Sagittarius Ascendant. All emotions may feel threatening to you now because your early experiences gave little nourishment, either to your discriminating Saturn or your independent air-fire spirit.

Audience: Yes, that is so. My Mother's Sun is in 25° Aquarius, square my Saturn and opposition my Jupiter-Pluto conjunction. I suppose she felt I was just as demanding of her as I felt she was of me. Her Saturn is in 25° Scorpio, so I was born under her Saturn return. Her Neptune is in 23° Leo, square her Saturn and mine, trine my Moon, and conjunct my Jupiter-Pluto. Evidently we have the same problem. So, as you can see, the situation I've managed to get myself born into is not just my subjective perception.

Liz: It's for real.

Audience: Yes, it's for real. What you were saying about the threat of invasion is not just my interpretation.

Liz: Looking at the Moon-Neptune opposition across the meridian of the chart, I would assume there is a great deal of reality in your view of things. When family issues are reflected in the birth chart, they are almost always a mixture of subjective perception and actual behaviour, and even if the former is more dominant, the latter is never wholly absent. It's not just the inherent mistrust of Saturn in Scorpio that makes you suspect other people's motives in close relationships; there is a family inheritance suggested here, of emotional invasiveness and lack of boundaries. A mother who is herself a desperately needy emotional child would certainly frighten the wits out of you, in terms of your ability to allow emotional closeness. If we add this Moon-Neptune opposition to Saturn in Scorpio, with its implied lack of emotional honesty in the early environment, we have a recipe for a very painful wound. You must have been desperately lonely as a child. You probably felt smothered by an emotional outpouring that you didn't experience as love. I suspect you still have a very hard time believing anyone who professes to love you.

Audience: It's not a problem that has ever arisen.

Liz: Do you mean you have never believed it, or no one's ever said it?

Audience: I don't give anyone a chance to say it. I discourage that sort of declaration.

Liz: That kind of denial is one of Saturn's characteristic defences. There are other chart factors involved as well. Looking at Venus in Cancer in the 7th, I would be even more inclined to disbelieve any statement you made about not needing closeness in a relationship.

Audience: Ah.

Liz: Because Venus is in the 7th, you probably rely on the other person to express all the feeling. Despite the cleverness and wit of Mercury in Gemini square Mars, there is enormous shyness and diffidence reflected in the chart. Mercury is opposition Saturn and square Pluto, and however sharp and amusing you might be in a social situation, you probably find it extremely hard to say what you really feel. Planets in the 7th house tend to get projected onto others, and someone else has to express Venus in Cancer qualities and thaw your emotional chill. But on the plus side, you seem to understand a great deal about your emotional dynamics, whatever you might say in this group setting. This means that you are a lot further in working on the more painful Saturn issues than many people might be, because you are conscious of your own dichotomy. Even though it isn't fun to be tested all the time by a suspicious Saturn in Scorpio, I wouldn't expect you to unleash Saturnian defences in the really destructive ways that some people do. Also, what you are doing at this very moment may prove to be helpful, because talking about such charged emotional issues in front of a large group takes a lot of courage.

Audience: I've wanted to do it here, rather than in a one-to-one situation. Is this what you mean when you talk about working at Saturn problems directly?

Liz: In part, yes. Discovering that other people have experienced similar hurts and fears, and that they are not all going to rush out of the room screaming, might make some difference to you. Although you said at the beginning that talking about your chart didn't make you part of the group, of course it does. Although the spotlight is on you, everyone here has the Moon, Saturn, Neptune, Chiron, Venus, and Pluto somewhere in the birth chart, and everyone has had a mother. It is also probable that everyone here needs to be loved, and that most people in this group have been disappointed, at one time or another, as a result of that need. The experience of being wounded through emotional needs, while unique to you in the particular form you experienced it, is not unique in itself; it is archetypal, and one of the great universal sources of human suffering. Every person with Saturn in a water sign or house, or in aspect to a watery planet, will know something about this archetypal hurt.

Being able to discuss it can help the restrictions of Mercury-Saturn, and knowing that others understand might also make some difference. One of the most important sources of healing, with Saturn in Scorpio, is the realisation that the emotional isolation you have imposed upon yourself is not quite what you think it is. It is not an emotional failing or a sign of lack of feeling, but a defence to protect the propensity to love deeply.

Audience: Yes, but what I am going through is really just the ordinary experience of what everybody goes through, in one way or another.

Liz: Be careful. When I said that emotional wounding is archetypal, I did not mean that it is "ordinary". You've just demeaned it, which is another of Saturn's defences. You seem to be saying, "Oh, well, my unhappiness isn't such a big deal, because everybody is unhappy. It's just the usual common or garden variety human mess, and therefore it's not that important." But it's extremely important; your feelings matter. They are unique, and nobody else has experienced exactly what you've experienced. But loneliness and betrayal are archetypal themes which have formed the basis of myth, poetry, fiction, and drama over many centuries – *because* these experiences are so important and matter so much. There may be enough understanding, amongst quite a few people here, to allow you to recognise that you are human, and not some sort of emotional misfit, as your family seem intent on insisting you are.

Saturn in the water signs may defend its vulnerability by shutting other people out. It may also demean the importance of feelings in general. That is what you are doing if you say, "Everybody goes through these things, and it's petty and indulgent to dwell on them." Wallowing in self-pity, or making a martyr of oneself, are also characteristic defences for Saturn in water; but you aren't showing any signs of that line of defence, perhaps because the strong bias in air and fire signs mitigates against it. You are doing the opposite. Quite a few people here know how you feel, at least enough to empathise – and that could help you to have some compassion for yourself. Also, not everyone in this room, or in any other room, will behave in the same way your mother did. Not everyone you meet will want to invade you, take you over, or turn you into a redeemer. Through giving other people a chance to be something other than your mother, you could work through some of the more intractable aspects of your wound. Friendships may be extremely important for this. Do you have any close friends?

Audience: Yes, but I don't see much of them, to be honest, which is my own fault. I've done a lot of withdrawing and holding my distance. Friendship is something I can relate to, but they are all hundreds of miles of way. Did I say *all?* They are *both* hundreds of miles away. What you describe is probably more appropriate to how I get along with my brother, whom I see a lot of, and who has direct experience of what I'm talking about.

Liz: Brothers can be friends. They don't have to be merely siblings.

Audience: That's the way it's worked out. It's ceased being a relationship between big brother and little brother, with all that entails on the negative side. There is much more parity. We see each other because we want to, rather than because we're family. It suddenly struck me that Uranus might actually be helping this situation. Usually I think of a 7th house Uranus as being extremely problematic in relationships, but it may help Saturn's mistrust through friendships, which are easier. Uranus could act as Saturn's ally.

Liz: They can be friends, as they are co-rulers of Aquarius, and in your chart they are in trine. So they would probably work as allies. Uranus helps to alleviate Saturn's loneliness through relationships which don't involve a lot of overt emotional dependency, but do permit mutual respect, concern, and intellectual affinity. That allows you to enjoy a sense of contact with other people. Saturn in Scorpio isn't as isolated as it might be without Uranus' support. But like everything else in the horoscope, this is a double-edged gift. Trines can often provide a defence against more difficult chart placements. Friendships of a Uranian kind can take just enough of the sting out of your isolation to allow you to avoid the pain. Also, this Uranus is not really in the 7th house; it is within a degree of the 8th house cusp, and I would interpret it as an 8th house Uranus. An ability to abruptly disengage from close emotional involvements may actually exacerbate your defences against emotional closeness. With Uranus in the 8th, you may also have experienced sudden losses or emotional shocks quite early in life, such as the death of a loved family member, or the sudden emotional withdrawal of one of your parents. The expectation of sudden loss may contribute to your fear of deep emotional involvement.

Chiron in the 2nd house

Audience: What about Chiron in the 2nd house?

Liz: Yes, we have been focusing almost wholly on Saturn, and have ignored Chiron. Chiron is in the 2nd house, which is concerned with self-worth. It makes only one major aspect, a trine to the Sun.

Audience: Could it be concerned with money as well as self-worth?

Liz: Money is often an issue with Chiron in the 2nd. But money is the concrete symbol of the value we place on people, objects, and qualities. When material difficulties are suggested by Chiron, they are usually important because in some way they reflect back on the individual's sense of what he or she is worth as a person. What was your family's material situation during your childhood?

Audience: We were never a poor family. My mother is a teacher, my father was middle management in industry. For some reason we got by. We were never madly rich either. The thing that springs to mind as having been a problem, regarding my own experience and battle with money, is that, when I finished university, I could have carried on to do a post-graduate degree, if I could have got a grant. They said, "If you get a grant, we'll give you a place." It occurred to me then, and to some extent it still does, that if my father had been more supportive, I might have a PhD now. But he wasn't, so I'm not.

Liz: We can all blame some failure or omission in our lives on someone else's lack of support. Somehow I am not convinced. You don't sound very distraught about not having letters trailing after your name.

Audience: I suppose not. But I can't really think of any other issues around money which might be linked with Chiron.

Liz: Chiron in the 2nd doesn't automatically indicate financial problems. As I said before, money in context of the 2nd house is a symbol, and it may be terribly important to one individual and not another because of its connotations as a measure of self-worth. If we took a sample group of a hundred people and gave them all ten thousand pounds, some would say it was enough, some would say it was insufficient, and some would say it was too much and they didn't deserve it. Money can be a concrete means of defining identity, and for people who are identified with their personal possessions and their bank accounts, their sense of self-value rises or falls according to what they own. Losing one's money, or finding oneself out of work, can serve as a spur to make some people develop new talents, but others may descend into depression and apathy, or jump in front of trains. This reflects the very different value different people place on money, and on themselves.

We should also remember that the 2nd house is also related to resources – the talents and skills we possess that represent our inner "wealth" – and also to our physical bodies. Money is only one area in which a 2nd house Chiron may reflect early wounds. Your Chiron is in Aquarius, an air sign, and this suggests that the area where there has been wounding is not material. It is more likely to be intellectual or social, and probably the latter, because this echoes Saturn in the 11th, which is Aquarius' house. I think the sense of social isolation, of not belonging or "fitting", may be a more accurate description of Chiron's wound.

Audience: Simply being incarnated seems to me to be an incurable wound. Not belonging is only part of that. You can find all sorts of ways of surviving incarnation, but you may never learn to really like it.

Liz: You seem to be describing not only Chiron's sense of deep alienation, but also the lack of earth in the birth chart, which would make Chiron's placement in an earthy house more "global" in its feelings of injury and isolation. Without earth, you can't easily avail yourself of the pragmatism necessary to contain and balance Chiron's sense of injustice and hurt. Also, Neptune is very powerful in the chart, not only because of its opposition to the Moon and sesquiquadrate to the Sun, but also because it is culminating at the MC. Neptune resents incarnation, because existence in a physical body necessitates separation from the source. In this respect you have something in common with your mother. The pain of separation seems to have afflicted both of you. But Chiron in Aquarius in the 2nd isn't the same as Neptune's anguish about being mortal and alone. It describes something quite different. Chiron in Aquarius may reflect the feeling that you aren't really part of the human race. Perhaps Chiron's wounding is connected with being excluded – being an anomaly, an outsider, an alien. Are there feelings like this which are part of the family myth?

Audience: Yes, that goes back through the family. Both my parents have a sense of being outsiders, not being part of the common run of humanity. There's a kind of arrogance, a sort of overcompensating which makes them insist on being special. My father talks of his father in similar terms as well. His father's family were always very poor, and spoken of as, well, a "shower of shit" was his term, whereas his mother's family were full of "geniuses" who were probably overcompensating in just the same way. But the only real indication of family genius is an uncle who died at age 19, at the end of the First World War. Certainly the message was that you have to be special to be loved.

Liz: Peopling the family with imaginary genuises is a powerful defence against a dreadful sense of being socially inferior and unacceptable. Glamorising one's differentness is a fairly common compensation for such feelings of exclusion, in families as well as individuals. It also happens in national and racial groups. "We're different, we're special, that common lot out there are too stupid to appreciate us, and that's why they have rejected us." This seems to be linked with Chiron in Aquarius in the 2nd. You are only really worthwhile if you are special, a "genius" with a PhD after your name. Your sense of self-value secretly depends on it. Without it you aren't anything, you are a failure to your family, and it is undermining to your confidence. Were there heavy expectations placed on you to be brilliant and exceptional?

Audience: Not in an obvious way. But being reminded of the family genuises constitutes an expectation, even if it isn't explicitly stated. We were expected to do well academically, within the context of where we were brought up, which tended to be below average academically, for one reason or another. So I got double messages about being deserving. One message said, "Do something really spectacular." The other said, "Don't do anything spectacular, or you'll surpass us."

Liz: It sounds a very curious setup. With all those geniuses in the family, why did your parents choose to live in an area where the academic standard was below average? You are in a no-win situation; you are damned if you do and damned if you don't. And behind your personal dilemma is the whole thorny problem of the inequalities in education, and the way in which diversity of educational background, as well as diversity in innate intellectual ability, divides families and social groups, and creates appalling injustices. There is no nice ideological solution to the problem, either. In theory, everyone should have the right to the same level of education, but in practise, people have different intellectual aptitudes and aspirations, and if they are all educated together in the same way, than someone will inevitably suffer. The slow will suffer if the bright are catered for, and the bright will suffer if the slow are catered for.

Audience: There was a local ethos in my school, that excellence is a crime against the collective. You are right, I couldn't win. The message from my peers was, "Don't show us up, or we'll do you. Don't be too clever, or you'll show the rest of us up as thick." Even my own parents seemed to say, "Yes, yes, go out and be brilliant, but don't you dare to be too brilliant, or we'll rip it to bits."

Liz: The sad thing is that this condemnation of intellectual excellence is a pervasive malady everywhere. It is a collective problem, not limited to your school or your parents. It is the old cry, "If I can't have it, you shouldn't have it either." As a Gemini, you would probably experience this intellectual "double bind" as deeply wounding, and your sense of self-worth has been badly injured by it. Chiron is trine the Sun, which is promising in terms of what these early experiences can contribute to your sense of individual meaning and purpose. Chiron's propensity to seek understanding as a defence against pain is probably connected with your involvement in psychological astrology. Also, you may have an unusual degree of empathy for people who have suffered similar difficulties in early education, and you might make an excellent teacher because of it.

Chiron in Aquarius in the 2nd, with its sense of social isolation and compassion for other "outcasts", could become a valuable resource giving focus to a 6th house Sun's need to be useful. But it sounds as though your sense of self has been deeply undermined, in subtle ways that are not immediately visible. "Don't show everybody else up as thick" is a pretty awful message to give a Gemini, since the desire to develop the intellect and communicate ideas is fundamental to Gemini. You are supposed to pretend to be thick, but you are also supposed to be a genius. You are supposed to be the devoted redeemer and surrogate husband of your mother, without having any emotional needs of your own. In adulthood, it isn't surprising that you're shy and that your defences have been mobilised, both emotionally and intellectually.

What about the darker feelings which might be associated, not only with Chiron, but also with Mars square Saturn and opposition Pluto? You have been describing extremely painful experiences with a kind of clinical detachment. What do you do with your rage?

Audience: Block it up, on the whole. I have a horror of directing rage against the person who has triggered it. I tend to go home and then go completely potty. At least a little bit of it comes out, even if it is directed at inanimate objects at inappropriate times. I'm sure that's better than not expressing it at all. I am certainly conscious of it.

Audience: I am very interested in the transits at the moment. Transiting Pluto has been squaring the natal Jupiter-Pluto conjunction, and will be coming over Saturn soon. Then it will oppose Mercury and square Mars.

Liz: Yes, there are some very interesting transits going on. The grand cross is being triggered by Pluto. There is also a lunar eclipse in four days, which will fall across natal Saturn. Transiting Jupiter is creeping up to set off the grand cross as well; it will conjunct Pluto in 28° Scorpio on 2 December. Saturn is being rooted out of its bunker with great force. Transiting Neptune is presently square the Moon. And transiting Uranus is approaching the opposition to its own place.

Audience: And the progressed Sun is at 20° Cancer.

Liz: So it is square the natal Moon, and transiting Neptune is opposition progressed Sun as well as square natal Moon. It sounds as though two things are happening. On the one hand, you are struggling to break out of your emotional prison. Your way of interacting with other people is going through enormous change, and you are probably experiencing a breaking down of defences which, although extremely positive, may leave you feeling very frightened and vulnerable. There may also be a great deal of anger unleashed, as Pluto approaches the square to natal Mars, and you might not be satisfied with merely overturning chairs or smashing plates. Progressed Sun square natal Moon suggests a struggle to break free of the mother and the family past. But on the other hand, transiting Neptune square the Moon and opposition progressed Sun may invoke feelings of weakness, passivity, and yearning, and make you very reluctant to face the psychological, and perhaps actual, separation from the family which I think may be required of you. It is certainly a very fruitful time for working with these inner issues; there couldn't be a better one.

Audience: That's what frightens me. It is a very frightening time.

Liz: What frightens you about it?

Audience: A number of things. First of all, survival. There is a threat of death attached to all this; probably not literally, but it feels like that. And fear of closeness, of having to start again without any defence mechanisms. They may be hellish defence mechanisms, but they're mine and the ones I know.

Liz: I don't think you will lose them. Basic defences, whether they belong to particular planets or to the character of particular signs, are part of our nature, and we can no more lose them than we can lose the colour of our eyes. These defences are healthy and necessary as well as permanent attributes of the personality. Saturn in Scorpio quite rightly mistrusts the unconscious motives of others, because many people, without meaning to, carry some rather smelly emotional undercurrents which could prove very destructive to the openness and sensitivity of Moon-Neptune. Chiron in Aquarius, while making you feel "different" and excluded, may also prove of enormous value in encouraging you to develop your talents in highly individual ways. You won't lose the benefits of these defences, which are a fundamental part of your character.

Pluto transiting in aspect to Saturn

What you may lose is the more extreme expressions of your defences, which could make you feel very uncomfortable for a while. When Pluto reaches Saturn, you may go through certain experiences which you feel are in some way humiliating, or which make you feel very vulnerable and exposed. That may be a necessary stage in the process, since Pluto has a way of stripping away masks and revealing the real person beneath. As far as your sense of death is concerned, transits of Pluto often feel as though one is dying; people and situations which once meant a lot may lose their power to hold you, and attitudes and beliefs which once seemed right and true may seem shallow or past their sell-by date. With Pluto, there is often a feeling of wandering through a dark tunnel, without any sense of what lies at the other end. Fire and air signs tend to suffer more from this, because logic and intuition don't provide their usual insights and answers. One must simply wander blind. Depression is a frequent accompaniment to Pluto transits, and your emotional mood may hit bottom for a while. But it is important to remain quietly in the tunnel, and just keep going, without struggling to get out. The tunnel is a kind of birth canal, and it requires a deep letting go. It is possible that you may experience a real death, and if so, it is likely to be your mother, although this death may, in the end, turn out to be a deep change in your relationship with her, a true and healing separation, rather than her physical demise.

The myth of Inanna's descent into the underworld is often relevant to anyone going through a powerful Pluto transit. She proceeds into the dark realm in stages, and she is required to give up a bit of control with each step. The issue of control is very powerful in this chart. It is reflected in the aspects, particularly Saturn square Pluto and Mars opposition Pluto. There seems to be a need to control everything and everybody around you, and it is the breaking down of control, especially over your own feelings, which may feel so frightening. That also can feel like a kind of death, particularly if Moon-Neptune feelings rise to the surface and swamp you with a longing to go home. Probably there is a longing for oblivion in you, because there is in most Moon-Neptune people. You might not call it a death-wish, but that's essentially what it is.

Audience: Oh yes, I would call it that. Having said that, I also have a very strong will to live. There is a grand fire trine in the chart, between the Ascendant, Moon, and Jupiter-Pluto. There are times when I have my suicide moments, but at the end of it, there is a part of me that says, "I will not die."

Liz: Moon-Jupiter may also say, "I want to live because otherwise I might miss something exciting!" The element of fire, as well as strong aspects from Jupiter, can reflect an irrepressible feeling that something better and more interesting lies just around the corner. That feeling may not be as lively at the moment as it sometimes is, but it will probably be there sufficiently to help you recognise the potentials in whatever you experience. The death issues reflected by Pluto are concerned with the stripping away of that which no longer serves life. Surprisingly, or perhaps not surprisingly, the astrological signatures of literal death seem to involve Jupiter and Neptune more often than they do Pluto, because of the leaving behind of the body for more subtle realms. Pluto's deaths are usually psychological. I don't know what kind of experiences the psyche will require in order to move you into the next stage, but they may come through the 7th house because of the progressed Sun moving through this house, square natal Moon. You may be involved in a relationship in which your habitual defences don't work any more. That would be a very painful process for you, but probably a profoundly healing one.

Audience: I would love someone to take me forward in a time machine so that I could know that, five years from now, I will be able to look back on this period and say, "Well, that all worked out for the best." But I don't know what is going to happen. Whatever it is, I know I will not go into therapy. I am afraid of a one-to-one confrontation.

Part Two: Saturn and Chiron as Defence Mechanisms

Audience: I have my Sun in 24° of Scorpio, and I also have Chiron in the 2nd. With Pluto transiting over my Sun, I felt as though I was crawling around under the table, on all fours. Scorpio doesn't like to show what is there. The act of revealing oneself to another person can be humiliating. But it is the thing that allows you to crawl out from under the table, because you are still alive, and somebody has listened. So some kind of counselling or therapy could work out.

Audience: Yes, I know it could work out. But...

Audience: It's a very powerful business. When Pluto first hit my Sun, I realised that I didn't know how to grow up. But I had an incredible ally, and I'm glad for it. It was very frightening sometimes.

Liz: I think there is a difference between transiting Pluto conjuncting the Sun, and transiting Pluto conjuncting Saturn. The end result in both cases may be a confrontation with and integration of hidden aspects of the psyche. But the Sun in Scorpio usually recognises its home terrain, because Pluto rules this sign. The terror that Saturn experiences can be paralysing. Reassuring words don't really do much good. Time, and finding oneself on one's knees at last, are far more effective in overturning pride and getting around the corner. Saturn's terror at the advent of an outer planet transit is connected with loss of control and fear of humiliation. Nothing that anyone says will make that fear go away, because Saturn's nature is intrinsically defensive. No matter how reassuring the words are, Saturn doesn't hear them. Also, there may be an element in you that doesn't want anyone's help. You may need to know that you can get through this on your own. I don't know whether this is right for you or not. It may be that you do need to discover your survival capacities on the emotional level, without the benefit of counselling or advice. But it might be wise to explore what your terror of a one-to-one confrontation is really about. Try to be as honest with yourself as you can. As you yourself said at the beginning, these emotional conflicts are a life-and-death issue for you.

Audience: I don't want life-and-death issues. I just want everything to be nice.

Liz: I am sure you do. But that is not likely at the moment, with a Pluto transit over your grand cross. Your terror is worth exploring, and perhaps even sharing with someone else, because in it may lie the key to a new sense of connection with other people. This seems to be something you can't talk about, yet you feel locked in by it, as though you were living in a bell jar.

Audience: I also should perhaps add that I was a breech birth, and spent the first week or ten days of my life on a ventilator. I went straight from the womb to being completely isolated from the rest of the universe. My mother didn't touch me for about four days afterwards. I don't know what was the matter with her. I don't know what was the matter with me, either; it was something to do with my breathing. Everyone was asking whether I would live or die. There was something even then that was saying, "You are not going to die."

Liz: Yet being alive meant being in total isolation. They kept you alive, but at the cost of any human contact. Although your will to live is strong, there also seems to be a deep conviction that life means utter isolation and alienation. These are the sort of things which may lie at the bottom of that state of terror you describe, and which I think you ought to be exploring at the moment. Having made the courageous step of asking that this chart be discussed in front of the group, perhaps you might consider talking about it to one person. Your fears ultimately seem to be bound up with the sense of being human, the experience of being in a body, and the feeling of being connected with the rest of life. There is a part of you which makes me think of an autistic child, living in a state of paralysing terror. This terror of life is being constellated by the current transits. It needs to come to the surface, because otherwise it can't heal. But I would suggest that you don't try to do this on your own, unless you are very articulate with a pen or a paintbrush.

Audience: I would like to think I am.

Liz: Then try keeping a journal. But if that fails to help, I would suggest, with your natal Sun conjuncting the cusp of the 7th house, that you make the effort to talk with a qualified person about what you are feeling. You seem so afraid of it that I suspect it is exactly what you need.

Audience: Ouch.

Liz: Counselling and therapy are not "cures" for painful Chiron and Saturn issues. For some people, the discovery that one can manage on one's own may provide the deepest healing and self-respect. Some people are therapy "addicts", and use therapy as a kind of emotional masturbation, going around and around

Part Two: Saturn and Chiron as Defence Mechanisms

the same issues, and never really integrating their insights into life. Sometimes Saturn and Chiron require ordinary hard work in the outer world, or a reasoned recognition of life's uneven nature. These complex and fundamentally defensive planets are involved with some of our most painful and intractable problems. Yet it is the pain they generate, and the difficulties into which our defences lead us, which sometimes make us really come alive.

Do you all know the fairy tale about the prince and the thief? There once was a king who had three sons. His kingdom was rich, and he was a powerful ruler. But one night a thief crept into his orchard and stole some of the golden apples from his most precious tree. These apples were the real source of the king's power, and he knew that if he lost them, the kingdom would fall. The king sent his eldest and bravest son to keep watch over the orchard. But this prince fell asleep, and the thief managed to steal another of the precious golden apples. The king then sent his next son to keep watch. This prince was also brave and strong, although not as strong as his brother. But he too fell asleep during the night, and the thief crept away with another golden apple.

The king then fell into despair, because, although he had a third son, this young man was a fool. He rode his horse backwards, and was not handsome or elegant like his brothers; and usually he made a mess of everything he did. But this foolish and unprepossessing young prince told his father, "I will keep watch! I know how to catch the thief!" No one tried to discourage him, thinking that, although he would surely do no good, at least he could do no harm. The young prince went out to the orchard, and made himself a pillow of thorns. And each time he began to fall asleep, the pain woke him up; and so he caught the thief, and the apples were restored, and the king and his kingdom all lived happily ever after.

We have come to the end of the seminar now. Thank you all for participating.

About the CPA

Director: Liz Greene, Ph. D., D. F. Astrol. S., Dip. Analyt. Psych.

The Centre for Psychological Astrology provides a unique workshop and professional training programme, designed to foster the cross fertilisation of the fields of astrology and depth, humanistic, and transpersonal psychology. The main aims and objectives of the CPA professional training course are:

- To provide students with a solid and broad base of knowledge within the realms of both traditional astrological symbolism and psychological theory and technique, so that the astrological chart can be sensitively understood and interpreted in the light of modern psychological thought.

- To make available to students psychologically qualified case supervision, along with background seminars in counselling skills and techniques which would raise the standard and effectiveness of astrological consultation. It should be noted that no formal training as a counsellor or therapist is provided by the course.

- To encourage investigation and research into the links between astrology, psychological models, and therapeutic techniques, thereby contributing to and advancing the existing body of astrological and psychological knowledge.

History

The CPA began unofficially in 1980 as a sporadic series of courses and seminars offered by Liz Greene and Howard Sasportas, covering all aspects of astrology from beginners' courses to more advanced one-day seminars. In 1981 additional courses and seminars by other tutors were interspersed with those of Liz and Howard to increase the variety of material offered to students, and Juliet Sharman-Burke and Warren Kenton began contributing their expertise in Tarot and Kabbalah. It then seemed appropriate to take what was previously a random collection of astrology courses and put them under a single umbrella, so in 1982 the "prototype" of the CPA – the Centre for Transpersonal Astrology – was born, with the adminstrative work handled by Richard Aisbitt, himself a practising astrologer.

In 1983 the name was changed to the Centre for Psychological Astrology, because a wide variety of psychological approaches was incorporated into the seminars, ranging from transpersonal psychology to the work of Jung, Freud and Klein. In response to repeated requests from students, the Diploma Course was eventually created, with additional tutors joining the staff. The CPA continued to develop and consolidate its programme despite the unfortunate death of Howard in 1992, when Charles Harvey became co-director with Liz Greene. Richard Aisbitt continued to manage the administration with great ability and commitment until 1994, when the burden of increasing ill-health forced him to restrict his contribution to beginners' and intermediate classes. At this time Juliet Sharman-Burke took over the administration. Richard himself sadly died in 1996. Finally, in February 2000, Charles Harvey tragically died of cancer, leaving Liz Greene as sole director. In the new Millennium, the CPA continues to develop along both familiar and innovative lines, always maintaining the high standards reflected in the fine work of its former co-directors.

Qualifications

Fulfilment of the seminar and supervision requirements of the In-Depth Professional Training Course entitles the student to a Certificate in Psychological Astrology. Upon successfully presenting a reading-in paper, the student is entitled to the CPA's Diploma in Psychological Astrology, with permission to use the letters, D. Psych. Astrol. The successful graduate will be able to apply the principles and techniques learned during the course to his or her professional activities, either as a consultant astrologer or as a useful adjunct to other forms of counselling or healing. Career prospects are good, as there is an ever-increasing demand for the services of capable psychologically orientated astrologers. The CPA's Diploma is not offered as a replacement for the Diploma of the Faculty of Astrological Studies or any other basic astrological training course. Students are encouraged to learn their basic astrology as thoroughly as possible, through the Faculty or some other reputable source, before undertaking the In-Depth Professional Training Course. The CPA offers introductory and intermediate courses in psychological astrology, which run on weekday evenings.

THE CPA DIPLOMA DOES NOT CONSTITUTE A FORMAL COUNSELLING OR PSYCHOTHERAPEUTIC TRAINING. Students wishing to work as counsellors or therapists should complete a further training course focusing on these skills. There are many excellent courses and schools of various persuasions available in the United Kingdom and abroad.

Seminars in Zürich

Certain seminars from the CPA programme are available in Zürich. Please write to Astrodienst AG, Dammstrasse 23, CH-8702 Zürich-Zollikon, Switzerland, www.astro.com for details. However, those wishing to enter the In-Depth Training Course will need to attend seminars and supervision groups in London in order to obtain the Diploma, and should apply through the London address.

Individual Therapy

In order to complete the In-Depth Professional Training, the CPA asks that all students, for a minimum of one year of study, be involved in a recognised form of depth psychotherapy with a qualified therapist, analyst or counsellor of his or her choice. The fee for the CPA training does not include the cost of this therapy, which must be borne by the student himself or herself. The basis for this requirement is that we believe no responsible counsellor of any persuasion can hope to deal sensitively and wisely with another person's psyche, without some experience of his or her own. Although it is the student's responsibility to arrange for this therapy, the CPA can refer students to various psychotherapeutic organisations if required.

Criteria for Admission

The following guidelines for admission to the In-Depth Professional Training Programme are applied:

- A sound basic knowledge of the meaning of the signs, planets, houses, aspects, transits and progressions, equal to Certificate Level of the Faculty of Astrological Studies Course. The CPA's own introductory and intermediate courses will also take the student to the required level of knowledge.

- Being able and willing to work on one's own individual development, as reflected by the requirement of individual therapy during the programme. Although a minimum of one year is required, it is hoped that the student will fully recognise the purpose and value of such inner work, and choose to continue for a longer period.

- Adequate educational background and communication skills will be looked for in applicants, as well as empathy, integrity, and a sense of responsibility.

Enrolment Procedure

Please write to the Centre for Psychological Astrology, BCM Box 1815, London WC1N 3XX, for fees, further information, and an application form. Please include an SAE and International Postage Coupon if writing from abroad. The CPA may also be contacted on Tel/Fax +44 20 8749 2330, or at www.cpalondon.com.

PLEASE NOTE:

- The CPA does not offer a correspondence course.
- The course does not qualify overseas students for a student visa.
- The course is for EU and Swiss residents only, although exceptions may sometimes be made.

About the CPA Press

The seminars in this volume are two of a series of seminars transcribed and edited for publication by the CPA Press. Although some material has been altered, for purposes of clarity or the protection of the privacy of students who offered personal information during the seminars, the transcriptions are meant to faithfully reproduce not only the astrological and psychological material discussed at the seminars, but also the atmosphere of the group setting.

Since the CPA's inception, many people, including astrology students living abroad, have repeatedly requested transcriptions of the seminars. In the autumn of 1995, Liz Greene, Charles Harvey and Juliet Sharma-Burke decided to launch the CPA Press, in order to make available to the astrological community material which would otherwise be limited solely to seminar participants, and might never be included by the individual tutors in their own future written works. Because of the structure of the CPA progrmme, most seminars are "one-off" presentations which are not likely to be repeated, and much careful research and important astrological investigation would otherwise be lost. The volumes in the CPA Seminar Series are meant for serious astrological students who wish to develop a greater knowledge of the links between astrology and psychology, in order to understand both the horoscope and the human being at a deeper and more insightful level. The hardback volumes in the series are not available in most bookshops, but can be ordered directly from the CPA or purchased from Midheaven Bookshop, 396 Caledonian Road, London N1, Tel. +44 20 7607 4133, Fax +44 20 7700 6717, www.midheavenbooks.com.

Hardback volumes available in the CPA Seminar Series:

The Astrologer, the Counsellor and the Priest by Liz Greene and Juliet Sharman-Burke

The Family Inheritance by Juliet Sharman-Burke

Venus and Jupiter: Bridging the Ideal and the Real by Erin Sullivan

The Astrological Moon by Darby Costello

The Art of Stealing Fire: Uranus in the Horoscope by Liz Greene

Incarnation: The Four Angles and the Moon's Nodes by Melanie Reinhart

Water and Fire by Darby Costello

Where In the World? Astro*Carto*Graphy and Relocation Charts by Erin Sullivan

Planetary Threads: Patterns of Relating Among Family and Friends by Lynn Bell

Relationships and How to Survive Them by Liz Greene

Earth and Air by Darby Costello

Astrology, History and Apocalypse by Nicholas Campion

Paperback volumes available in the CPA Seminar Series:

The Horoscope in Manifestation: Psychology and Prediction by Liz Greene

Apollo's Chariot: The Meaning of the Astrological Sun by Liz Greene

The Mars Quartet: Four Seminars on the Astrology of the Red Planet by Lynn Bell, Darby Costello, Liz Greene and Melanie Reinhart

Saturn, Chiron and the Centaurs: To the Edge and Beyond by Melanie Reinhart

Anima Mundi: The Astrology of the Individual and the Collective by Charles Harvey

Direction and Destiny in the Horoscope by Howard Sasportas

Barriers and Boundaries: The Horoscope and the Defences of the Personality by Liz Greene